FORENSIC EXAMINATION
OF INK AND PAPER

FORENSIC EXAMINATION OF INK AND PAPER

By

RICHARD L. BRUNELLE, M.S.

Chief, Scientific Services Division
Bureau of Alcohol, Tobacco and Firearms
Department of the Treasury
Rockville, Maryland

and

ROBERT W. REED, M.F.S.

Shore Walk Road
Riva, Maryland

CHARLES C THOMAS • PUBLISHER
Springfield • Illinois • U.S.A.

Published and Distributed Throughout the World by

CHARLES C THOMAS • PUBLISHER

2600 South First Street

Springfield, Illinois 62717

© *1984 by* CHARLES C THOMAS • PUBLISHER

ISBN 0-398-04935-1 (cloth)

ISBN 0-398-06039-8 (paper)

Library of Congress Catalog Card Number: 83-18039

With THOMAS BOOKS *careful attention is given to all details of manufacturing and design. It is the Publisher's desire to present books that are satisfactory as to their physical qualities and artistic possibilities and appropriate for their particular use.* THOMAS BOOKS *will be true to those laws of quality that assure a good name and good will.*

Printed in the United States of America

Q-R-3

Library of Congress Cataloging in Publication Data

Brunelle, Richard L.
    Forensic examination of ink and paper.

    Bibliography: p.
    Includes index.
    1. Chemistry, Forensic.   I. Reed, Robert W.
II. Title.
HV8073.B73   1984   363.2'562   83-18039
ISBN 0-398-04935-1. — ISBN 0-398-06039-8 (pbk.)

To the ink and paper industry
whose help
has contributed significantly
to the forensic application
of ink and paper analyses and,
consequently,
the administration of justice.

PREFACE

PROBABLY no other field of forensic science has had more of an impact on the detection of white collar crimes or has stirred as much interest as the forensic examination of ink and paper. Over the past fourteen years, law enforcement agencies, nationwide and at all levels of government, have turned to the forensic examination of ink and/or paper for assistance in determining the authentic or fraudulent nature of questioned documents. The investigation of Spiro Agnew, Watergate, the Howard Hughes (Mormon) Will, and Juan Corona are just a few headline cases that relied heavily on the forensic examination of ink and paper.

Forensic science is rapidly becoming a field of many specialties. Rapidly developing technology and the application of this technology to the examination of many types of physical evidence makes it very difficult for anyone to keep current and be truly an expert in all areas of forensic examination. Forensic ink and paper examination is such a specialty.

Advancements in the ability to distinguish, identify, and date questioned documents through ink and paper examination over the last fourteen years have paved the way for a completely new approach to the examination of questioned documents. Document examiners have extended the scope of their traditional examinations to include the comparison and dating of inks and papers; or, in some laboratories, document examiners work closely with forensic chemists to perform these examinations. Barriers preventing minimal damage to documents have been broken and the laboratory procedures used are now routinely admissible as evidence in federal and local courts of law.

This book was prompted by the need to convey the many advancements that have occurred in the field of forensic examination to the forensic science community and to provide a suitable text for courses in the forensic examination of ink and paper at universities with graduate or undergraduate degree programs in forensic science. Apart from the value this book will have to the forensic and academic communities, we feel that prosecuting and defense lawyers, investigators, and anyone associated with the criminal justice system will also benefit. The laboratory methodology will be of interest to the ink and paper industries as well.

The Forensic Examination of Ink and Paper is complete in itself. That is, in addition to a complete discussion of laboratory procedures and forensic applications for the examination of ink and paper, the history of the development of ink and paper, their chemical and physical properties, and court admissibility of the techniques used are also addressed. Several forensic cases are included in the text to help explain how the procedures described can be applied to real-life criminal and civil investigations. Every attempt was made to write this text in a style that can be understood by forensic chemists, document examiners, lawyers, judges, investigators, industrial scientists, students, or anyone with an interest in the subject matter.

The authors are indebted to many people for their generous assistance and advice so essential to the successful completion of this book. In the field of questioned document examination we would like to express our gratitude to the large number of examiners who provided excellent feedback regarding our paper analysis and watermarks sections. To the ink industry, we would like to thank those companies who allowed and encouraged our interest in the production of writing and printing inks. We are grateful for the generous assistance of the research and library staff at the Institute of Paper Chemistry for providing invaluable materials and information regarding the production of paper, paperboard, and watermarks. Our thanks too to a number of individuals from varying disciplines incorporated within the framework of forensic science for their critiques on the forensic sections in this textbook. The Writing Instruments Manufacturers Association, Inc., contributed materials on the nomenclature of writing instruments which are considered "state of the art" for that industry. The authors are indebted to the hundreds of individuals whose kindness and patience encouraged the completion of this work.

Particular thanks are given to Doctor Antonio A. Cantu, former ATF ink specialist, for his valuable input to this text. The authors also acknowledge the help of Larry F. Stewart and Albert Lyter, III, former employees of the ATF Forensic Science Branch. Special thanks are also given to Roland Wilder and Tony Wadsworth, photographers employed by the Forensic Science Branch of the Bureau of Alcohol, Tobacco and Firearms, for their assistance in the preparation of photographs for the text.

The authors are indebted to the Bureau of Alcohol, Tobacco and Firearms for giving permission to publish this book and for contributing photographs and illustrations.

We also want to express our sincere appreciation to our families, Dawn, Desiree, Holly, Heidi, and Barbara; Wayne and Eileen for inspiring the writing of this book and for tolerating moods—sometime good, but often frustrating—during the preparation of the manuscript.

The views and opinions expressed in this book are those of the authors and do not necessarily reflect those of the Bureau of Alcohol, Tobacco and Firearms.

CONTENTS

FORENSIC EXAMINATION
OF INK AND PAPER

CHAPTER 1

INTRODUCTION

UNDERSTANDING and application of the material in this text requires a brief explanation of the overall approach to the forensic examination of ink and paper and a brief comparison of modern approaches with procedures followed in the past.

PHILOSOPHY BEHIND FORENSIC EXAMINATION
OF PAPER AND INK

The approach to conducting a forensic examination of ink and paper differs in several respects from the traditional analysis of these products by ink or paper chemists. Traditionally, these materials are examined primarily for reasons of quality control to insure inks or papers are being made according to a prescribed formulation or to evaluate the various physical properties such as drying properties of inks or the strength or whiteness of paper. When these examinations are conducted by manufacturers, the precise formulas of the products are known and quantity of material for analysis is abundant.

Forensic examination of ink and paper are normally performed for three reasons:

- Comparison of two or more samples to determine whether they are the same or different. This would be done for example to determine whether a particular ink entry on a check or ledger had been altered.
- Determination of whether two or more similar samples have a "common" origin. As for inks, the "commonness" or "rarity" of their formula defines the degree of their "common" origin. In paper, once the manufacturer can be identified, as through a watermark, one can make statements on the degree of their "common" origin.

• Determination of the date a document was executed. While the absolute dating of ink, in general, is not yet possible with any reliable accuracy, it is possible to (a) determine the earliest a particular ink formulation could have been used for writing purposes, (b) in some instances, estimate the length of time an ink has been written on a document, and (c) in some situations, determine that an entry was written subsequent to other entries on a page. Similarly, paper can be dated by the identification of a watermark or formula changes prior to which these specific changes did not exist. More on this will be explained later.

Major differences involved with the forensic approach to the examination of ink and paper rather than the traditional approach include the following:

• Only limited sample of ink and paper is available for analysis lest the document be destroyed. Therefore, methods of analysis used must of necessity be changed to accommodate this fact.
• The precise formula of the ink and paper is seldom known to the forensic examiner. From this, it is obvious that the support of the ink and paper industry is required in many instances where it is necessary to obtain information pertaining to formula changes in their products. Such is often the case when the situation requires the dating of ink or paper.
• The results of the examinations require that the examiner interpret the evidentiary value of the results rather than an evaluation of the quality of the product or to determine whether the prescribed ingredients have been added according to a specified formula.
• In the absence of some unique ingredient or combination of ingredients in the products, such as a tag in an ink or the use of new synthesized or natural dye, positive identifications are seldom possible. Such is the situation with most types of trace evidence such as paint, soil, glass, metal, etc. Positive determinations as to origin are not always possible with this type of evidence either.

From the above discussion it can be seen that the forensic approach to the analysis of ink and paper is considerably different from the traditional analysis of these products. The forensic scientist interprets the results of the examination relying on experience and knowledge of the material being analyzed, and the conclusion rendered is an opinion, not fact. Nevertheless, the criminal justice system is relying more and more on the forensic scientist to arrive at the truth in cases adjudicated in or out of court. A forensic expert's testimony has been generally proven to be more reliable than that of an eye-witness. The well-trained, experienced, and ethical forensic scientists will objectively limit the extent of their conclusion to be consistent with the facts available from the similarly ethical ink and paper manufacturers with which we, in the forensic community, have dealt.

COMPARISON OF MODERN APPROACHES TO PAPER AND INK EXAMINATION WITH TRADITIONAL METHODOLOGY

The establishment of the Standard Ink Library at the Bureau of Alcohol, Tobacco and Firearms and its use for the matching and dating of writing inks in 1968 is generally accepted by forensic scientists as the beginning of the modern approach to ink examination. Therefore, pre-1968 methodology will be arbitrarily referred to as traditional methods, recognizing that many pioneering efforts during the early 1960s made possible what are referred to in this text as the modern methods for the analysis of ink and paper.

Prior to 1968, due to the basic structure of most crime laboratories, analysis of ink and paper fell under the purview of the examiner of questioned documents. Any problem concerned with a questioned document, be it handwriting, typewriting, alterations to ink, paper, etc., was given to the examiner of questioned documents for examination. Forensic chemists were more concerned with analysis of trace evidence such as drugs, soil, paint, glass, blood, and other types of evidence that clearly required chemical analysis. Examiners of questioned documents were therefore responsible, for the most part, for the little forensic ink and paper examination that was conducted by traditional methods.

Little research and development of methodology for ink and paper analysis was accomplished prior to 1968 because —

- Examiners of questioned documents had, with few exceptions, nontechnical backgrounds, which understandably inhibited their research in these areas.

- Traditionally, no damage to a questioned document, no matter how little, was permitted. This philosophy prevailed throughout the profession of questioned document examination and obviously prevented any significant research on chemical methods of analysis of ink and paper that does require some, although very minimal damage to the document.

- Forensic chemists traditionally left matters dealing with documents to the examiner of questioned documents, and there was very little interaction between the forensic chemist and the examiner of questioned documents. This reality served as a barrier to progress to the application of chemical and physical methods for the forensic examination of paper and ink.

TRADITIONAL METHODS FOR THE FORENSIC EXAMINATION OF PAPER AND INK

To examine inks, examiners of questioned documents relied almost totally on nondestructive methods for comparison. Examinations primarily used various wavelengths of light, dichroic filters, and infrared photography, and these were sometimes successfully able to distinguish different samples of inks. Subtle differences in chemical formulation could not be detected, however, by these methods. During the 1960s, however, a few examiners began experimenting with destructive techniques such as spot tests, paper chromatography and electrophoresis for the comparison of ink samples. These researchers deserve a great deal of credit because their pioneering efforts helped to pave the way for later developments. They began the gradual acceptance of minimal damage to documents.

Dating of inks by the traditional techniques was limited to (a) the identification of a type of ink not available at the time the document was purportedly prepared (for example, the presence of ballpoint ink on a document dated 1935 would not be possible since, for all practical purposes, ball-point inks were not generally available comercially until 1945) and (b) the identification of a gross change in an ink formulation (such as the change of ball-point inks from oil base to glycol base about 1950) or the use of a new ingredient (such as copper phthalocyanate dyes introduced about 1956.)

In summary, whereas, traditional methodology was often sufficient to distinguish inks, it was not adequate to match questioned and known samples, or date questioned inks with any significant degree of scientific certainty. Traditional methods for the examination of paper were limited to the measurement of physical properties of paper, such as weight, thickness, fluorescence properties, and opacity and, of course, the identification and dating of paper by watermark examination. Coded watermarks provide an excellent means of determining the date the paper was manufactured by a specific manufacturer. However, the physical measurement could only serve as a means to distinguish papers or indicate similarity. Without chemical analysis of the ingredients in paper and a fiber analysis, questioned and known samples of paper cannot be matched with any degree of certainty.

MODERN METHODOLOGY FOR THE FORENSIC EXAMINATION OF PAPER AND INK

Modern approaches to the comparison and dating of ink and paper extend the premodern techniques to include chemical analysis of the ingredients in these products. Micro quantities of ink and paper are removed from the questioned document to perform the tests.

Techniques such as TLC, HPLC, solubility tests, and densitometry enable the direct comparison of many colored and invisible components of inks to differentiate or match questioned and known samples. The acquisition of a comprehensive Standard Ink Library including samples of changes in formulations as they occur in industry allows questioned inks to be matched with standards to determine manufacturer, formula, and the first date the formula of ink could be used for writing purposes. For example, a document dated 1977, containing an ink not available commercially until 1979 must of necessity be a backdated document. On the other hand, if an ink first introduced in 1974 was used to prepare the document, no conclusion can be reached as to whether the document was backdated.

In 1975 another improvement occurred in the dating of inks. At the request of the Bureau of ATF, several ink manufacturers began to voluntarily add taggants to their inks during the manufacturing process. This enabled the precise year of manufacture of the ink on a questioned document to be determined. About 40 percent of all inks manufactured in the United States are now tagged in this manner.

Recent research by Doctor Antonio Cantu, chemical physicist with the Bureau of ATF, has led to the determination of relative aging of inks with the potential for aging. This technique is extremely helpful on documents such as ledger records or expense and income records where (a) several ink entries with known dates and one or more questioned entries on the same page or pages are involved and (b) these inks are of the same formula. Doctor Cantu has established that a relationship exists between the age of ink on paper and its solubility in various organic solvents. The relationship is that the longer an ink has been written on paper, the slower it will dissolve in various solvents, which means that recent entries will dissolve faster than older entries.

The relative and absolute aging of inks has opened a whole new era in the dating of inks on questioned documents. While research is still underway in this area, as will be explained later in this text, this approach to dating has already had its impact on the detection of backdated fraudulent documents.

Modern forensic paper examination has been expanded to include not only the traditional nondestructive physical measurements used during the premodern era, but also includes determination of the fiber composition of paper, pulping processes, coatings, fillers, and whiteners and their elemental compositions. Altogether these examinations provide a large number of identifying characteristics that can be applied to the comparison of questioned and known samples of paper. When agreement exists on all tests, then common origin is a high degree of certainty.

The dating of paper is conducted in three ways: (a) identification of a coded watermark or the identification of a change in the design of a watermark on a specific date, (b) the comparison of the questioned paper with standards with known production dates, as well as the (c) elemental composition of the questioned paper obtained from the manufacturer. Obviously, the presence of a watermark is essential to the identification of the manufacturer of the questioned paper. Since the trace elemental composition of paper from a manufacturer will change with time due to changes in raw materials, often the approximate period of manufacture of the questioned paper can be determined by matching the questioned paper with a standard sample that has a known production date. A major change in the composition of the paper that occurred on a specific date (for example, a change in the type of coating, fluorescent whiteners, filler material) is also a means of dating paper.

All of the above approaches to dating paper require close contact with and the cooperation of the paper manufacturing industry. The paper industry is much too large to attempt to accumulate a comprehensive standard paper collection. As a result, close liaison with industry is essential to obtain information pertaining to formulation changes and their corresponding dates.

As with ink analysis procedures, chemical and physical examination of paper is often helpful to the detection of fraudulent documents. Modern procedures that add chemical methods to traditional physical methods allow the forensic scientist to greatly extend the scientific certainty of conclusions regarding the common origin of two or more samples of paper and the dating of paper.

CHAPTER 2

THE HISTORY OF THE DEVELOPMENT
OF WRITING INKS
Their Properties and Compositions

The Palest Ink Is Better Than A Capricious Memory
An Ancient Chinese Proverb

INTRODUCTION

A SEARCH of the available literature reveals that the history and development of ink is closely bound to the development of writing, writing instruments, and paper. Some believe that the origin of ink began about 2698 BC during the reign of the emperor Huing-ti in China. Huing-ti utilized the talents and inventive genius T'ien Chen to create this new writing medium.[1] The truth is that nobody knows for certain when and who is responsible; however, it can be stated, with some certainty, that the Chinese deserve the credit for this accomplishment. Frank B. Wiborg has written extensively on the subject of the history of ink.[2] Wiborg has stated that the mental attitude of the Chinese toward the arsenal of the learned is well crystallized; paper, brush, ink, and ink slab are the four great emblems of scholarship and culture and are inventions Wiborg feels the Chinese may justly claim as their own.[3]

The historical development of inks is a fascinating subject and a complete treatise on the subject would require several volumes of text. This chapter attempts only to cover the major developments in the chronology of ink development. It describes when and where they were developed and who was responsible for their conception. History has shrouded these early discoveries with ambiguity; therefore, we present this material, as devoid as possible, of these uncertainties.

9

VARNISH

According to the unanimous opinion of all competent scholars of China, varnish was the earliest vehicle of committing thoughts to writing.[4] What the composition and preparation of this ancient varnish was, however, is not known; but it is more than probable that it was a product obtained from the sap of the lacquer or varnish tree (*Rhus Vernicifera* D. C., family *Anacaroiaceae*), a sumach indigenous to China.[5]

INDIA OR CARBON INKS

Under the great T'ang dynasty (AD 618 – 906) the manufacture of ink took an unprecedented development.[6] Political expansion led to the predominance of Chinese civilization all over Asia. This epoch marks China's Augustan age in literature and printing. It was the then new invention of printing books by means of wooden blocks that gave a fresh impetus to further progress in the production of ink.[7] The most significant departure during the T'ang sovereignty was the emergence of a large number of ink factories that sprung up under the guidance of highly trained specialists, the mo we Kwan, or "official of ink affairs."[8] With this expansion, Chinese governmental affairs increased in volume, and state correspondence assumed unparalleled proportions. The business of ink manufacture was taken out of private hands and began to be industrialized and commercialized. The mo we Kwan was held responsible to send an ever-increasing supply of ink to the metropolis for the feeding of the administrative machine. No less than twenty-five names of manufacturers of ink have been handed down from this epoch.

Carbon ink was essentially produced from the smoke of green pine. Lampblack was extracted from this pine and placed in the form of cakes. These cakes could be sent easily on to the administrative offices.

The Koreans advanced the cause of ink and conveyed its manufacture to the Japanese. According to the *Nihongi (Annuals of Japan),* the king of Korea sent in AD 610 two Buddist priests to Japan. One of these priests, Tam-ch'i, was skilled in preparing painters' pigment, paper, and ink.[9] This industry was ardently advocated and promoted by the Japanese royalty.

The misnomer "India" ink should be clarified at this point. Among the Brahmans of ancient India, it was not the written, but the spoken, word that was looked upon as all inclusive. The hymns of the Veda (knowledge) were memorized and transmitted for ages from generation to generation strictly from memory. In the Mahabharata it is said that those who sell, forge, or write the Veda are condemned to hell.[10] In a society where, for thousands of years, an aversion to writing prevailed, it is not likely that there existed an interest in the production and perfection of writing materials. Despite its close contact geographically to China, India did not adopt paper and ink until well after the birth of Christ. The term *India ink* grew in popularity as the result of caravan trades from east to west that traversed through India. Therefore, the term India ink is a misnomer.

Composition

Carbon ink is one of the oldest forms of writing ink and is commonly referred to as India ink. This class of ink is still widely used in the Far East and by artists worldwide. In its simplest form, carbon ink consists of amorphous carbon shaped into a solid cake with glue. It is converted into a liquid for writing by grinding the cake and suspending the particles in a water – glue medium. Occasionally a pigmented dye is added to improve the color. Also available are liquid carbon inks in which the carbon is kept in suspension. Shellac and borax are used in place of animal glue and a wetting agent is added to assist the mixing of the shellac and carbon.

Carbon inks are very stable and are not decomposed by light, air, moisture, or microbiological organisms. They are insoluble in water and can be removed from paper only by abrasion. Therefore, the ink will endure as long as the paper. This class of inks is usually unsuitable for fountain pens, but is used extensively as drawing inks and printing inks.

Carbon Inks and Antiquity

Antiquity produced several manufacturing methods regarding inks. The names of many dyestuffs have come down to us, some of them in use today while others are long since obsolete. The variety of pigments and dyes used by the Ancients was very considerable.[11] The peoples bordering the Mediterranean employed a variety of colors to their writing medium. For white colors, they were acquainted with white lead; blacks were obtained through various kinds of charcoal and soot. Browns were made by blending differing kinds of ochre or impure iron ores. Pastel-woods gave off a blueish dye. Weld and saffron (*Crocus Sativus*), as well as other plants of similar origin, gave off yellowish pigments.

The Ancients also used a number of tinctures as ink, among them a brown color, sepia. As a natural ink, its origin antedates every other ink in the world, artificial or otherwise.[12] It is a black – brown liquor, secreted by a small gland into an oval pouch, and through a connecting duct is ejected at will by the cuttlefish, which inhabits the seas of Europe, especially the Mediterranean. The pigment most valued was that obtained from the Mediterranean cuttlefish, *Sepia Officinalis,*[13] as it is the most lasting of all natural ink substances.

This is not to suggest that the ancient Egyptians did not utilize carbon inks. The carbon ink of ancient Egypt was prepared in solid sticks and cakes, as in

China, and were used down to the fifth century AD; remains found in inkstands would seem to confirm that it was available in fluid form as well.[14] History provides us with another account of these early carbon inks; Dioscorides, physician to Antony and Cleopatra (40 BC – 30 AD), in a dissertation on the medicinal use of herbs, gives the proportion of lampblack and oil to be used in the manufacture of ink (*atramentum*).[15]

The inks that have previously been described consisted of an insoluble pigment suspended in a vehicle which merely bound the coloring matter to the surface of the sheet. In the first century, AD, we see the first mention of encaustic inks, that is, inks that penetrated the body of the sheet rendering erasure much more difficult. The word *ink* was derived from the Latin *encaustum*, the name given to pigment first used in baking tiles. Later it was restricted to the purple ink with which Roman emperors signed their names, the black ink being called *atramentum*.[16] This was an era in which emerged the first "vitriolic" inks, that is, inks that embraced suspensions of copper sulphate and lampblack in water. This suspension found favor with the priests who used it for their religious manuscripts for two to three hundred years.

Beginning with AD 200, the employment of inks became more and more constant and popular. The Europeans began to import Chinese carbon inks as well as rediscovering ancient formulas belonging to their own ancestors.[17]

The destruction of Rome by Alaric, King of the Western Goths, AD 410, and the subsequent dismemberment of the entire Roman Empire announced that ancient history had come to an end. It may be truly said as well that the ending of the ancient history of the black and colored writing inks was also contemporaneous with these events.[18]

The eclipse of ink-written literature for a least 500 of the 1000 years which followed, known as the Middle or Dark Ages, was complete, except in the Church alone, which seems to have kept up the production of manuscript books principally for ecclesiastical and medical purposes.

The sixth century marked the invention of the quill pen; a wider degree of latitude in writing never before known resulted.[19] Inks were made thinner and, unfortunately, were less durable in character. This is not to suggest that these inks were of an inferior grade; regarding the longevity of these formulas, they exceed many modern formulations.

IRON GALLOTANNATE INKS

The transition of ink made from carbon to that made from iron and galls was a very gradual one. In all probability, gall ink was invented in the Anterior Orient, from the species of oak (chiefly *Quercus lusitanica* var. *infectoria*), on which the gall-wasp deposits its ova that form the excrescences known as galls.[20] The utilization of galls for ink is mentioned by Philo of Byzantium in the second century (AD), in a description of sympathetic ink, and by Martianus Capella in the fifth century.[21] The earliest extant document, to date, written with iron ink is an Egyptian parchment of about the seventh century A. D.[22]

It is to the female wasp that we are beholden for gall ink. As C. A. Mitchell once observed

> Curious abnormal excrescences, known as galls, are frequently formed upon the branches, shoots and leaves of plants and trees, notably upon the oak. They are produced by the introduction of a foreign organism which sets up an irritant action within the plant, resulting in the development of a growth which, possibly, stands in some form of symbiotic relationship to the causal organism. The female gall-wasp punctures the young tissues of the leaves and deposits their eggs. Under this stimulus the plant juices accumulate at the point of puncture, and a gall is gradually formed, which serves as the home of the larva.[23]

Every nation has nut galls that are indigenous to their respective regions, so there are literally thousands of differing types of galls produced. These galls vary in shape and size and, perhaps most importantly, color.[24] The amounts of tannin and gallic acid vary according to these colors. For centuries to come, the utilization of nut galls in ink making would be a vital one. Fountain pen inks were eventually derived from these substances.

The fifteenth century saw the rebirth of learning and along with it a strong need for these iron gallotannate inks. The inks of the Renaissance required greater fluidity than those of an earlier period. This could only be obtained by the reduction of the quantity of gummy vehicles blended with an increase in the use of acids. These new, emerging nation-states required uniformity of these ink formulations. France, in 1626, concluded an arrangement for the manufacture of a gall ink that guaranteed and insured more reproducibility in respect to desirable ink qualities.[25] This first step pioneered the European wave of regulation of the industries that were considered vital to the growth of the state.

In 1765, the English chemist William Lewis publicly announced that he proposed to investigate the subject of ink chemistry. Doctor Lewis was the first to advocate logwood as a tinctorial agent in connection with iron and gall compositions.[26]

The year 1831 witnessed the Academy of Sciences in France designate a committee composed of chemists with instructions to study the subject of a permanent ink. This committee reported that it was in favor of the tanno-gallate of iron inks then in use, but stressed that it was essential to be uniform in its compounds, once again for "the good of the state."[27]

William I. Clark, in 1879, submitted a thesis, to the Edinburg University entitled, "An Attempt to Place the Manufacture of Ink on a Scientific Basis." The introduction of blue – black ink as a phase of the development towards modern methods was the essential point he was trying to make.

Finally, in 1890, Schluttig and Newman, in their *Edition Dresden,* discussed the subject of iron and gall inks, which served as the definitive work on the subject of tanno-gallate of iron inks.[28]

During those mid to late 1880s, ink classifications became a commercial success. To capture the ever-growing public's eye, ink chemists developed different coloring substances. Previous to the discovery of the soluble anilines, indigo, madder, logwood, and other dyeing components were added to the iron tanno-gallates for basically a twofold purpose: to lower the costs of production and to add to the color selection of inks.

Nigrosine was developed as a form of inexpensive ink and became immensely popular due to its blueish color. Another popular favorite was the use of vanadium, which is fairly permanent. These ingredients were utilized in an extremely popular ink utensil known to us as the fountain pen.

FOUNTAIN PEN INKS

There are two basic types of fountain pen inks — iron-gallotannate type and aqueous solution of synthetic dyes. These iron-gallotannate types are essentially iron salts in combination with gallotannic acid in an aqueous solution. This solution is colorless when first applied to paper, but darkens quickly when oxidized by air. Modern inks of this type contain a synthetic blue dye to provide an immediate blue color to the ink which turns black after oxidation on paper. This explains the origin of the name blue-black fountain pen ink. Blue-black inks are very stable. Unlike carbon ink which remains essentially on the surface of the paper, blue-black inks are absorbed into the fibers of the paper so that the iron compound formed when the ink ages becomes an integral part of the paper. The ink is insoluble in water and cannot be erased effectively by abrasion.

The most popular fountain pen ink is the type that consists of an aqueous solution of synthetic dyes. These inks have a bright color and produce attractive writing; however, they are not nearly as stable as the blue-black inks. Synthetic dyes fade and are soluble in water. The most recent inks of this type, however, contain pigmented dyes such as copper phthalocyanate blue which contributes much more permanence to the ink.

BALL – POINT PEN INKS

In 1888 John Loud invented and received a patent for what he called a ball-point pen. Loud's invention proved a trifle premature; the country was not ready for a pen with a ball point. Seventeen years after Loud had his invention patented, it entered into the public domain without having been exploited.[29] G.

A. Werner and A. W. Askew patented a ball point in 1895 and, for a time, actually produced and sold it commercially, using an ink made from lampblack and castor oil.[30] Another ball-point writing device was patented by Van Vechten Riesberg in 1916; his patent, like Loud's, expired without exploitation.[31] In 1935, a pair of Czechoslovakians named Paul V. Eisner and Wenzel Klimes attempted to market a ball-point pen in Europe. The German war machine rolled over Czechoslovakia in 1937 and flattened out the prospect of any future production.[32]

Ladislao Biro, in conjuction with his brother George, began to experiment with the ball-point pen. Ladislao Biro moved from Hungary in 1939 to Paris where he developed a ball-point pen that operated on a new ink-feed system based on capillary action instead of gravity flow . . . and it worked! The Biro pen differed from the conventional fountain pen in three important respects: first, instead of a nib it had a minature socket that held a ball bearing one millimeter in diameter; second, instead of using ordinary ink, it contained a gelatinous dye with an oil base that, rolled onto a writing surface by the ball bearing both lubricated and dried almost instantly; and, third, it held enough of this unconventional ink to perform for several months without refilling.[33]

During the closing months of WW II, the United States Air Force showed interest in the idea of the ball-point pen and sent a few of these Biro pens to key American manufacturers. To add some icing to the cake, the Air Force let it be known that they were interested in the purchase of this pen. The big three in pen manufacturing concerns in the United States at that time — Parker, Sheaffer, and Eversharp — began looking into the question of patent rights. Although Eberhard Faber, the pencil manufacturing firm, had contracted for those rights, Eversharp won out; and, in the spring of 1945, had matters well in hand, or so they thought.[34] While Eversharp's engineers worked on "cleaning up" the Biro pen, a man named Milton Reynolds saw a golden opportunity and seized it. Reynolds and his engineers devised a way of feeding the ink to the ball bearing by the simple and unpatentable law of gravity.

Reynolds, the P. T. Barnum of the ink industry, knew that with the ending of the war with Japan the American public would be ripe for a postwar wonder. Late one rainy evening Reynolds hit upon an idea for the promotion of his pen. While dining one rainy night Reynolds mindlessly began doodling on a damp newspaper. Gradually he became conscious that, soggy as the newspaper was, the lines of his scribbling stood out clearly. Returning to his shop, he put a piece of paper on the bottom of a basin of water, which led to his coining of the phrase, "It writes under water."[35]

With no factory in which to produce his pens Reynolds, shortly after V-J day, talked the then all-powerful Office of Price Administration into raising the ten-dollar per unit ceiling up to twelve-fifty. Reynolds then took his pen into

Gimbel's department store in New York City and came away with an order for twenty-five hundred pens. Eversharp got wind of the deal and threatened to sue Gimbels on the basis of patent infringements. Gimbels turned around and raised their order for the Reynolds' pen to fifty thousand. The response by the "innovation starved" American public was overwhelming.[36]

The ball-point pens developed shortly after WW II were a far cry from perfection. The Reynolds pen had a number of things that fouled up the mechanism. The pen gooped (or the deposition of large droplets of ink) and was faced with the problems of skipping and directionality as well. Because the parts of the pen often fitted together imperfectly, it plainly leaked, to name but a few of its problems.[37]

Within a few short years, the majority of the imperfections of the ball-point pen had been worked out. By 1950, excluding the Reynolds pens, the ball-point pen had arrived as an acceptable writing instrument. Around 1950, a new type of ball-point ink had been developed by a Hungarian chemist named Fran Seec. Seec's ink was instant drying and nontransferable. He sold his formulations to Patrick Frawley, Jr., who owned the Frawley Pen Company located in Los Angeles, California. Frawley turned around and introduced the Paper Mate ball pen, using the ink developed by Seec. Eventually Frawley sold his concerns to Gillette Company.[38]

Composition

Ball-point inks consist of synthetic dyes in various solvents. The dyes are soluble in the solvents, but the inks also may contain insoluble pigments in suspension. The dyes in ball-point inks can contain as much as 50 percent of the total ink formulation that produces a very viscous ink with a consistency similar to honey or molasses.

A number of additional ingredients usually are included in the ink to impart specific characteristics, and these materials generally are kept secretive by ink manufacturers.[39] Basically, these secret ingredients are acidic materials, resins, surface active agents, and viscosity adjustors. The acid materials are normally fatty acids that act as a lubricant for the ball of the pen, help the starting characteristics of the ball-point, and solubilize (neutralize) dyes. Resinous materials consist of natural resins or synthetic polymers and are used primarily to adjust the viscosity of the inks and to reduce the cost. These polymeric materials affect properties such as adhesiveness, tackiness, and elasticity. Some resins also serve to lubricate the ball in the socket of the pen. Surface active agents promote and adjust the wetting characteristics of the ink. Other organic additives serve as corrosion inhibitors or improve the solubility of the dyes in the various possible solvents.

Ball-point ink made prior to about 1950 used oil-based solvents such as mineral oil, linseed oil, recinoleic acid, methyl and ethyl esters of recinoleic acid, glycerine monoricinoleate, coconut fatty acids, sorbital derivatives, and plasticizers such as tricresylphosphate. Modern ball-point inks (those made after 1950) are referred to as glycol-based inks because of the common use of ethylene glycol as a solvent for the dyes. The following are commonly used solvents:

ethylene glycol

1, 2-propylene glycol

1, 3-butylene glycol

hexylene glycol

octylene glycol

di and tri ethylene glycol

di propylene glycol

glycerin

phenoxyethylene glycols

benzyl alcohol

ethylene glycol monomethylether

diethylene glycol monomethylether

The dyes used in the early oil-based inks were primarily basic dyes for the colored inks and nigrosine for the black inks. The colors, which faded quickly, consisted primarily of methyl violet, victoria blue, rehodamine red, victoria green, and ausamine. Some of these early inks also contained carbon or graphite to provide permanence. Modern glycol-based inks contain chelated metalized dyes that are specially treated to effect solubility in glycol or similar solvents. The most popular dyes are the blues based on the compound copper phthalocyanine. These dyes are prepared by sulfonating or chlorosulfonating copper phthalocyanine pigment and reacting the sulfonic acid salts or sulfonamides. The resulting dyes are durable to light and have excellent solubility properties. Other premetalized dyes — reds, greens, yellow, etc. — are similarly made to produce a variety of colored inks. Other commercial names for the metalized dyes are Azosol®, Luxol Fast®, and Spirit Soluble®. However, nonmetalized basic dyes utilized in the oil-based inks are still extensively used — provided they are first made into organic salts soluble in glycols by mixing (dissolving) in organic acids (oleic, etc.). Some dyes used in glycol-based inks are referred to as "Spirit Soluble" instead of "Oil Soluble" because they are soluble in spirits (alcohol).

Pressurized ball-point pen inks were developed about 1968. In 1969, Paul Fisher developed the pressurized cartridge using ink that was very heavy, with the consistency of chewing gum. Fisher used nitrogen pressure to force the ink forward; and, when applied to a surface, the ink liquifies and flows smoothly.

The physical characteristics of these inks are quite different from standard ball-point pen inks. Compositionally they are similar except the ink is a thixotropic material that is essentially nonfluid until disturbed by rotation of the ball-point in the socket. Cartridges containing these inks are usually under the pressure of nitrogen or some other inert gas. The positive pressure on the ink allows the pen to write in all positions and in a vacuum: these pens were used by American astronauts during space travel.

FIBER OR POROUS TIP PEN INKS

The fiber tip pen entered the marketplace in 1963 when Japan Stationery Companies' Pentel introduced its 49-cent model. Pentel heralded this device as a revolutionary "third way" to write.[40] This soft tipped pen became very popular in the United States during the 1960s, and the number of units of these instruments sold had surpassed the number of ball-point pens during that time period.

As far back as 1500 BC the Chinese were using soft tip pens made from fine animal hairs.[41] The early Egyptians used a kind of porous point pen made from rushes, and both the Greeks and Romans used writing instruments that employed similiar principles.[42]

The market for modern markers had its beginning in the early 1940s. At that time, only a handful of manufacturers in the United States were making a complicated instrument called the "brush pen." It was sold primarily to industrial users for factories, warehouses, and shipping rooms. It also became a favorite of artists and art studios. Those first markers were blunt instruments. Their felt points (called nibs) were too thick for fine writing. The "brush pen" came with a kitful of components that included the pen itself, several chisel or bullet-shaped felt tips and washers, cans of ink and ink cleaner, and several fine-line tips with an adapter. Selling for around three dollars per unit, it was the genesis of our modern marker.[43]

In 1951, the first canister type marker was introduced. The newly-designed marker was a firm, wedge-shaped felt nib or tip attached to an ink-saturated wick that was housed in an airtight, leak-proof, metal or plastic barrel. By the mid 1950s Carter's Ink Company produced a device that was actually called a "marker," but you practically had to be an engineer to assemble and operate the device.[44]

Redeveloped in 1962 in Japan, the marketability of the product in its homeland suggested the overnight success it was to enjoy in the United States. These pens produce very attractive, smooth, and bold writing strokes and are commonly used for writing signatures. The major disadvantage of many of these pens is that the fiber tip wears quickly, and the writing stroke becomes wider and wider until it has the appearance of a marker pen.

Composition

Fiber tip inks are usually water – or xylene – based and contain dyes and additives similar to those used in fluid inks (fountain and rolling ball marker inks). The early pens of this type had problems with the tip drying out. New formulations contain formamide and/or glycol additives which adjust the surface tension to allow the tip to remain wet even when uncapped. The water based fiber tip inks are water soluble and are, therefore, not durable. The xylene based inks, however are water resistant and are quite permanent on paper. The inks that contain metalized chelated dyes are relatively light fast.

ROLLING BALL MARKER INKS

Rolling marker pens first appeared at the marketplace in 1968. Consumers had two models from which to choose: the Uni-Pen, manufactured by Mitsubshi Pencil Company and distributed in the United States by Yasutomo & Company; and the Pentel Rolling Writer, manufactured by Pentel of Japan (a subsidiary of the Japan Stationery Company) and distributed by Pentel of America.

There had been previous attempts to produce and market writing instruments of a similar disposition. Harrison[45] makes note of a ball-point pen using ordinary writing ink. "one such pen has been marketed in which the ball consists of a tiny sphere of sapphire working in a housing of platinum."[46] The instrument mentioned aboved lacked popularity with the writing public and drifted into obscurity.

R. M. Dick,[47] in a presentation prepared for the 1973 annual meeting of the American Society of Questioned Document Examiners, mentions still another attempt to market such an instrument:

> Sometime in 1959 or 1960, the Pan Fountain Jewel Pen was marketed, to some extent in this country, by the Merschmann Pen Company, Inc., of Chicago, Illinois. This pen was manufactured in West Germany and was on the market in Europe and Canada for approximately ten years prior to its introduction in the United States. It featured a rolling synthetic ruby tip fed by ordinary writing ink held in a partially transparent chamber. The chamber was filled by dipping the pen in an ink bottle and rotating a knob on the top of the pen which in turn activated a plunger in the chamber.[48]

Autoball Pen Company, in 1965, attempted to market a rolling ball marker type of instrument. Autoball found it more profitable to sell their idea to Pentel of Japan, who further developed the pen prior to its introduction on the market.[49]

Composition

The rolling ball marker inks are water based and usually contain organic liquids such as glycols and formamide to retard the drying of the ball-point. The dyes in these inks are water soluble or acidic dye salts. Since these dyes are the type used in the textile industry, there are a large number available for use in ink compared to the standard ball-point inks. The light fastness of these dyes range from good for the metalized acid dyes to poor for some of the basic dye salts. Water fastness is usually poor, but some of the dyes have an affinity for cellulose paper fibers, which produce a certain degree of water fastness.

The writing produced by these fluid rolling ball marker inks resembles the writing of a fountain pen ink more than standard ball-point ink because the fluid nature of the ink causes it to flow into the capillary surface of the paper. The concentration of dyes in fluid rolling marker inks is substantially less than in standard ball-point inks, but is higher than the amount of dyes in fountain pen inks. Rolling ball marker pens are very comfortable to write with, but the ink is used up much more rapidly than standard ink in the ball-point pens.

NOTES

1. F. Wiborg, *Printing Ink — A History* (New York, Harper & Brothers, Pub., 1926), pp. 3-62.
2. See note 1 above.
3. See note 1 above.
4. See note 1 above.
5. D. N. Carvalho, *Forty Centuries of Ink* (New York, Banks Law Pub. Co., 1904), pp. 5-62.
6. See note 2 above.
7. See note 2 above.
8. See note 2 above.
9. See note 2 above.
10. C. Ellis, *Printing Inks — Their Chemistry and Technology* (New York, Reinhold Pub. Corp., 1940), pp. 37-45.
11. See note 5 above, p. 288.
12. See note 5 above, p. 288.
13. See note 5 above, p. 5
14. See note 10 above, pp. 37-46
15. T. Davids, *The History of Ink* (New York, Thaddeus Davids & Co., 1860), pp.7-72.
16. See note 15 above.
17. See note 15 above.
18. See note 15 above.
19. See note 1 above, p. 75.
20. See note 15 above.
21. T.M. Fisher, *The Calligrapher's Handbook* (London, Faber & Faber Lim., 1968), pp. 65-75.
22. C. A. Mitchell, *Inks, Their Composition and Manufacture* (London, C. Griffin & Co., 1937), p. 41
23. See note 22 above.

24. See note 5 above, pp. 100-130
25. See note 5 above, pp. 100-130
26. See note 5 above, pp. 100-130
27. See note 5 above, pp. 100-130
28. See note 5 above, pp. 100-130
29. "The Ball Ben Story—History of a Success," *The Counselor Magazine,* March: 15-24, 1962
30. T. Whiteside, "Where Are They Now? The Amphibious Pen" *The New Yorker Magazine,* Feb.: 39-61, 1951.
31. See note 30 above.
32. D. Wharton, "The Battle of the Ball Point Pen," *The Reader's Digest,* Dec.: 59-62, 1946.
33. See note 30 above.
34. Material extracted from the private collections of David Purtell, Questioned Document Examiner, Chicago, Ill., 1980.
35. See note 34 above.
36. See note 30 above.
37. See note 32 above.
38. G. S. James, "A History of Writing Instruments," *The Counselor Magazine,* July: 96-99, 1978.
39. Private communications with P. Daugherty, Director of Chemical Research, Anja Engineering Co., Monrovia, California, Sept., 1980.
40. S. D. Strauss, "The Soft-Tip Revolution," *The Counselor Magazine,* Nov.: 16. 1967.
41. T. Dubois, "The Fibre-Tip Phenomenon," *The Counselor Magazine,* Nov.: 20-21, 76, 1967.
42. See note 41 above.
43. "The Marker Revolution," *Office Products Dealer,* May:1-3, 1966.
44. J. Joseph, "A Plethora of Pens," *Mechanix Illustrated,* Dec.:1-2, 1965
45. W. R. Harrison, *Suspect Documents—Their Scientific Examination,* (London, Sweet & Maxwell Lim., 1966), p. 24
46. See note 45 above.
47. R. M. Dick, *Rolling Marker Pens.* Read before the annual meeting of the 1973 American Society of Questioned Document Examiners.
48. See note 47 above.
49. Private communication with A. A. Cantu, BATF, Rockville, MD, Sept., 1981.

CHAPTER 3

THE MANUFACTURE OF WRITING INKS

INTRODUCTION

THE purpose and scope of this chapter is to bring into perspective certain questions that have arisen regarding the manufacturing of writing inks. The material within this chapter has been gathered through a series of interviews and inspections of certain key manufacturers. The authors posed a series of questions to these manufacturers in the hopes that their answers might shed additional light on specific problems pertaining to the forensic identification of writing inks. With three exceptions, the writing ink and instrument manufacturers we contacted requested anonymity. Consequently we have elected to grant anonymity to all; the exceptions will be designated companies A, B, and C.

Publications that have included the composition and manufacture of writing inks are precious few in number[1-4] and do not attempt to address the problems encountered by the forensic scientist: our interest lies with ink that has dried on the surface of paper or other suitable writing mediums. Ink, therefore, in its written form is the underlying consideration of the material that will follow.

INK CLASSIFICATIONS

For the purpose of clarification, the following question was addressed to various members within the writing inks manufacturing framework: "Just by visual observation is this a proper characterization of writing inks in written form?"

Having been deemed a proper characterization of writing inks we proceeded with the following broad question: "Is it correct to state that, in general, inks consist of two components—the volatile or vehicle components and the nonvolatile or dry components?

MODERN WRITING INKS AND WRITING INSTRUMENTS

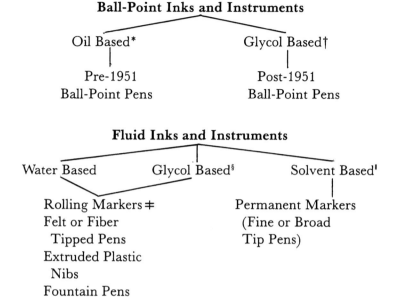

There existed a common agreement that *basically* inks consisted of these two components. In addition to the above statement, the consideration of certain semivolatile components such as resins, oils, oleic and other fatty acids, corrosion control ingredients, etc., with the understanding that these semivolatile components should be considered as essentially nonvolatile.

THE PROBLEM OF CHANGES WITHIN INK FORMULATIONS

A formula is a combination of ingredients that represents the composition of a substance. The first step in deriving the formula of any compound lies in the determination of its percentage composition; this percentage composition indicates the ratio of numbers of the different kinds of atoms present followed by the actual number and kind of molecules present. Formulation, as it applies to

---

* Chiefly oleic acid ink.

† Glycol plus resin components yielding high viscosity ink.

* Fluid or liquid ball point ink.

§ Glycol plus water and other components yielding a low viscosity ink.

ǀ Such as Xylene ink.

SOURCE NOTE: From A.A. Cantu and R.L. Brunelle, "Modern Writing Inks and Writing Instruments." A chart developed for B.A.T.F. Forensic Laboratory procedures.

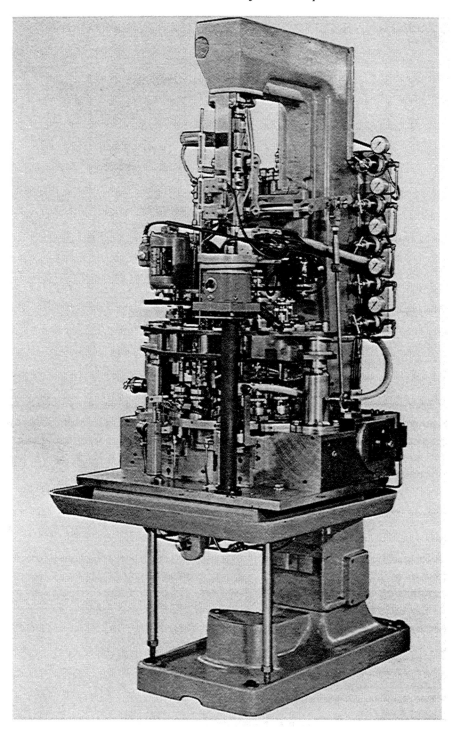

Figure 3-1. Automatic Ball-point Machine. From the Anja Engineering Corp., Monrovia, California.

the writing inks industry, is nothing more than a good recipe — a set of instructions for making inks from a list of specified materials. The ink chemist lends a close eye towards the given specifications of a given formula and the end result should produce a standard ink formulation.

When we addressed the problem of changes within ink formulations to the manufacturer, we received a number of varying answers; however, there were several responses we considered to be a consensus. The question was the following, "What are the major considerations involved in changing standard ink formulations?" Their consensus may be characterized as the following:

1. To necessitate adjustments of specific flow properties.
2. To necessitate adjustments of specific drying times.
3. To necessitate adjustments to the availability of pen parts.
4. The availability of raw materials/dyestuffs.
5. The consideration of the particular climate in which the finished pen will be purchased.
6. To necessitate adjustments of any new innovations that suggest possible improvement of either product or performance.
7. To necessitate adjustments to customer needs and specifications.

The authors will now elaborate further on a few of these points.

The Availability of Pen Parts

The manufacturers of pen parts specialize in, among other things, ball points, balls, and various components designed for both ball point pens and marker components. Some of these manufacturers have pioneered innovations in the field of manufacturing ball point pen components. Company A's ballpoint blank back drilling machine has been designed and built to drill the back holes in ball point blanks, with the necessary chambering and turning of diameter done at the same time. Essentially, blank slugs of brass, stainless steel, or bronze are either chopped to length, or chopped to length and preformed. The chopped, or preformed, blanks are then automatically loaded into the automatic back drilling machine and the back holes are drilled in the blank. These blanks are then ready to be finished in the automatic ball point finishing machine (see Figure 3-1).

The ball point is made from special metal alloys on automatic equipment. It is necessary to machine and hold tolerances that, in many of the dimensions, are closer than the tolerances held in guided missile parts that cost millions of dollars when assembled. The point may start out as a brass or bronze blank, which is then thoroughly cleaned, tumbled, and degreased until it takes on a

---

˙For a detailed description of the myriad of components that goes into the making of writing instruments, the manufacturers suggest that the interested reader contact the *Writing Instruments Manufacturers Association (WIMA) referred to in teh following chapter.*

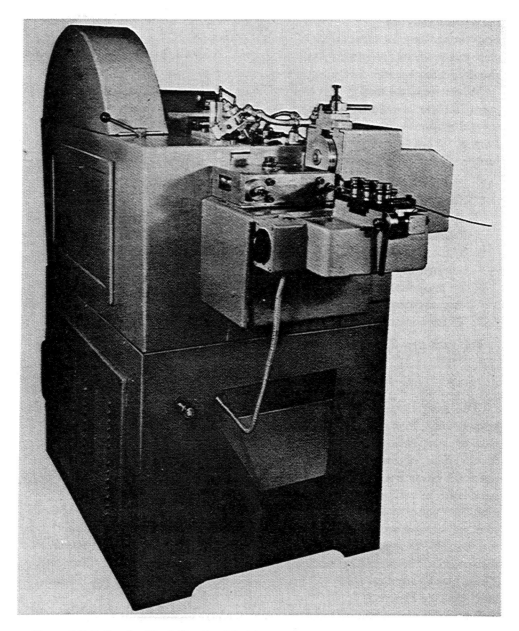

Figure 3-2. Ball-point Blank Heading Machine. From the Anja Engineering Corp., Monrovia, California.

jewel-like lustre. Company A holds a patent on an automatic point machine that is so sophisticated the finished points come from the machine clean and ready for assembly. This machine, used extensively throughout the industry, is a twelve station indexing machine that performs the following operations: It automatically feeds and orients the blanks into the collets. The machining operations then turn the O. D. to size, holding tolerances of 0.0003 in; the cone is formed; the ball socket drilled; the capillary or ink hole drilled through to meet the back holes already in the blanks.

Each point is then automatically inspected to make sure the holes are perfect and no metal chips remain. Following this inspection, the ink channels are broached; the ball is inserted and seated; finally, a rim is spun around the ball, and the finished points are ejected (see Figure 3-2). The complete machining process is done dry, with each station of the operation encased in a vacuum housing that sucks out the metal chips as fast as they are cut. Tolerances are held within fractions that are thousandths of an inch. To give the reader some basis for comparison, the rim that holds the ball in its socket is one-thousandth of an inch thick.

Points 3 and 7 of the major considerations involved in changing standard ink formulations now come into the forefront (3 being to necessitate adjustments to the availability of pen parts; 7 being to necessitate adjustments to customer needs and specifications). Many in this industry state that it is possible to tailor ink "laydown" to suit any unusual customer requirements. Company A has gone on the record as stating that this ink laydown of a given point can be controlled to within 10 milligrams of ink for a thousand feet of writing.[5]

For ball-point pens, a perfectly spherical ball is required to insure a good writing instrument. The balls used in early ball-point pens were made principally of chrome steel and stainless steel. Today these balls may be made of anything from tungsten carbide to plastics to sapphire or ruby jewel balls. There are four basic sizes, 0.062 inch, 0.039 inch, 0.031 inch, and 0.027 inch.

The making of a ball-point pen writing tip is an exercise in perfection. Every serious corporation/company in this industry exacts tremendous quality control standards prior to their respective products reaching the marketplace. As a rule of thumb, the heavier the necessary laydown of ink the more ink that unit will require in reserve. Consequently, the finer the ball point and its textured surface, the less likelihood of "build-up," "gooping," or "nosebleeding" (point seepage).

The assembly of ball pen cartridges is generally composed of either brass or plastic tubing. Company A holds the patent on an automatic cartridge assembly machine that can handle either brass or plastic tubes. Roughly, the tubes are "hoppered" and automatically fed onto an indexing drum. This drum indexes and the machine automatically inks the tubes and joins the points into the tube to a precise overall length, and the finished cartridges are ejected into a receiving tray. These assembled cartridges, either of brass or plastic origin, are "pinch crimped" in another company A innovation, an automatic cartridge crimping machine, for the retention of the retractable spring. Visual quality control follows immediately after the assembly and crimping of the cartridge. Following the cartridge assembly and crimping, the cartridge is centrifuged.

The writing inks and instrument manufacturer will then insist that the finished product (cartridge and pen mechanism) be subjected to additional testing to insure to the customer that the pen will operate reasonably trouble free. The "write test" of all writing instruments will effect this purpose. This is done to test the cartridge for the amount of ink laydown as well as the cartridge's propensity towards gooping. Normally the machine is set for approximately 11 feet of writing per minute, which is considered "normal" handwriting speed, and at 22 feet of writing per minute, which is considered "check writing speed." The machine is run for the desired number of feet in the counter, to be followed by removal of the cartridges being tested (being careful not to lose any/all potential goop present). The cartridges are then reweighed and subtracted from the original weight measured prior to the initial testing; the difference is the amount of ink laydown for the number of feet run for all the cartridges measured during the course of testing. One can divide by the number of cartridges utilized during the testing process to obtain laydown for one cartridge. The goop is then removed from the point(s), and the cartridges are reweighed again; the difference is goop for all cartridges. One can divide by the number of cartridges to obtain goop per cartridge.

The preceeding discussion of the pains exacted by members of the writing inks manufacturers profession are, admittedly, somewhat simplified. For a more detailed discussion of the manufacture and quality control essential to this industry, the authors suggest the reader contact the appropriate manufacturer of the specific writing inks of interest.

The Availability of Raw Materials/Dyestuffs

Writing ink manufacturers, within the past four years, have been faced with a number of problems. One such problem surfaced when two of the "giants" of the dye/raw materials industry elected to either withdraw completely from that industry, as is the case with DuPont de Nemours & Co., Inc., or to substantially reduce their production efforts by more than 50 percent, as was the case with the American Cyanamid Company.[6] The reasons are easy to understand; "small clients" represented by these writing ink manufacturers could not provide a sufficient amount of business to warrant the troubles involved in obtaining the necessary raw materials.

The writing ink manufacturers' quality control office(s) are responsible for the necessary "adjustments" when a raw materials/dyestuffs supplier submits their material. The feedback that the authors have received from several quality control offices can be crystalized into a few sentences: the dyestuffs submitted in recent years are, reportedly, not as "clean" as in the recent past; for instance, one manufacturer informed us that the oil concentration was so heavy in one of his water-based ink lines that, large concentrations of oil surfaced during the mixing.[7] With water-based dyes one has to be careful because the first place this oil will appear, in the finished product state, is with the nib or the tip of the writing instrument. This will, of course, greatly increase that instrument's propensity toward gooping. In recent years, a significant percentage of dyestuffs have switched from actual raw materials to synthetics but, reportedly, this has not affected the quality of the finished product to any great extent.

When a shipment of dyestuffs arrives from a supplier, the typical writing inks manufacturer may exact the following testing procedures:

1. Measurement/analysis for chloride content.
   (The manufacturer does not need salt in their insoluble dyes.)
2. Measurement/analysis for the absorption of the materials through spectrophotometric analysis.
3. Solvent components are measured/analyzed by gas chromatography.
4. Parametric testing
   a. Weight loss tests. A sample is weighed, dried in an oven, and measured for potential weight loss.
   b. Tests to determine additional insoluble materials in the dyestuffs. If the insoluble materials cannot be "filtered" out they are returned to the distributor.
   c. Surface tension tests. These tests observe the control of the flow of the ink (or the properties of the ink) and the penetration of that ink into or onto the paper surface.
   d. pH tests.
   e. Color strength tests. Viscosity tests are run here as well, to insure "sameness" from batch to batch.
   f. "Point" determination. There are some dyes with certain insolubles that cause the point of the writing instrument to wear out ahead of schedule.
5. TLC examination. This insures that the dyes are in the right proportion; the examiner can visually examine the material and compare its quality to previous dye samples.

Climate Compensation

The consideration of the particular climate in which the finished pen will be purchased (point 6) is an interesting factor involved with standard ink formulation. For example, if the finished product is shipped into an area where the temperatures are somewhat colder than the area in which this product is produced and this factor is not compensated properly, the ink in that writing instrument will dry out considerably faster than normal. Quality control will perform these necessary viscosity adjustments. Ordinarily these compensations are very minor, the coefficients of viscosity adjustment being part of the work of the quality control staff. Often this factor is brought to the attention of the potential customer. Company A, for instance, attempts to make all of their formulas work in extreme weather conditions; directed towards that end they prefer to make their inks somewhat thicker, reasoning that it is easier to thin out the inks to meet the necessary requirements of a particular customer. Their (company A) sales department informs the customer which of their inks are or are not hydroscopic and allows the customer to make the decision as to what meets their specific needs.

Company B has in the neighborhood of 60 percent of its business in water-based inks. Company B makes these adjustments in viscosity as the exception rather than the rule. For example, if company B dispenses their water-based inks in the standard marker format to an arid area, they will produce that ink with more plasticizers than the marker designated for more humid environments. The marker in the arid area would dry out faster if not for the increased amounts of plasticizers added to it and visa versa — the plasticizers being the key as far as the dyes or vehicles employed.[8]

Company C gives us still another illustration of the "problem" regarding climate compensation. Company C acknowledges the necessity of these adjustments in their finished products; for example, they make viscosity adjustments in their writing inks designed for sale in the arid regions of Nevada.

STABILITY OF INK WHILE IN THE BULK STATE

The bulk state of inks — prior to the placement of this ink in cartridge form (ball point) — brings up the question of uniform stability. Ball pen inks are not very volatile; they become volatile when they meet the fiber of the surface of the paper. By and large the writing ink manufacturers will exact caution in watching the aging of the ink while in bulk state.

STABILITY OF INK WHILE HOUSED IN THE CARTRIDGE STATE

"Shelf life" is the question in the forefront here. What, if anything, takes place while an ink cartridge is placed on the shelf awaiting its purchase by the potential customer? Ideally the ink cartridge will be purchased within one year after it leaves the manufacturer: often this is not the case. What changes, if any, await within this neglected ink cartridge? The main consideration on the part of the manufacturer is, of course, the potential that his product will dry out prior to its sale. Deterioration occurs first in the solvent within the ink causing the ink to dry; following that there may be some chemical alteration leading to a potential loss of vehicle "punch," occurring generally, if at all, within a twelve- to twenty-four-month period after reaching the shelf. Another problem is the preservation of light fastness, e.g. a transparent pen rail or a transparent cartridge will lend difficulties with certain dyes incorporated within that cartridge, since not all dyes have the same degree of light fastness. With the writing instrument in mind, the possibility of trouble with corrosion factors versus cartridges while on the shelf is another point of consideration. An example would be that of the possibility of changes within the ink as the result of its contact with the type of material used as the mechanism's writing point; for instance, if the dye has in it some type of copper complex, a brass point with zinc may effect a subtle change within that ink formulation. It should be stressed however, that, while all of these changes are subtle, they can easily be detected in the laboratory.

INK AND THE PAPER'S SURFACE — A QUESTION OF POSSIBLE DETERIORATION

This question is dependent upon a number of significant factors:

1. the composition of the ink utilized
2. the composition of the surface of the paper in question
3. the type of writing instrument used
4. The host of ambient conditions to which the document is subjected:
   a. air
   b. light
   c. heat/cold
   d. humidity/moisture
   e. microbiological organisms

When we addressed this question to the various manufacturers of writing inks and instruments, we were promptly informed that the question would be better directed to those individuals interested in the examination of questioned documents. Nonetheless a number of valid responses were elicited.

The question raised was voiced in the following manner: "In the dried or written state — when there are only the dry volatile components of the ink remaining and these are found on the surface, such as paper — is there any deterioration?

One such possibility would lie with the nature of the dye utilized within that specific formulation. Some dyes have the characteristic of sublimation. Sublimation may be defined as the changing of a substance from the solid state (or phase) directly to the vapor phase, which condenses a solid on a relatively cooler surface. Iodine is the best example for this phenomena; you heat it and it doesn't become liquid: it vaporizes.[9] Malachite green is a prime example of a dye that sublimes. Company B reported that some of the dyes that are particularly bad for sublimation were some of the oil-soluble dyes they were using in aromatic types of markers. Company B initially used dyes originally conceived for the tinting of gasoline; those dyes measured roughly one ounce per thousand gallons of gasoline. Company B utilized this same dye but their concentration measured roughly one ounce per gallon of ink. The result was a classic study in the phenomena of sublimation. Pieces of paper marked with those inks, when placed in a normal filing system, would "go through" eight to ten pieces of paper. Needless to point out company B made the necessary changes prior to placing this product on the market.

Some of these manufacturers utilize carbon or nigrosine in the formulation in an attempt to reduce sublimation. Carbon or nigrosine, given the right set of circumstances, will not fade. Fading is nothing more than the changing of strength or color dependence upon exposure to ambient conditions. A manufacturer will use this factor as a selling point to the potential customer; fading or light resistance depends, for the most part, on the quality of the ink the manufacturer formulates. Light fastness, or the lack of the same, may raise the question of the possibility of some form of oxidation occurring while the ink is drying upon the paper's surface or underneath the paper's surface dependent on the nature of the writing instrument used. Nonetheless, this question seemingly revolves around the nature of the dyes utilized in the formulation designed by the manufacturer, and the response of these dyes to the forces of ambient conditions at work.

THE BASIC DIFFERENCES IN THE MANUFACTURING PROCESSES BETWEEN FLUID PEN INKS AND BALL PEN INKS

To protect the proprietary nature of this information, discussion of the "art of manufacture" will be limited to *basic* descriptions. With that end in mind we have elected to discuss only the *basic* differences in the manufacturing processes between fluid and ball pen inks, devoid of the potential danger of revealing industrial secrets.

By way of a review, ball pen inks consist of coloring materials, usually spirit soluble dyes with the occasional insoluble pigment thrown in. These coloring materials are present in high concentrations; dyes constituting roughly 20 to 50 percent of the total ink formulation. The solvents or carriers represent the major portion of the remaining materials in the ball pen ink. The other materials present in the composition of ball pen inks may be characterized in a few large areas: acidic materials (i.e. fatty acids), resinous materials (naturally occurring or synthetic polymers), surface active agents (to adjust or promote wetting properties), and corrosion control ingredients.[10]

The manufacturing of ball pen inks is somewhat more sophisticated than that of its fluid ink counterparts. Initially the solvents are heated to a specified temperature. If the temperature of the solvent is too high, the introduction of the dyestuffs will be affected; for instance, 200° F is too hot for some dyes —

the result being the destruction of that dye. Once the solvent is properly heated, the introduction of the dyestuffs follows. The dyes involved in the production of ball pen inks are much thicker than those involved with fluid inks. These dyes, generally speaking, require some measure of filtration. The manufacturer will purify these dyestuffs by one of two methods: one, centrifuging the material; or two, by standard filtration methods. Once the dyes are subjected to either method, the viscosity of the liquid is measured and any/all adjustments are then made.

One has to exact extreme caution when adding the dyestuffs. The material isn't just "dumped" into the kettles; if they were, half of the dyes would be thrown up into the exhaust fans, which, in turn, would provide the community with some beautiful puddles (on a rainy day), not to mention some breathtaking rainbows.[11]

With the addition of the dyes to the heated solvents, visual checks are noted so that the material will acquire the proper "thickness." Once this thickness is deemed satisfactory, the material is then strained and filtered once again. The mixture is then permitted to cool. Once the temperature reaches a predetermined level, additional dyes, solvents, or volatile materials are added as needed. When the manufacturer adds these additional materials, the adjustment of the high-speed mixers is next on the agenda. This adjustment is in accord to the proper blend desired for the finished ink.

A host of control tests are brought into play. The manufacturer will check the finished product for proper pH, surface tension, and viscosity. A "color strike out" will follow and a thin layer chromatogram will be run to make sure that the dyes introduced are in the right proportion. Finally the links will be subjected to an "eyeball" test and compared with previous ink samples. If all meets with satisfaction, the finished ink is either shipped to its destination or properly stored until needed.

The manufacture of fluid inks can be far less sophisticated. Generally, these stamp pad inks, marker inks, etc., are less viscous, more free flowing solutions. They are, for the most part, not as concentrated or the percentage of dyestuffs is not as high as with ball pen inks. The majority of these fluid inks can be manufactured devoid of additional heating sources (outside of the steam-jacketed kettle). The advantage of being able to mix these inks at "room temperature" cannot be overemphasized.

For water-based inks the procedure is relatively simple. First, the desired amount of water is placed in a kettle; this may or may not be heated depending upon the specific formulation required and whether the dyes necessitate an increase in temperature in order to dissolve. The solvent(s) are then added, followed by the introduction of various surfactants, corrosion inhibitors, plasticizers, or any type of "add ins" required for a particular type of ink. The dyes are then introduced, followed by the stirring or mixing until the materials are dissolved and integrated together. The finished product is cooled and then filtered. During this step of the process, the same type of quality control measures for ball pen inks are exacted towards the fluid inks.

The finished fluid inks are pumped through additional filtrations into fifty-five-gallon drums, sealed and either stored or shipped to the customer.

FORMULAS AND THEIR BATCHES

The definition of a batch of ink is largely dependent upon two factors:

1. The ink-making capabilities of the manufacturer or of the plant's physical infrastructure.
2. The ink requirements of the customer. This will be determined by —
   a. the writing instrument designated for that ink
   b. the quality of the ink
   c. the quality of ink manufactured to effect 1 and 2

The Manufacturer's Capabilities

At present there are two methods of manufacturing that are embraced by the majority of the manufacturers of writing inks: the steam-jacketed kettle and the flow reactor (a sealed unit with agitation and heated by the traditional steam-jacketed kettle). These two kettles come in a variety of sizes, from as small as fifty gallons to as large as ten thousand gallons. In conjunction with these kettles are the mixers, which are normally two speed in design; ball pen inks requiring the higher speeds because of the thicker nature of the dyes involved in their production and the necessary increase in agitation involved for the introduction of resins. Fluid inks, by comparison, require little mixing.

Smaller batch requirements (one- to ten-gallon orders) are normally handled "inside" the plant, away from the larger machinery.

The Ink Requirements of the Customer

The nature of the writing instrument will determine the quality and quantity of the ink to be manufactured. For example, company C has thee grades of ball pen inks: economy inks, high quality inks, and premium inks. These different grades of ink are carefully monitored by company C's quality control department. The single most important factor in the determination of the differences between these three grades of ink is the amount of raw materials/ dyestuffs incorporated within a specific formulation. The premium inks receive significantly larger amounts of dyes, followed by the high quality inks and so on. After the different grades of inks are explained to the customer, he makes the decision as to which ink to incorporate into the writing instrument.[12]

The larger manufacturer of writing inks will often produce the pen parts for those inks. A large company that contracts for writing inks will normally permit the manufacturer of both ink and pen parts to make all the decisions necessary for the impeding "marriage" between these two factors.

The quantity of the ink produced is dependent upon the nature of the cartridge housed within the instrument designated by the customer. For example, if a customer places an order for ten thousand ball-point pens, the manufacturer can determine the specific amount (in pounds or gallons) of ink required to complete the job. The manufacturer will compute the size of the cartridge, allowances for loss during the processing, etc., and arrive at the "bottom line" for the customer. For example, company A may produce 1000 pens of a ball type per pound of ink; if the customer desires a smaller capillary type of cartridge for the instrument, that figure might run as high as 1270 units. Preparation for this smaller capillary type of cartridge may equate to as little as 0.4 gm of ink per unit. Ideally between 1.1 and 1.7 gm of ink per pen is the desirable range in the industry but, as we have pointed out, that is customer requirement dependent.

If the customer is interested in water-based inks, a small marker may yield the manufacturer in the neighborhood of a million units per thousand gallons, or roughly 0.3 gm per unit. With larger markers, something in the nature of a water-based sketching unit or a metal marker, the manufacturer may yield around 350 units per gallon. Ideally, water-based inks will yield the manufacturer around one thousand units per gallon, or 1.3 to 1.5 gm per unit, dependent upon the reservoir housed within the instrument.

The definition of a batch is dependent on both the capabilities of the manufacturer to produce the ink and that of the needs of the customer. A number of interesting questions arise at this point. For instance, what happens to "leftover" inks — those inks that, for a host of reasons, are not consumed by the intended customer? In short, is it permissible for the manufacturer to mix these leftover inks into different formulations in an attempt to salvage the costs of production?

If the manufacturer of writing inks has produced a quantity that exceeds the demands of the customer; or the manufacturer, for one reason or another, makes an error during the mixing of the formulation, what happens to the inks? The key here is one of compatibility. If the components in the batch in question are compatable with those of another batch, the manufacturer is well within his rights to incorporate the two batches. Normally the ink is stored and the manufacturer awaits the next order whose formulation is close to this batch after all the necessary corrections and adjustments are made. If the reformulated ink meets the standards of the manufacturer's quality control department then "all's well that ends well."

EXAMPLES OF CLASSICAL AND MODERN INK FORMULATIONS

Examples of Classical Iron Gallotannate Inks

A[14]*

Ferrous sulphate cryst	15.0 g
Tannic acid	11.7 g
Gallic acid	3.8 g
Phenol	1.0 g
Soluble blue	3.5 g
Hydrochloric acid	10%
Water	Variable

B[15]

Extract of oak apple	120.0 g
Glycerine	0.6 g
Hydrochloric acid	2.5 g
Salicylic acid	1.0 g
Ferrous sulfate	50.0 g
Oxalic acid	0.9 g
Glucose	20.0 g
Dye blue-ink	10.0 g
Sulfuric acid	2.0 g
Nitric acid	3.1 g
Phenol	1.0 g

Early Ball-point Pen Ink Formulations

Patents

Hungary #138248   *1/2/43*   *To Ladislao Biro*

Glue

Dextrin or polysaccharide

glycerol or cholesterolized oil containing dye

U. S. #2427921   *9/23/47*   *Pfaeizer to Milton Reynolds*

Methyl violet	0.72 parts
Victoria blue	1.68

---

*Gum arabic (about 10 g/1) as well as glycerol and glycol ethers or polyglycols, may be added as a means to improve the ink flow.

Oleic acid	2.42
Mineral oil	0.84

U. S. #2623827	*12/30/52 (thixotropic)*		*Moos to Eversharp*
Victoria blue oleate	56.0		
Carbowax 1500 + polyoxy- ethylene glycol 400	15.0		
Victoria blue phospho- tungstic toner (pigment)	15.0		
Tween 20 (Surface active agent)	2.0		

Examples of Fountain Pen Ink Formulations*

A

Blue	% (+ or − 5%)
Water	96.33
Ethylene glycol	3.97
Methylene blue	0.81
Glucose	0.41
Phenol	0.31

B

Red	% (+ or − 5%)
Water	96.33
Glycerine	3.97
Acid dye bright-red	0.53
Glucose	0.41
Phenol	0.31
Acid dye red #2	0.28

C

Green	% (+ or − 5%)
Water	96.33
Glycerine	3.97
Acid dye green	0.81
Glucose	0.41
Phenol	0.31

*The manufacturer may elect to either add or substitute ethyl alcohol to these formulations

Examples of Modern Ball Point Ink Formulations

A

Royal Blue	%
A-1 Resin Solution	36.0
Oleic Acid	11.4
Carbitol Solvent	12.5
1,3 Butylene Glycol	11.8
Victoria Blue Base (V. B. Base)	8.7
Spirit Solvent Fast Blue BGO Ex	9.1
Victoria Pure Blue BGO Ex	4.9
Methyl Violet 2B Base	2.7
Polyvinylpyrrolidone (PVP) K30	1.6
Spirit Solvent Fast Yellow Tx	1.3
	100.0

B

Blue	%
A-2 Resin Solution	35.9
Oleic Acid	11.3
Carbitol Solvent	12.5
1,3 Butylene Glycol	11.6
Victoria Blue Base	5.4
Victoria Blue Base BGO	8.6
GG (Dye materials)	9.1
Methyl Violet 2B Base	2.6
Polyvinylpyrrolidone (PVP) K30	1.6
Yellow Tx	1.4
	100.0

C

Blue	%
A-3 Resin Solution	55.5
Glyceryl Monoricinoleate	35.3
Oleic Acid	3.7
Methyl Violet 2B Base	3.7
Victoria Blue B Base	1.8
	100.0

D

Blue	%
Hexylene Glycol	25.0
50% MHP/C90	15.5
Victoria Pure Blue BGO Ex	16.6
MBSN	16.6
Oleic Acid	4.9
Diethylene Glycol	7.5
Phenyl Methyl Carbinol	1.5
Acetopheone	0.5
Glyceryl Monoricinoleate	3.2
Carbitol	5.4
Methyl Violet 2B Base	1.1
Black NJ (Dye material)	1.2
GRL	1.0
	100.0

E

Black	%
Oleic Acid	5.7
Diethylene Glycol	2.5
Phenyl Methyl Carbinol	8.8
Glyceryl Monoricinoleatae	5.0
Hexylene Glycol	26.5
Carbitol	9.3
Victoria Blue 2B Base	8.5
Orange Luxol Fast	16.6
GG (Dye materials)	12.8
Yellow Tx	4.3
	100.0

F

Blue	%
Oleic Acid	2.4
Methyl Hexylene Glycol/ Cellulube GO	13.9
Diethylene Glycol	6.1

Phenyl Methyl Carbinol	1.9
Glyceryl Monoricinoleate	4.1
Hexylene Glycol	20.6
Carbitol	5.1
SSF Blue GG (Dye materials)	20.5
Victoria Blue BGO Ex	20.6
Victoria Blue 2B Base	1.0
Black NJ (Dye materials)	1.1
GRL	0.9
	100.0

G

Red	%
Oleic Acid	4.5
Diethylene Glycol	7.0
Phenyl Methyl Carbinol	1.9
Glyceryl Monoricinoleate	4.1
Hexylene Glycol	22.2
50% Santolite MHP/Cellulubego	14.6
Spirit Soluble Fast Red G (Allied)	17.7
Spirit Soluble Fast Red 3R (Allied)	14.5
Rhodamine B Base (du Pont) (Allied)	5.2
Azosol Fast Red 3 BA (General)	2.3
Ink Red G (Dye materials)	—
	100.0

H

Red	%
Oleic Acid	4.5
Diethylene Glycol	7.0
Phenyl Methyl Carbinol	1.9
Glyceryl Monoricinoleate	4.1
Hexylene Glycol	22.2

50% Santolite MPH/Cellulubego	14.6
Spirit Sol. Fast Red G (Allied)	—
Spirit Sol. Fast Red 3R (Allied)	14.5
Rhodamine B Base (du Pont) (Allied)	5.2
Azosol Fast Red 3 BA (General)	2.3
Ink Red G (Dye materials)	17.7
	100.0

MANUFACTURERS OF WRITING INKS

Presented below is a list of the major manufacturers of writing inks within the borders of the United States of America:

American Writing Ink Company, Inc.
35 Farnsworth Street
Boston, Massachusetts 02210

Anja Engineering Corporation
1017 South Mountain Avenue
Monrovia, California 91016

Berol USA
Eagle Road
Danbury, Connecticut 06810

Bic Pen Corporation
Wiley Street
Milford, Connecticut 06460

Chromex Chemical Corporation
19 Clay Street
Brooklyn, New York 11222

Denison Manufacturing Company
Building 26-2
300 Howard Street
Framinghan, Massachusetts 01701

Eberhard-Faber
Crestwood
Wilkes Barre, Pennsylvania 18703

A. W. Faber Castell Pencil Company
P. O. Box 7099
Newark, New Jersey 07107

Fisher Pen Company
711 Yucca Street
Boulder City, Nevada 89005

Formulab, Incorporated
529 West 4th Avenue
P. O. Box 1056
Escondido, California 92025

The Hartley Company
P. O. Box 1027
1987 Placentia Avenue
Costa Mesa, California 92627

Hedra, Incorporated
475 Fifth Avenue
New York, New York 10017

Jensen's Incorporated
P. O. Box 320
Shelbyville, Tennessee 37160

David Kahn, Incorporated
Route 61
Deer Lake, Pennsylvania 17961

Koh-I-Noor Rapidograph, Inc.
100 North Street
Bloomsburg, New Jersey 08804

National Ink
9395 Cabot Drive
San Diego, California 92126

Paper Mate Division
(Gillette Co.)
1681 26th Street
Santa Monica, California 90406

Parker Pen Company
Writing Instrument Group
219 East Court Street
Janesville, Wisconsin 53545

Pentel of America, Incorporated
2715 Columbia Street
Torrance, California 90503

Sanford Corporation
2740 Washington Boulevard
Bellwood, Illinois 60104

Sheaffer Pen
301 Avenue H
Fort Madison, Iowa 52627

Techform Laboratories, Incorporated
215 West 131st Street
Los Angeles, California 90061

NOTES

1. C. A. Mitchell, *Inks — Their Composition and Manufacture* (London, C. Griffin & Co., 1916).
2. C. A. Mitchell, *Inks — Their Composition and Manufacture* (New York, Lippincott, 1937).
3. C. E. Waters, *Inks* (National Bureau of Standards, C 426) (Washington, D.C., U. S. Govt Print Office, 1940).
4. D. N. Carvalho, *Forty Centuries of Ink* (New York, Banks Law Publ. Co., 1904).
5. Material extracted from the Anja Engineering Corporation, Monrovia, California, Sept., 1981.
6. Personal communication with F. E. Gilbert, Sanford Corporation, Bellwood, Illinois, Sept., 1980.
7. See note 6 above.
8. See note 6 above.
9. Personal communication with S. Heiman, Laboratory Director, Sanford Corporation, Bellwood, Ill., Dec., 1980.
10. P. M. Daugherty, "Composition of Ball Pen Inks" (Unpublished material, 1970).
11. Personal communications with P. M. Daugherty and T. Bailey, Anja Engineering Corp., Monrovia, California, Sept., 1981.
12. Personal communication with F. Taracon, M. Mellin, and J. Dumont, Chromex Chemical Corp., Brooklyn, N.Y., August, 1980.
13. See note 9 above.
14. O. Schluttig and G. S. Neumann, *Die Eisengallustinten* (Dresden, Zahn and Jaensch, 1890).
15. Communication between A. A. Cantu and C. R. Principe, questioned document examiner, Northern Illinois Police Crime Laboratory, Highland Park, Illinois, Sept., 1977.

CHAPTER 4

WRITING INSTRUMENTS:
DEFINITIONS AND NOMENCLATURE

BASIC DEFINITIONS

Handwriting Instrument

A hand-operated device designed for and normally used in making the alphanumeric symbols associated with common handwriting (as opposed to similar marking devices used for preparing graphic representations, marking cartons, etc.), having a reserve supply of writing media, which automatically supplies the writing tip of the device with the writing media.

Line

Writing media deposited on writing surface by a handwriting instrument with such media forming a geometric shape in which its length is substantially greater than its width.

Handmarking Instrument

A hand-operated device designed for and used primarily for preparing graphic representation, labeling cartons, and other marking tasks not normally

The information in this chapter was submitted, upon request, from the Writing Instrument Manufacturers Association, Incorporated (WIMA). The Executive Vice President of WIMA, Mr. Frank L. King, and his Executive Secretary, Ms. Dawn White, may be contacted by those individuals who have a sincere desire to further understand the nature of writing instruments, their physical composition, and the nature of the writing instrument business in general. All materials received are the property of the WIMA unless otherwise designated.

The authors wish to thank Mr. King and Ms. White for all of their help in the collection of current data regarding writing instruments.

*The definitions are based upon the findings of the Nomenclature Subcommittee of the WIMA Test Standardization Study Committee.

considered common handwriting (as opposed to similar writing devices used for making alphanumeric symbols generally associated with common handwriting), having a reserve supply of marking media, which automatically supplies the marking tip of the device with the marking media.

Mark

Marking media deposited on marking surface by a handmarking instrument with such media forming a geometric shape in which its length is substantially greater than its width and in which its width is noticeably greater than the maximum practical width of a line (such maximum practical width for a line to be established at a later date).

Ink and Writing Fluid

The words *ink* and *writing fluid* are interchangeable as to definition; however, the term *writing media,* being broader in its meaning, is not necessarily interchangeable as to definition with *ink* and *writing fluid.*

Ink and Marking Fluid

The words *ink* and *marking fluid* are interchangeable as to definition; however, the term *marking media,* being broader in its meaning, is not necessarily interchangeable as to definition with *ink* and *marking fluid.*

Paper, Writing Surface, and Marking Surface

The words *paper, writing surface,* and *marking surface* are interchangeable as to definition, unless otherwise specified.

DEFINITIONS PERTAINING TO HANDMARKING INSTRUMENTS

Structure and Components

1. *Marker*—A handmarking instrument, complete with all auxiliary components (such as barrels, caps, clips) required to make it suitable for usage as desired by its purchaser and having as its distinguishing characteristic a point made of a material conducive to conducting a marking fluid to the surface to be marked and said mark having a minimum line width of 2 mm.
2. *Nib*—The member used for the application of the marking fluid to the marking surface.
3. *Nib Shape*
   a. Bullet—A member that is round in cross section, and the mark

generating portion is shaped to a conical or parabolic form parallel to the longitudinal axis of the nib.

    b. Parallelogram — A member that is rectangular in cross section, and the mark generating portion is slanted in relation to the longitudinal axis of the nib.

    c. Chisel — A member that may be round or polyhedric in cross section, and the mark generating portion is slanted and wedge-shaped in relation to the longitudinal axis of the nib.

4. *Nib Material*

    a. Porous Plastic Nib — The term for the type nib made from granules of plastic that are formed into the desired form.

    b. Oriented Fiber Nib — The term for a nib made from a bundle of oriented fibers.

    c. Felt Nib — The term for a nib made from nonoriented fibers.

    d. Extruded Plastic Nib — The term for a nib made from extruded and/or molded plastic, having machine-made capillary devices to transfer the ink.

5. *Nib Holder* — The separate member that adapts to the exterior or outer diameter of the nib to the inner shape of the barrel.

6. *Nib Stop* — That member within the barrel used to prevent the nib from receding to the barrel.

7. *Vent* — An orifice that provides for maintaining the reservoir at atmospheric pressure.

8. *Reservoir* — The component in which the reserve ink supply is stored.

9. *Staking* — That method of securing a nib by driving a metal pin through the nib.

General Definitions

1. *Mark* — A deposit of ink substantially longer than wide made by the handmarking instrument.

2. *Marking* — The act of generating a mark.

3. *Marking Speed* — The rate of mark generation.

4. *Mark Test Machine* — A device for mechanically generating a mark with a marking instrument.

5. *Performance Testing Paper* — Paper for test marking performance.

6. *Ink Testing Paper* — Paper used in determining the level of excellence for certain properties that are inherently related to the marking fluid. May or may not be identical with performance testing paper.

7. *Nib Load* — The vertical component of the force applied to the marking nib during mark generation.

8. *Marking Angle* — The included angle measured from the plane of the marking surface to the longitudinal axis of the marker when in a mark-

ing position.

9. *Compatibility*—The ability of the individual elements to collectively serve their intended purpose satisfactorily.

10. *Shelf Life*—Manifestation of functional stability when stored over periods of time and/or environmental changes.

11. *Marking Smoothness*—Frictional resistance, or lack thereof, encountered during mark generation.

12. *Nonmarker*—A marking instrument that fails to deposit a mark regardless of the rate at which is is moved along the marking surface.

Definitions Related to Performance and Inherently Related to Ink

Handmarking instruments have essentially the same applicable definitions as those of ball-point, fountain, and porous writing instruments.

DEFINITIONS INHERENTLY RELATED TO INK*

1. *Waterfast*—The ability of a line written on appropriate testing paper to withstand change on immersion in water for a given length of time.

2. *Water Resistant*—The ability of a line written on appropriate testing paper to remain legible on immersion in water for a given length of time.

3. *Nonwater Resistant*—The inability of a line written on appropriate testing paper to remain legible on immersion in water for a specified length of time.

4. *Lightfast*—The ability of a line written on appropriate testing paper to withstand change on exposure to light of a specified nature and intensity for a specified length of time.

5. *Light Resistant*—The ability of a line written on appropriate testing paper to remain legible on exposure to light of a specified nature and intensity for a specified length of time.

6. *Nonlight Resistant*—The inability of a line written on appropriate testing paper to remain legible on exposure to light of a specified nature and intensity for a specified length of time.

7. *Water and Lightfast*—The ability of a line written on appropriate testing paper to withstand change on immersion in water for a specified length of time and subsequent exposure to light of a specified nature and intensity for a specified length of time.

8. *Water and Light Resistant*—The ability of a line written on appropriate testing paper to remain legible on immersion in water for a specified

---

*The following definitions are recommended for adoption by the WIMA (Writing Instruments Manufacturers Association) Test Standardization Study Committee.

length of time and subsequent exposure to light of a specified nature and intensity for a specified lenth of time.

9. *Nonwater and Light Resistant*—The inability of a line written on appropriate testing paper to remain legible on immersion in water for a specified length of time and subsequent exposure to light of a specified nature and intensity for a specified length of time.

10. *Eradicator Resistant*—The ability of a line written on appropriate testing paper to remain legible after treatment by a specified ink eradicator for a specified number of times.

11. *Wash Resistant*—The ability of a line to resist complete removal (remain legible) from fabrics made from natural or synthetic fiber or combinations thereof by specified test procedures representative of common laundry procedures.

12. *Washable*—The inability of a line to resist complete removal from fabrics made from natural or synthetic fiber or combinations thereof by specified test procedures representative of common laundry procedures.

13. *Reproducible*—The ability of a line to be reproduced by a specified machine process from an original deposit.

14. *Nonreproducible*—The inability of a line to be reproduced from an original deposit without the use of a separate or special master.

15. *Erasable*—The inability of a line to resist erasure from the writing surface under specified procedures, but without rendering the surface unwriteable.

16. *Nonerasable*—The ability of a line to resist erasure from the writing surface under specified procedures without rendering the surface unwriteable.

17. *Microbial Resistance*—The ability of the ink to resist attack by molds, yeasts, and bacteria.

18. *Stability*—The ability of an ink to maintain its original properties over periods of time and/or environmental changes.

19. *Crystal Growth*—That characteristic of an ink that promotes excessive accumulation on or near the nib, resulting in the formation of crystals or amorphous dye deposits.

DEFINITIONS PERTAINING TO BALL-POINT PENS*

Structures and Structural Components

1. *Ball-point Pen*—A handwriting instrument complete with all of the aux-

---

*The following nomenclature is recommended for adoption by the WIMA (Writing Instrument Manufacturers Association) Test Standardization Study Committee.

iliary components, such as barrels, caps, clips, etc., required to make it suitable for usage as desired by its purchaser and having as its distinguishing feature or characteristic a writing tip containing a rotatable ball for contacting the writing surface for the purpose of depositing the writing fluid on the writing surface.

2. *Cartridge*—Identifiable assembly of components, usually removable from the complete pen, independently capable of performing all of the handwriting functions of a complete pen but lacking in either dimensional characteristics or auxiliary components that would make it suitable for usage as a pen per se.

3. *Ball Housing*—The component that holds the ball.

4. *Point Assembly*—The ball housing plus the ball.

5. *Reservoir*—The component (or section or area thereof) in which the reserve supply of ink is stored.

6. *Follower*—Slideable member or structure, either rigid or nonrigid, in continuous contact with the top of the writing fluid column, and which moves forward as the writing fluid is depleted.

7. *Plug*—A nonslideable structure at the rear end of the reservoir.

8. *Ink Control Plug*—A plug to control back-leaking.

9. *Adapter*—A device used to ensure an adequate connection between the point assembly and reservoir.

General Definitions

1. *Line*—A deposit of ink substantially longer than wide made by a ball point pen or cartridge.

2. *Writing*—The act of generating a line.

3. *Writing Speed*—The rate of line generation.

4. *Write Test Machine*—A device for mechanically generating a line with a ball-point pen or cartridge.

5. *Performance Testing Paper*—Paper for testing writing performance.

6. *Ink Testing Paper*—Paper used in determining the level of excellence for certain properties that are inherently related to the ink used in a ball-point pen or cartridge. May or may not be identical with performance testing paper.

7. *Point Load*—The vertical component of the force applied to the writing tip during line generation.

8. *Writing Angle*—The included angle measured from the plane of the writing surface to the longitudinal axis of the pen when in a writing position.

9. *Compatibility*—The ability of the individual elements to collectively serve their intended purpose satisfactorily.

10. *Shelf Life*—Manifestation of functional stability when stored over periods of time and/or environmental changes.

Definitions Related to Performance

1. *Lay-down*—The amount of ink delivered to the writing surface per unit of line length.
2. *Flow Rate*—The amount of ink removed from the reservoir as a result of writing out one ink fill.
3. *Ink Writeout*—The amount of ink removed from the reservoir as a result of writing out one ink fill.
4. *Blobbing*—The accumulating of ink on the exterior of the point assembly, with the ink so accumulated dropping intermittently to the surface being written upon.
5. *Dotting*—The deposit of small amounts of extraneous ink on the paper, occurring with predictable regularity under given conditions.
6. *Skip*—The self-recoverable, temporary interruption (no deposition of ink in an otherwise continuous line.
7. *Directional Skipping*—That skip that may occur after an abrupt (90% or more) change in the direction of line generation.
8. *Directional Error*—Variation in lay down occurring with changes in relative direction of line generation.
9. *Starving*—A condition in which there is an inadequate flow of writing fluid to the writing surface.
10. *Splitting*—Division of a line into two more or less equal portions by a noninked area running generally parallel to the direction of line generation
11. *Starting Characteristics*—Those characteristics reflecting the instrument's ability to begin generating its typical line.
12. *Starting Point*—The point along a line at which a writing instrument begins to generate a consistent line.
13. *Starting Distance*—The linear distance from initial contact of the writing instrument and the writing surface to the starting point.
14. *Line Quality*—The level of excellence in the peculiar and essential characteristics of the written line.
15. *Beadiness*—A line appearing as a series of uniformly spaced discrete dots as opposed to a continuous deposit of ink.
16. *Feathering*—The condition in which the writing fluid has spread laterally in an irregularly-shaped pattern on the surface being written upon.
17. *Strike-through*—The condition in which the writing fluid has traversed vertically through the paper so as to appear on the underside of the written line.
18. *Seepage*—The accumulating of ink on any exterior portion of the cartridge.
19. *Point Seepage*—The accumulating of ink on or around the tip of the point during periods of nonuse and while the point is not in contact with any

other materials.

20. *Point Wicking* — The accumulating of ink on or around the tip of the point when the tip is in contact with a second material and/or transfer of such into the second material.

DEFINITIONS PERTAINING TO FOUNTAIN PENS

Structures and Structural Components

1. *Fountain Pen* — A handwriting instrument having the following characteristics:
   a. It has a solid, generally bifurcated member contacting the writing surface during the act of writing.
   b. During the act of writing, it is supplied with ink from a reservoir.
   c. It has provisions for either refilling the reservoir from a bulk ink supply or replacing the reservoir with a pre-filled container when ink supply is depleted.
2. *Filling Mechanism* (totally enclosed)
   a. Plunger Filler — Piston type mechanism that is alternately depressed and released to fill the pen.
   b. Inner Filling Bar — Bar acting along the long axis of the reservoir that is alternately depressed and released to fill the pen.
3. *Filling Mechanism* (totally or partially exposed)
   a. Filling Lever — Exposed lever that is alternately raised and lowered to fill the pen.
4. *Ink Supply Containers*
   a. Sac — Permanently affixed, flexible structure to accommodate ink supply. Such structure is intended to be refilled from a bulk ink supply by use of appropriate mechanism.
   b. Reservoir — Permanently affixed, rigid structure to accommodate ink supply. A reservoir is intended to be refilled from a bulk ink supply by use of appropriate mechanism.
   c. Cartridge — Disposable container for the ink supply and intended to be detached when empty and replaced by a new full container. No mechanisms are provided to refill this structure.
   d. Converter — Optionally detachable but not necessarily disposable structure serving to accommodate an ink supply that is refillable from a bulk ink supply. Used interchangeably with a cartridge to contain the ink supply.
5. *Structures Connecting the Tip of the Pen with the Ink Supply*
   a. Feed — Structure or series of interrelated structures serving to deliver ink from the supply to the tip of the pen.
   b. Feed Channel — The groove or grooves in a feed forming routes for

ink passage from the reservoir to the point.

    c. Collector—That structure serving to store limited quantities of ink that would otherwise flood the nib.

6. *Writing Point Elements*

    a. Nib—That structure, nonporous and usually bifurcated, that conveys ink to the writing surface during the act of writing.

    b. Tines—The separate bifurcations of the nib formed as the result of a longitudinal slit in the forward portion of the nib.

    c. Pierce Hole—That hole at the rearward end of the slit that forms the tines.

    d. Tip—Small area of the nib, often of added thickness, actually in contact with the writing surface during the act of writing.

    e. Pellet—Small quantity of separate material permanently positioned on the nib so as to contact the writing surface during the act of writing.

7. *Barrel*—The rearward portion of a two-part, frequently separable, exterior housing for a fountain pen.

8. *Gripping Section*—The forward portion (other than the cap) of a two-part, separable exterior of a fountain pen.

General Definitions

1. *Line*—A deposit of ink substantially longer than wide made by a fountain pen.

2. *Writing*—The act of generating a line.

3. *Writing Speed*—The rate of line generation.

4. *Writing Test Machine*—A device for mechanically generating a line with a fountain pen.

5. *Performance Testing Paper*—Paper for testing writing performance.

6. *Ink Testing Paper*—Paper used for determining the level of excellence for certain properties inherently related to the ink used in a pen. May or may not be identical with performance testing paper.

7. *Point Load*—The vertical component of the force applied to the writing tip during line generation.

8. *Writing Angle*—The included angle measured from the plane of the writing tip during line generation.

9. *Nonwriter*—Writing instrument that fails to deposit a written line, regardless of the rate at which the writing instrument is moved over the writing surface.

10. *Shelf Life*—Manifestation of functional stability when stored over periods of time and/or environmental changes.

11. *Compatibility*—The ability of the individual elements to collectively serve their intended purpose satisfactorily.

Definitions Related to Performance

1. *Lay-down* — The amount of ink delivered to the writing surface per unit of line length.
2. *Flow Rate* — The amount of ink delivered to the writing surface per unit of time per unit of line length.
3. *Ink Writeout* — The amount of ink removed from reserve ink supply as a result of writing out one ink fill.
4. *Skip* — The self-recoverable, temporary interruption (no deposition of ink) in an otherwise continuous line.
5. *Directional Skipping* — The skip that may occur after an abrupt (90% or more) change in the direction of line generation.
6. *Directional Error* — Variation in lay-down occurring with changes in relative direction of line generation.
7. *Starving* — A condition in which there is an inadequate flow of writing fluid to the writing surface.
8. *Splitting* — Division of a line into two more or less equal portions by a noninked area running generally parallel to the direction of line generation.
9. *Starting Characteristics* — Those characteristics reflecting the instrument's ability to begin generating its typical line.
10. *Starting Point* — The point along a line at which a writing instrument begins to generate a consistent line.
11. *Starting Distance* — The linear distance from initial contact of the writing instrument and the writing surface to the starting point.
12. *Line Quality* — The level of excellence in the peculiar and essential characteristics of the written line.
13. *Beadiness* — A line appearing as a series of uniformly-spaced discrete droplets as opposed to a continuous deposit of ink.
14. *Feathering* — The condition in which the writing fluid has spread laterally in an irregularly-shaped pattern on the surface being written upon.
15. *Strike-through* — The condition in which the writing fluid has traversed vertically through the paper so as to appear on the underside of the written line.
16. *Drying Time* — The length of time required for an inked line to become nonsmearing, nonsmudging, nontransferable or otherwise displaced from the original position when tested under specified conditions.
17. *Weiring* — The upward passage of air into the ink supply structure.
18. *Airlock* — The blockage of ink transport from the ink supply to the nib by bubbles.
19. *Nonwriter* — Fountain pen that fails to deposit a written line regardless of the rate at which the pen is moved along the writing surface.
20. *Line Intensity* — Contrast between a written line and the writing surface

when viewed under specific lighting conditions.

21. *Flooding* — A condition characterized by an excessive amount of writing fluid being delivered to the writing surface during writing.

22. *Cap-off Life* — The length of time required for the instrument to become a nonwriter due to dryout, when left in an unused state with the nib exposed.

23. *Recoverability* — The ability of the writing instrument, when recapped and left in a static condition to again generate a line of predetermined quality.

24. *Dryout* — Loss of volatiles from the writing fluid by evaporation.

DEFINITIONS PERTAINING TO POROUS POINTED WRITING INSTRUMENTS

Structures and Structural Components

1. *Porous Point Pen* — A handwriting instrument complete with all of the auxiliary components, such as barrels, caps, clips, etc., required to make it suitable for usage as desired by its purchaser and having as its distinguishing characteristic or feature a nib made of a porous material for contacting the writing surface for the purpose of depositing the writing fluid on the writing surface.

2. *Cartridge* — Identifiable assembly of components, generally removable from the complete pen, independently capable of performing all of the characteristics and/or auxiliary components that would make it suitable for usage as a pen per se.
   Note: In some instances the cartridge may serve in the same capacity as a cartridge for fountain pens. In such cases the cartridge will not be independently capable of performing all the handwriting functions of a complete pen.

3. *Nib* — The member used for the application of the writing fluid to the writing surface.

4. *Nib Holder* — The separate member that adapts the O. D. of the nib to the I. D. of the barrel.

5. *Vent* — An orifice that provides for maintaining the reservoir at atmospheric pressure.

6. *Reservoir* — The component in which the reserve ink supply is stored.

General Definitions

We refer the reader to the general definitions featured in the section under ballpoint pens.

Definitions Related to Performance*

1. *Ink Fill*—Amount of ink originally contained in the writing instrument.
2. *Wear*—A measurable change in a specific dimensional geometry and/or finish, resulting from abrasion.
3. *Nib Wetout*—The ability of the nib to become initially wetted with the ink.
4. *Capillary Rise Capacity*—The amount by weight of a predetermined fluid that is taken up into a capillary reservoir under specified conditions.
5. *Nib Stability*—The ability of the nib to retain its initial configuration and firmness and to resist deformation, cracking, or splitting under predetermined conditions.

BALL-POINT PEN PARAMETERS†

DEFINITIONS RELATED TO PERFORMANCE	TEST RESULTS EXPRESSED	PARAMETERS
Lay Down—The amount of ink delivered to the writing surface per unit of line length	Weight per linear unit	Writing Speed Writing Angle Point Load Ambient Conditions‡ Performance Test Paper Precision of Measuring Equipment
Flow Rate—The amount of ink delivered to writing surface per unit of line length	Weight/time unit/ linear unit	Writing Speed/Duration Writing Angle Point Load Ambient Conditions
Ink Writeout—The amount of ink removed from reserve ink supply as a result of writing out one ink fill	Weight	Writing Speed Writing Angle Point Load Ambient Conditions
Blobbing—The accumulating of ink on the exterior of the point assembly, with the ink so accumulated dropping	Against predetermined acceptance levels	Writing Speed/Duration Writing Angle Point Lead Ambient Conditions Performance Test Paper Precision of Measuring Equipment

---

*The definitions related to performance associated with porous writing instruments are essentially the same as with fountain & ball point pens, with the following additions.

†The authors wish to thank the Writing Instruments Manufacturers Association (WIMA) for the information listed here.

‡For the purposes of this document, *ambient* is understood to mean preselected conditions of temperature and humidity.

DEFINITIONS RELATED TO PERFORMANCE	TEST RESULTS EXPRESSED	PARAMETERS
Dotting — The deposit of small amounts of extraneous ink on the paper, occurring with predictable regularity under given conditions	Against predetermined acceptance levels	Writing Speed/Duration Writing Angle Point Load Ambient Conditions Performance Test Paper Precision of Measuring Equipment
Skip — The self-recoverable, temporary interruption (no deposition of ink) in an otherwise continuous line	Against predetermined acceptance levels	Writing Speed/Duration Writing Angle Point Load Ambient Conditions Performance Test Paper Precision of Measuring Equipment
Directional Skipping — That skip which may occur after an abrupt (90° or more) change in the direction of line generation	Against predetermined acceptance levels	Writing Speed/Duration Writing Angle Point Load Ambient Conditions Performance Test Paper Precision of Measuring Equipment
Directional Error — Variation in lay-down occurring with changes in relative direction of line generation	Against predetermined acceptance levels	Writing Speed/Duration Writing Angle Point Load Ambient Conditions Performance Test Paper Precision of Measuring Equipment
Starving — A condition in which there is an inadequate flow of writing fluid to the writing surface	Against predetermined acceptance levels	Writing Speed/Duration Writing Angle Point Load Ambient Conditions Performance Test Paper Precision of Measuring Equipment
Splitting — Division of a line into two more or less equal portions by a non-inked area running generally parallel to the direction of line generation	Against predetermined acceptance levels	Writing Speed/Duration Writing Angle Point Load Ambient Conditions Performance Test Paper Precision of Measuring Equipment
Starting Characteristics — Those evaluatable characteristics reflecting the in-	Qualitatively as Excellent	Recognition of Starting Point

DEFINITIONS RELATED TO PERFORMANCE	TEST RESULTS EXPRESSED	PARAMETERS
strument's ability to begin generating its typical line	Good Fair Poor Hard Start Nonstart	Starting Distance Writing Speed Point Load Writing Angle Ambient Conditions Performance Test Paper Storage Time Storage Environment Predetermined Qualitative Rating Scale Predetermined Acceptance Level for Typical Line
Starting Point — The point at which a writing instrument begins to generate its typical line	Not applicable	
Starting Distance — The linear distance from initial contact of the writing instrument and the writing surface to the starting point	Linear units to starting point	Recognition of Starting Point Writing Speed Point Load Writing Angle Ambient Conditions Performance Test Paper Storage Time Storage Environment
Line Quality — The level of excellence in the peculiar and essential characteristics of the written line	Not applicable	
Beadiness — A line appearing as a series of uniformly spaced discrete dots as opposed to a continuous deposit of ink	Against predetermined acceptance levels	Writing Speed Writing Angle Point Load Ambient Conditions Performance Test Paper Precision of Measuring Equipment
Feathering — The condition in which the writing fluid has spread laterally in an irregularly-shaped pattern on the surface being written upon	Against predetermined acceptance levels	Writing Speed Writing Angle Point Load Ambient Conditions Performance Test Paper Precision of Measuring Equipment
Strike-through — The condition in which the writing fluid has traversed vertically through the paper so as to ap-	Against predetermined acceptance levels	Writing Speed/Duration Writing Angle Point Load

DEFINITIONS RELATED TO PERFORMANCE	TEST RESULTS EXPRESSED	PARAMETERS
pear on the underside of the written line		Ambient Conditions Performance Test Paper Precision of Measuring Equipment
Seepage—The accumulating of ink on any exterior portion of the cartridge or pen	Weight per cartridge or pen	Writing Speed Writing Angle Point Load Ambient Conditions Performance Test Paper Precision of Measuring Equipment Storage Environment Position and distribution of test units in storage Storage time
Point Seepage—The accumulating of ink on or around the tip of the point during periods of nonuse and when the point is not in contact with any other material	Weight per cartridge or pen	Writing Speed Writing Angle Point Load Ambient Conditions Performance Test Paper Precision of Measuring Equipment Storage Time Storage Environment Position and distribution of test units in storage
Point Wicking—The accumulating of ink on or around the tip of the point when the tip is in contact with second material and/or the transfer of such onto the second material	Weight per cartridge or pen	Writing Speed Writing Angle Point Load Ambient Conditions Performance Test Paper Precision of Measuring Equipment Storage Time Storage Environment Position and distribution of test units in storage Contacting material
Back Leaking—The condition of ink, follower, or ink and follower moving rearwardly so as to leave the reservoir	Pass/Fail	Writing Speed Writing Angle Point Load Ambient Conditions Performance Test Paper Precision of Measuring Equipment

Definitions Related to Performance	Test Results Expressed	Parameters
		Storage Environment
		Position and distribution of test units in storage
		Front end seal
		Storage Time
Gooping—The accumulating of ink on the exterior of the point assembly as a result of writing, with the bulk of the ink so accumulating continuing to adhere to the point	Against predetermined acceptance levels	Writing Speed/Duration Writing Angle Point Load Ambient Conditions Performance Test Paper Precision of Measuring Equipment
Drying Time—The length of time required for an inked line to become nonsmearing, nonsmudging, nontransferable, or otherwise displaced from the original position when tested under specified conditions	Unit of Time	Performance Test Paper Ambient Conditions Point Load Flow Rate Prearranged Technique for determining when the line is dry
Nonwriter—Ball-point pen or cartridge that fails to deposit a written line regardless of the rate at which it is moved along the writing surface	Pass/Fail	Writing Speed/Duration Writing Angle Point Load Ambient Conditions Performance Test Paper Precision of Measuring Equipment
Line Intensity—Contrast between a written line and the writing surface when viewed under specified lighting conditions	Against predetermined acceptance levels	Writing Speed/Duration Writing Angle Point Load Ambient Conditions Performance Test Paper Precision of Measuring Equipment Predetermined Lighting

FOUNTAIN PEN TEST PARAMETERS*

Definitions Related to Performance	Test Results Expressed	Parameters
Lay-down—The amount of ink delivered	Weight per linear	Writing Speed

*The authors wish to thank the Writing Instruments Manufacturers Association (WIMA) for the information listed here.

DEFINITIONS RELATED TO PERFORMANCE	TEST RESULTS EXPRESSED	PARAMETERS
to the writing surface per unit of line length	unit	Writing Angle Point Load Ambient Conditions† Performance Test Paper Precision of Measuring Equipment
Flow Rate— The amount of ink delivered to the writing surface per unit of time per unit of line length	Weight/time unit/ linear unit	Writing Speed/Duration Writing Angle Point Lead Ambient Conditions Performance Test Paper Precision of Measuring Equipment
Ink Writeout— The amount of ink removed from reserve ink supply as a result of writing out one ink fill	Weight	Writing Speed Writing Angle Point Load Ambient Conditions Performance Test Paper Precision of Measuring Equipment
Ink Load— The limit in writing fluid that can be loaded into a reservoir without jeopardizing previously determined stability and/or performance characteristics	Weight	Ambient Conditions Precision of Measuring Equipment
Skip— The self-recoverable, temporary interruption (no deposition of ink) in an otherwise continuous line	Against predetermined levels	Writing Speed Writing Angle Point Load Ambient Conditions Performance Test Paper Precision of Measuring Equipment
Directional Skipping— The skip that may occur after an abrupt (90° or more) change in the direction of line generation	Against predetermined levels	Writing Speed Writing Angle Point Load Ambient Conditions Performance Test Paper Precision of Measuring Equipment
Starving— A condition in which there is an inadequate flow of writing fluid to the writing surface	Against predetermined acceptance levels	Writing Speed/Duration Writing Angle Point Lead

---

†For the purposes of this document, *ambient* is understood to mean preselected conditions of temperature and humidity.

DEFINITIONS RELATED TO PERFORMANCE	TEST RESULTS EXPRESSED	PARAMETERS
		Ambient Conditions
		Performance Test Paper
		Precision of Measuring Equipment
Splitting—Division of a line into two or more or less equal portions by a non-linked area running generally parallel to the direction of line generation	Against predetermined acceptance levels	Writing Speed
		Writing Angle
		Point Load
		Ambient Conditions
		Performance Test Paper
		Precision of Measuring Equipment
Starting Characteristics—Those characteristics reflecting the instrument's ability to begin generating its typical line	Qualitatively as Excellent Good Fair Poor Hard Start Nonstart	Recognition of Starting Point
		Writing Speed
		Writing Angle
		Point Load
		Ambient Conditions
		Performance Test Paper
		Storage Time
		Storage Environment
		Predetermined Qualitative Scale
		Predetermined Acceptance Level for a typical line
Starting Point—The point along a line at which a writing instrument begins to generate its typical line	Not Applicable	
Starting Distance—The linear distance from initial contact of the writing instrument and the writing surface to the starting point	Linear units to starting point	Recognition of Starting Point
		Writing Speed
		Writing Angle
		Point Load
		Ambient Conditions
		Performance Test Paper
		Precision of Measuring Equipment
Line Quality—The level of excellence in the peculiar and essential characteristics of the written line	Against predetermined acceptance levels for starving, skipping, intensity, etc.	Writing Speed/Duration
		Writing Angle
		Point Load
		Ambient Conditions
		Performance Test Paper
		Precision of Measuring Equipment
Beadiness—A line appearing as a series	Against predeter-	Writing Speed/Duration

DEFINITIONS RELATED TO PERFORMANCE	TEST RESULTS EXPRESSED	PARAMETERS
of uniformly spaced discrete droplets as opposed to a continuous deposit of ink	mined acceptance levels	Writing Angle Point Load Ambient Conditions Performance Test Paper Precision of Measuring Equipment
Feathering—The condition in which the writing fluid has spread laterally in an irregularly-shaped pattern on the surface being written upon	Against predetermined acceptance levels	Writing Speed/Duration Writing Angle Point Load Ambient Conditions Performance Test Paper Precision of Measuring Equipment
Strike-through—The condition in which the writing fluid has traversed vertically through the paper so as to appear on the underside of the written line	Against predetermined acceptance levels	Writing Speed/Duration Writing Angle Point Load Ambient Conditions Performance Test Paper Precision of Measuring Equipment
Drying-time—The length of time required for an inked line to become nonsmearing, nonsmudging, nontransferable, or otherwise displaceable from the original position when tested under specified conditions	Unit of time	Ambient Conditions Performance Test Paper Time Flow Rate Prearranged technique for determining when line is dry Point Load
Weiring—The upward passage of air into the ink supply structure	Against predetermined acceptance levels	Writing Speed Writing Angle Point Load Ambient Conditions Performance Test Paper Precision of Measuring Equipment
Air-Lock—The blockage of ink transport from the ink supply to the nibi by air bubbles	Pass/Fail	Writing Speed/Duration Writing Angle Point Load Ambient Conditions Performance Test Paper Precision of Measuring Equipment
Nonwriter—Fountain pen that fails to deposit a written line regardless of the rate at which the pen is moved along the writing surface	Against predetermined acceptance levels	Writing Speed/Duration Writing Angle Point Load Ambient Conditions

DEFINITIONS RELATED TO PERFORMANCE	TEST RESULTS EXPRESSED	PARAMETERS
Line Intensity — Contrast between a written line and the writing surface when viewed under specific lighting conditions	Against predetermined acceptance levels	Performance Test Paper Precision of Measuring Equipment Writing Speed/Duration Writing Angle Point Load Ambient Conditions
Flooding — A condition characterized by an excessive amount of writing fluid being delivered to the writing surface during writing	Pass/Fail	Performance Test Paper Precision of Measuring Equipment Predetermined Lighting Writing Speed Writing Angle Point Load Ambient Conditions
Cap-Off Life — The length of time required for the instrument to become a nonwriter due to dryout when left in an unused state with the nib exposed	Unit of time	Performance Test Paper Precision of Measuring Equipment Barometric Pressure Writing Speed Writing Angle Point Load Ambient Conditions Performance Test Paper Precision of Measuring Equipment Storage Time Storage Conditions Position and distribution of test units in storage
Recoverability — The ability of a nonwriter, as defined previously, to again generate a line of predetermined quality when recapped and left in a static condition	Unit of Time	Writing Speed Writing Angle Point Load Ambient Conditions Performance Test Paper Precision of Measuring Equipment Storage Time Storage Conditions Position and distribution of test units in storage
Dryout — Loss of volatiles from the writing fluid by evaporation	Weight	Ambient Conditions Time Precision of Measuring Equipment Capped/Uncapped

POROUS POINTED PEN TEST PARAMETERS*

DEFINITIONS RELATED TO PERFORMANCE	TEST RESULTS EXPRESSED	PARAMETERS
Lay-down — The amount of ink delivered to the writing surface per unit of line length	Weight Per Unit of length	Writing Speed Writing Angle Point Load Ambient Conditions† Performance Test Paper Precision of Measuring Equipment
Flow Rate — The amount of ink delivered to the writing surface per unit of time per unit of length	Weight Unit of Time Unit of Length	Writing Speed Duration Writing Angle Point Load Ambient Conditions Performance Test Paper Precision of Measuring Equipment
Ink Load — The limit of writing fluid that can be loaded into a reservoir without jeopardizing previously determined stability and/or performance characteristics	Weight	Ambient Conditions Precision of Measuring Equipment
Ink Writeout — The amount of ink removed from the reservoir while writing to a condition whereby the pen no longer writes a line of preestablished acceptability	Weight	Writing Speed Writing Angle Point Load Ambient Conditions Performance Test Paper Precision of Measuring Equipment
Starving — A condition in which there is an inadequate flow of writing fluid to the writing surface	Against predetermined acceptance levels	Writing Speed Duration Writing Angle Point Load Ambient Conditions Performance Test Paper Precision of Measuring Equipment
Ink Fill — Amount of ink originally contained in the writing instrument	Weight	Precision of Equipment

---

*The authors wish to thank the Writing Instruments Manufacturers Association (WIMA) for the information listed here.

†For the purposes of this document, *ambient* is understood to mean preselected conditions of temperature and humidity.

DEFINITIONS RELATED TO PERFORMANCE	TEST RESULTS EXPRESSED	PARAMETERS
Starting Characteristics — Those characteristics reflecting the instrument's ability to begin generating its typical line	Qualitatively as Excellent Good Fair Poor Hard Start Nonstart	Recognition of Starting Point Starting Distance Writing Speed Writing Angle Point Load Ambient Conditions Performance Test Paper Storage Time Storage Environment Predetermined Qualitative Scale of Acceptance Predetermined Acceptance Level for Typical Line
Starting Point — The point at which a writing instrument begins to generate its typical line	Not Applicable	
Starting Distance — The linear distance from initial contact of the writing instrument and the writing surface to the starting point	Linear Units to Starting Point	Recognition of Starting Point Writing Speed Writing Angle Point Load Ambient Conditions Performance Test Paper Storage Time Storage Environment
Line Quality — The level of excellence in the peculiar and essential characteristics of the written line	Not Applicable	
Line Intensity — Contrast between a written line and the writing surface when viewed under specified lighting conditions	Against predetermined acceptance levels	Writing Speed Duration Writing Angle Point Load Ambient Conditions Performance Test Paper Precision of Measuring Equipment Predetermined Lighting
Beadiness — A line appearing as a series of uniformly spaced discrete dots as opposed to a continuous deposit of ink	Against predetermined acceptance levels	Writing Speed Writing Angle Point Load Ambient Conditions Performance Test Paper

DEFINITIONS RELATED TO PERFORMANCE	TEST RESULTS EXPRESSED	PARAMETERS
Splitting — Division of a line into two more or less equal portions by a non-inked area running generally parallel to the direction of line generation	Against predetermined acceptance levels	Precision of Measuring Equipment Writing Speed Writing Angle Point Load Ambient Conditions Performance Test Paper Precision of Measuring Equipment
Feathering — The condition in which the writing fluid has spread laterally in an irregularly-shaped pattern on the surface being written upon	Against predetermined acceptance levels	Writing Speed Duration Writing Angle Point Load Ambient Conditions Performance Test Paper Precision of Measuring Equipment
Strike-through — The condition in which the writing fluid has traversed vertically through the paper so as to appear on the underside of the written line	Against predetermined acceptance levels	Writing Speed Duration Writing Angle Point Load Ambient Conditions Performance Test Paper Precision of Measuring Equipment
Flooding — A condition characterized by an excessive amount of writing fluid being delivered to the writing surface during writing	Pass/Fail	Writing Speed Writing Angle Point Load Ambient Conditions Performance Test Paper Precision of Measuring Equipment Barometric Pressure
Wear — A measurable change in a specific dimensional geometry and/or finish, resulting from abrasion	Change in tip length per unit length	Writing Speed Duration Writing Angle Point Load Ambient Conditions Performance Test Paper Precision of Measuring Equipment
Cap-off Life — The length of time required for the instrument to become a nonwriter due to dryout when left in an unused state with the nib exposed	Unit of time	Writing Speed Writing Angle Point Load Ambient Conditions

Forensic Examination of Ink and Paper

DEFINITIONS RELATED TO PERFORMANCE	TEST RESULTS EXPRESSED	PARAMETERS
		Performance Test Paper
		Precision of Measuring Equipment
		Storage Time
		Storage Conditions
		Position and distribution of test units in storage
Recoverability — The ability of the writing instrument when recapped and left in a static condition to again generate a line of predetermined quality	Unit of time	Writing Speed
		Writing Angle
		Point Load
		Ambient Conditions
		Performance Test Paper
		Precision of Measuring Equipment
		Storage Time
		Storage Conditions
		Position and distribution of test units in storage
Dryout — The loss of volatiles from the writing fluids of evaporation	Weight	Ambient Conditions
		Capped
		Uncapped Time
		Precision of Measuring Equipment
Capillary Rise Capacity — The amount by weight of a predetermined fluid that is taken up into a capillary reservoir under specified conditions	Weight	Ambient Conditions
		Time
		Barometric Pressure
		Precision of Measuring Equipment
Drying Time — The length of time required for an inked line to become nonsmearing, nonsmudging, or otherwise displaced from the original position when tested under specified conditions	Unit of Time	Ambient Conditions
		Performance Test Paper
		Flow Rate
		Prearranged technique for determining when the line is dry
Nib Stability — The ability of the nib to retain its initial configuration and firmness and to resist deformation, cracking, or splitting under predetermined conditions	Qualitatively as Excellent Good Fair Poor Unacceptable	Point Load
		Writing Speed
		Writing Angle
		Performance Test Paper
		Storage Time
		Storage Environment
		Ambient Conditions
		Prearranged evaluation scale of line quality
Drainback — Failure of writing element to sustain adequate ink volume	Qualitatively as Excellent	Ambient Conditions
		Storage Time

DEFINITIONS RELATED TO PERFORMANCE	TEST RESULTS EXPRESSED	PARAMETERS
after being placed in point-up position for a specified period of time	Good Fair Poor	Environment Position

A CHRONOLOGY OF THE DEVELOPMENT OF WRITING INSTRUMENTS

BC

56   Pens cut from the quills of geese were in use in the Mediterranean area. The Latin word for feather, *penna*, was shortened to *pen* to denote a writing instrument.

50   The majority of writing was done with either the quill or reed pen from this date until 1650 AD. Monks of the Middle Ages are said to have used reed pens for normal manuscript writing and quill pens when they wanted their writing small in size. Occasionally, in Roman times and later in Europe, a pen was made of metal. Bronze, steel, iron, silver, and gold were used. Bronze and steel were hard enough to be used for both the stem and point of the pen. When a craftsman made an instrument of iron, silver, or gold, he added a precious stone cut to a point to provide a pen point hard enough for writing.

AD

1650   Books written during the seventeenth century described pens that could carry a supply of ink in an attached well or "fountain." It was during this period that the name "fountain pen" was first used. A British bookseller's trade card printed about 1714 stated that he had for sale "ink horns, fountain pens, wax wafers . . . " but did not explain the writing instrument.

1748   Individual steel nibs were first made in France by Johann Jansen. They were stiff, inflexible, and very expensive.

1803   Steel pens were made and sold in London. These were homemade.

1809   Makers of quill pens began making separate points to be inserted in the stem of the quill.

1818   Charles Watt tipped quill nibs with gold to make them more durable.

1820   Joseph Gillott began to mass-produce steel slip pens in England. Gillott also mechanized making of nibs by a process that had been started by his brother-in-law, John Mitchell.

1828   James Perry, a craftsman, and Joseph Mason, an inventor, improved the machinery invented by Mitchell and began manufacturing nibs with a central slit and ink-hole that gave greater flexibility.

1839   Charles Goodyear of New Haven, Conn., discovered a hot vulcanization process for rubber. This presaged the manufacture of rubber tubes that would serve as inkwells for fountain pens.

1851   An alloy called irium was first combined with gold to make a pen point that was strong and long-lasting. The pen industry was gaining momentum.

1858   The first American factory for the manufacture of steel pens was established by Richard Esterbrook at Camden, N. J.

1884   A fountain pen considered the first practical instrument of its type was invented by Lewis Edson Waterman, an American businessman who almost lost a sale when the dip pen being used splattered ink all over the contract. In Waterman's pen, ink was poured into the barrel with a dropper and its flow to the nib was controlled by a feed. First manufactured by hand, these pens were later produced on machines designed by Waterman. Fountain pens today still have the same basic parts, which work on the concept he developed.

1888   A patent for a ball-point pen was issued to John Loud, an American inventor. The pen was not produced commercially, however, because suitable ink could not be developed.

1895   G. A. Werner and A. W. Askew produced and sold a ball-point pen using an ink comprised of castor oil and lampblack.

1903   L. E. Waterman invented a pump-type filler involving a rubber sac that drew in ink when squeezed. This was followed by the Conklin pen in which the sac was depressed by inserting a coin through a slot in the barrel.

1908   W. A. Sheaffer, an Iowa jeweler, invented the lever-fill principle for filling a fountain pen, terminating a long search for a way to make a practical and satisfactory self-filling pen.

1913   The W. A. Sheaffer Pen Company was established and began the manufacture of lever-fill pens.

1916   Van Vechten Riesbery patents a ball-point pen writing device; his invention suffers the same fate as that of Louds'.

1922   The first nonsediment ink for use in fountain pens (Skrip) was developed by the Sheaffer Pen Co.

1935   Paul V. Eisen and Wenzel Klimes attempt to perfect the ball-point pen; two years later World War II ends its production.

1943   A ball-point pen was invented by Ladislas Biro, a Hungarian living in Argentina, manufactured and sold in South America until American flyers introduced the product to the United States (in a very limited sense).

1945   Milton Reynolds, a Chicago entrepreneur, introduced "the pen that will write under water" to an innovation-starved American public.

1947   The ball-point pen bubble burst because of poor-quality ink that contained particles that clogged the writing ball, corroded the cartridge, ruined the tip, and persisted in leaking in the owner's pocket when not in use.

1949   Fran Seec, a Hungarian chemist living in the United States, invents an ink that made the ball-point pen a practical invention.

1950   Patrick J. Frawley, Jr., introduces the Paper Mate retractable ball-point pen, first of its kind and the first pen to appear with a nonsmear ink.

1960s   A second "new" wave of writing technology swept on the scene in the early 1960s, as the porous tip marker joined other writing instruments as a stable writing aid. Originally conceived as an industrial marking device that could write on any surface by means of a wick-type felt tip that actually painted on the writing fluid, the marker has undergone rapid and effective refinements. One such improvement was the development of new long-lasting tip materials that could be produced in any degree of fineness.

1968   Uni-Pen and Pentel of Japan introduce the rolling ball marker into the United States.

1969   Paul Fisher develops the pressurized cartridge using ink that has the consistency of chewing gum. Fisher used nitrogen pressure to force the ink forward and when applied to a surface the ink liquefies and flows smoothly. This type of ball pen has been used in the American Space Program and is known to all as the "Space Pen."

1970s   The single most significant development to the writing industry proved to be the perfection of erasable inks. These inks were housed in ball-point pen mechanisms, after modifications were effected. Credit for the conception of erasable inks is shared by Doctor Phillip Daugherty and Henry Peper, Jr.

THE MAJOR MANUFACTURERS OF WRITING AND MARKING INSTRUMENTS, PARTS, AND ACCESSORIES

A PARTIAL LISTING (NORTH AMERICA)

Anja Engineering Corporation
1017 South Mountain Avenue
Monrovia, California 91016

Artistic Desk Pad & Novelty Comapny, Incorporated
721-731 East 133rd Street
Bronx, New York 10454

Best-Rite Pen Corporation
15 Des Brosses Street
New York, New York 10013

Brooklyn Pen and Pencil Company
453 Greenwich Street
New York, New York 10013

Chromex Chemical Corporation
19 Clay Street
Brooklyn, New York 11222

Diecraft Automation Systems
177-10 93rd Avenue
Jamaica, New York 11433

DieMakers Limited
2700 De Miniac
Montreal, Quebec, Canada H4S 1K9

Glaro, Incorporated
735 Old Willets Path
Hauppauge, L. I., New York 11787

Harvey Machine Company, Incorporated
2916 Foster Creighton Drive
Nashville, Tennessee 32704

Swiss Albe, Incorporated
4 Broad Street
P.O. Box 788
Norwalk, Connecticut 06101

V-Mark Automation, Incorporated
11300 Hamon Street
Montreal, Quebec, Canada H3M 3A3

CHAPTER 5

PRINTING INKS

HISTORY

THE origin of the history of printing can be traced to the Assyrian civilization.[1] The Assyrians left a record of their existence in the form of inscriptions made upon damp tablets of clay. The cuneiform punches that made the inscriptions were forged in copper. We can say that the first books, as well as the first library, consisted of countless thousands of tablets of baked clay — devoid of a single drop of ink. With the advent of matching inks with writing, mankind found it possible not only to preserve and record facts of necessity, but the possibility to make works of beauty as well.

Chinese Buddhist missionaries introduced printing into Japan sometime during the eighth century (AD). The oldest known piece of printing comes from that island empire dating sometime between 768 and 800 AD.[2] The oldest printed book in existence is also of Buddhist origin. It is an edition of the *Diamond Sutra*, consisting of six sheets of text and one smaller leaf with a woodcut illustration; it was printed in 868 AD.[3] The Chinese deserve the credit for having printed from engraved wooden blocks, using applications of water-inks in the process.[4] As printing developed in both China and Japan, some method of mixing oils with the pigments took place. Certainly both the Chinese and Japanese had arrived at printing from wooden blocks with oil colors several hundred years preceding the invention of typography.

Although the Korean civilization was printing with a movable type as early as 1403, history has chosen Johannes Gutenberg of Mainz, Germany, as having the honor of inventing the printing press with movable types.[5] There are a select number of historians who have designated that honor to Lourens Janszoon Coster of Haarlem, Holland, as deserving that credit.[6] The problem is one of proof; none of Coster's work survived him so what he may or may not have contributed to the science of ink making and printing consists of nothing but speculation.

Gutenberg, whose real name translated into "Goose flesh," adopted the name of the village in which he gained his fame. Gutenberg has, to his credit, a host of authenticated examples from which modern examiners can draw a number of conclusions. The nature of Gutenberg's ink is of particular interest to the student of ink chemistry. Although printed during the period of 1450 to 1456, the inks utilized by Gutenberg appear as bright today as they must have been when they were first "hot off the press." During that century, and up until the mid nineteenth century, lampblack (soot) remained the principal pigment, and varnish made by boiling linseed oil remained the vehicle of choice.[7]

The first really important and instructive color printing was a book printed in 1457 by Johann Fust and Peter Schoffer, both of Mainz. This book is famous for its magnificent initial letters printed in blue on red and in red on blue. It is also the first book that bore a printer's name, date, and place, not to mention the first usage of colored printing ink (as well as the use of black ink).[8]

The students and disciples of Mainz spread throughout Europe, taking with them the secrets of the printing press. In a very short period of time the majority of the nation-states in Europe had the capability of printing the various works of their respective scholars.

The credit of having printed the first book in the English language belongs to William Caxton of London. Caxton learned the trade while serving as governor of the English nation in the Low Countries (Netherlands). The first book by Caxton, with a printed date, was *The Dictes or Sayengis of the Philosophres*, completed in 1477.[9]

To undertake a history of printing would exceed the capabilities of any single text. The remainder of this section will address itself to that of the composition of printing inks and modern printing practices.

PRINTING INKS

There are four interdependent components in the printing system: the press, which is the mechanical means; the type or plate, which provides the subject matter; the paper, which is the vehicle to carry the subject material; and the printing ink, which ties all of the other components together and gives visibility to the material.

The manufacture of printing inks today is a highly technological and specialized segment of the graphic arts industry. Basically, printing inks are colored coatings graphically applied to a given surface by differing mechanical printing processes. Today's printing ink manufacturer often has to formulate inks according to the expressed requirements of each job. Most printing inks, therefore, are custom made products. The NAPIM (National Association of Printing Ink Manufacturers, Inc.) estimates that approximately one million new ink formulae each year are prepared with that end in mind.[10] Often the success or failure of any ink company rests on its ability to develop ink formulae to meet customer needs.

There are, at present, several types of printing processes with inks being broadly classified by the method employed in each process. Briefly, the types of printing inks may be classified as the following:[11]

1. Letterpress
2. Lithographic
   a. Web Offset inks
   b. Sheet Offset inks
   c. Metal decorating inks
3. Flexographic
4. Gravure

Letterpress Inks

Letterpress is one of the oldest forms of printing. The following are some of the major types of letterpress inks currently in use:[12]

- Rotary ink
- Quickset ink
- Heatset ink
- High Gloss ink
- Moisture-set ink
- Waterwashable ink
- News ink

Letterpress inks are viscous, tacky systems. The vehicles are oil or varnish based and generally contain resins that cure by oxidation. News inks provide the major exception in this category; they generally consist of pigments dispersed in mineral oil, with its drying procedure accomplished by absorption.[13]

Lithographic Inks

Introduced in 1796 by Alois Senefelder, lithographic printing is a planographic process. Roughly, this means that the image, which prints, and the nonimage area, which does not print, both lie on the surface of the plate in the same plane.[14] Most lithographic printing is done with an offset blanket so the term *offset* is synonomous with lithography.

WEB OFFSET INKS: These inks require lower viscosities and tack, but high resistance to emulsification with water because of the process's higher running speeds. Web offset inks can be separated into two categories; nonheatset, which air dry and heatset, and heatset which dry with the assistance of drying ovens.[15]

SHEET OFFSET INKS: These inks set rapidly as the ink oil component penetrates the substrate, and subsequently dry as the vehicle cures by oxidation.[16]

METAL DECORATING INKS: These inks are specially formulated with synthetic resin varnishes to dry on metal surfaces with high temperature baking.[17]

Flexographic Inks

Flexography is a form of rotary letterpress printing that uses rubber plates and fluid inks.[18] Initially, this process was utilized primarily for printing on paper bags. With the introduction of plastic films for packaging, the market witnessed a phenomenal growth pattern that enabled this process to blossom.

Flexographic inks generally consist of pigments dispersed in a vehicle made by dissolving one or more resins in solvent. The resins utilized in this type of printing can be modified with a variety of plasticizers and waxes to impart flexibility, scratch resistance, and slip.[19]

Water-based flexographic inks are widely used on paper and paperboard, including bleached or brown kraft and corrugated. Vehicles for these water-based inks are usually made from ammonia or amine-solublized protein, casein, shellac, esterified fumarated rosin, acrylic copolymers, or their mixtures.

Gravure Inks

The gravure or intaglio process of printing is specifically different from other methods of printing in that the design to be printed is engraved or etched below and into the surface of the printing cylinder.

The printing image consists of many thousands of tiny recessed cells per square inch. These cells vary in depth and width so they may accurately meter the proper amount of ink to each tonal gradation of the desired reproduction. This is done in the acid etching process photographically by selectively hardening the screened resist to correspond to the tone densities of the transparent positives.[20]

The gravure press is one of the simplest printing mechanisms known. Its major elements are the gravure cylinder on which the design to be reproduced is etched; the impression roller that brings the web of paper, foil, or film into contact with the gravure cylinder; a doctor blade that removes excess ink from the surface of the gravure cylinder; and an ink pan or reservoir in which the cylinder is immersed.[21]

INGREDIENTS IN PRINTING INKS

Ingredients used in the manufacture of printing inks fall into three main classifications: fluid ingredients or vehicles; solid ingredients or pigments; and supplementary additives, principally driers and other compounds.

The function of the vehicle is to act as a carrier for the pigment and as a binder to affix the pigment to the printed surface. The nature of the vehicle determines in a large measure the tack and blow characteristics of a finished ink.

The printing process and the drying system involved determine the type of vehicle used in the manufacture of printing inks:[22]

Printing Process	Drying System	Type of Vehicle
Letterpress, offset	Oxidation	Drying oil
Letterpress, news	Absorption	Nondrying oil
Letterpress, offset	Quick-setting	Resin oil
Letterpress, letterset	Precipitation	Glycol-resin
Letterpress	Cold-setting	Resin wax
Gravure, flexographic	Evaporation	Solvent-resin

Care should be exercised in mixing and blending different types of inks. It can be seen that components of inks designed for different printing processes may not be at all compatible with each other.

COMPOSITION OF VARIOUS VEHICLES

As mentioned earlier, the printing process and the drying system involved determine the type of vehicle utilized in the manufacture of printing inks. These vehicles may be broadly enumerated as the following:[23]

- Nondrying Oil
- Drying Oil
- Solvent-Resin
- Glycol
- Resin-Oil
- Resin-Wax
- Water-Soluble
- Photo Reactive

NONDRYING OIL VEHICLE: Inks printed on soft absorbent papers, such as comic and news inks, dry by the absorption of the vehicle into the paper. The vehicle consists of nondrying, penetrating oils such as petroleum oils, rosin oils, etc., used in combination or modified with various resins to impart suitable tack and flow characteristics.

DRYING OIL VEHICLE: Oxidation drying is the type used in most letterpress and offset inks today.[24] The chemistry of oxidation is rather complicated. It consists, essentially, of the absorption of oxygen by drying oils. Added "driers" function as catalysts and speed up this action. Of the many types of drying oils in use today, linseed oil or litho is the most widely used. Numbers are used to describe the various viscosities of litho oil — from 00000, which is very thin; to #9 and #10, which are very heavy and sticky and are known as "body gum." Lindseed oil varnishes have excellent wetting properties for most pigments. They distribute well, have good transfer qualities, and provide good binding on paper. The following are some of the other oils used in printing inks: China wood oil, cottonseed oil, castor oil, perilla oil, soybean oil, petroleum drying oils, fish oil, rosin oil, and synthetic drying oils.[25] Many of these oils are combined with synthetic resins in order to obtain faster and harder drying inks.

SOLVENT-RESIN VEHICLE: Gravure and flexographic inks dry principally by the evaporation of the solvent in the ink, which leaves behind a solid film of pigment and resin. In gravure inks for paper, low-boiling hydrocarbon solvents are generally used in combination with gums and resins. Evaporation takes place rapidly with or without the use of heat.

Flexographic inks may contain either alcohols, water, or other fast-evaporating solvents in conjunction with suitable resins or gums. The exact nature of the surface to be printed determines the choice of specific ingredients.

GLYCOL VEHICLE: Moisture-set or precipitation inks are made from resins that are insoluble in water, but soluble in glycol-type solvents. The glycol is readily soluble in water. When moisture, in the form of steam, water spray, or even dampened paper, comes in contact with this type of ink, it solubilizes the glycol, and the resin is thus precipitated from the solution, taking the pigment with it.

A development of glycol-type inks comprises the "fast drying inks" that are based on a vehicle composed of an acidic resin, neutralized by an amine, and dissolved in a suitable glycol.

RESIN-OIL: These vehicles consist of a carefully balanced combination of resin, oil, and solvent. The solvent is rapidly absorbed by the paper, leaving a preliminary dry ink film of resin and oil that is subsequently hardened by oxidation. Such inks, for both letterpress and offset, are of a type that sets very rapidly on contact with paper, and are called "quick-setting."

RESIN-WAX: These inks are solid at room temperature and are liquefied by heating; the terms "cold set" or "hot melt" are derived from this. They can be used only in fountains on presses specifically designed for their use. Rollers, plates, and fountains are all heated to keep the ink liquid. The ink sets immediately on contact with the cold surface of the paper. These inks contain a relatively high percentage of waxes and resins.

WATER-SOLUBLE GUM: A final type of printing ink not included in any of the foregoing is known as watercolor ink. The vehicle consists of water-soluble gum such as gum arabic and other similar materials, dissolved in water and glycerine or other water-miscible solvents. These inks are used for wallpaper, greeting cards, and novelties.

PHOTO REACTIVE: UV-curing inks are essentially nonvolatile, and cure very rapidly by exposure to ultraviolet radiation. The vehicle consists of a complex, reactive monomer and a photoinitiator, or catalyst, which is activated by UV energy. UV inks cure almost instantly without the use of heat and with practically no emission of volatile substances.

Composition of Pigments

Pigments are the solid coloring matter in inks — whether black, white, or any of the common colors.[26] It is primarily the pigment we see when examining printed matter.

Pigments are also responsible for many of the specific properties of the inks, such as specific gravity to a large degree, opacity, or transparency, and permanency to light, heat, and chemicals; they usually determine whether or not a print will bleed in water, oil, alcohol, fats, acid, or alkali.

Pigments partially determine whether or not the ink is suitable for a specific printing process or for specific end uses, such as butter and meat wrappers or soap labels, and whether or not the finished job can be spirit varnished, lacquered, laminated, etc.[27]

The pigments involved in printing inks may be broadly characterized in the following manner:[28]

- Black pigments
- White pigments
- Inorganic color pigments
- Metallic powders
- Organic color pigments
- Flushed colors

Black Pigments

Black pigments are mostly furnace black and thermal black. There are, however, several other blacks used:[29]

FURNACE BLACKS — Produced by "cracking" oil in a continuous furnace and are much smaller in particle size than thermal blacks. Furnace blacks are now used in printing inks almost to the exclusion of other blacks. Each type of black has specific properties used in formulating various types of black inks for different printing processes.

THERMAL BLACKS — Composed in batch furnaces by "cracking" natural gas.

CHANNEL BLACKS — This black is bluer and provides outstanding flow properties. These inks are, for the most part, extinct in their usage in the United States. The Environmental Protection Agency has ruled that the utilization of channel black pigments add to the deterioration of our "clean air." These pigments may still be imported in certain cases but only where costs are of a secondary consideration.

MINERAL BLACKS — Used for special purposes such as magnetic recognition of printed characters.[30]

White Pigments

Opaque pigments reflect light from their outer surface and have the property of covering or hiding the background on which they are printed.[31] Opaque white pigments commonly used in printing inks are listed here in order of decreasing opacity:[32]

Titanium Dioxide — Cover white
Zinc Sulfide
Lithopones
Zinc Oxides

Each pigment has specific properties and is useful for certain types of inks. These pigments are used by themselves as opaque white inks, cover whites, or mixing whites and also in combination with any of the color pigments to add opacity or to lighten the color.

Transparent pigments do not reflect light at the surface, but rather "transmit" light or allow the light to pass through the film of the ink and be reflected from the surface on which it is printed. Transparent pigments do not hide the background material to be seen through the film. Those commonly used in inks are listed below in order of decreasing transparency:[33]

Alumina Hydrate or "Hydrate"
Magnesium Carbonate or "Magnesia"
Calcium Carbonate
Blanc Fixe
Barytes
Clays

Transparent whites may also be used to reduce color strength of inks, to aid dispersion of some of the color pigments, to help "carry" some of the heavier pigments and to make the "tints." However, the most important function of a transparent pigment is to "extend" the ink and decreases the concentration of the more costly materials in the formula. Transparent pigments are also called "extender pigments."

Inorganic Color Pigments

This group covers pigments in which color is derived primarily from mineral components. All chrome colors are quite fast to light, quite opaque, and heavy in gravity. They are nonbleeding in most solvents, oils, greases, wax, etc., and have varying degrees of alkali and acid resistance.[34] Some chrome colors tend to darken on exposure to light and darken considerably on exposure to sulfur gases in the air. Examples of these inorganic color pigments are as follows:[35]

CHROME YELLOW — Produced in a number of shades, from the greenish shades, all the way to the orange. It is generally lead chromate, modified with other lead compounds, especially lead sulfate.

CHROME GREEN — Largely a mixture of chrome yellow with iron blue.

CHROME ORANGE and MOLYBDATE ORANGE — Modified lead compounds similar in structure to chrome yellow.

CADMIUM-MERCURY REDS — Among the newest additions to the pigment color field. They range from bright red to deep red.

VERMILION — A red mercury sulfide pigment, very heavy in gravity but also very brilliant and very opaque. It is useful where extreme hiding is essential and where resistance to sulfur is important.

IRON BLUE — Also made in a number of shades such as milori, bronze blue, Prussian blue and toning blue, it is actually a complex chemical compound of iron. Iron blues are light in gravity, are quite transparent; and, when used in full strength as dark blues, are very permanent to light. They have good acid resistance, do not bleed in solvents, grease, or wax, but most have poor alkali resistance.

EARTH COLORS — Actually mined as such as consist of ochre, sienna, umber, and so forth and are generally not used in printing inks except for special purposes. They are dull and "dirty" in color.

Metallic Powders

"Silver" powder is actually aluminum. "Gold" is generally a mixture of brass flakes, copper flakes, and other metals mixed to obtain varying shades of "gold" such as Rich Gold and Pale Gold. These metallic powders are available in many different grades and finenesses, and ink formulators select the one best suited to the job, stock, and printing process being used. Special vehicles are required also to make powders "leaf" properly, give maximum brillance, and bind properly to the surface.

Organic Color Pigments

Organic color pigments are the largest group used in printing inks.[36] They are classified by color rather than by chemical composition. Examples of these organic color pigments are as follows:[37]

YELLOWS — Consist mainly of Yellow Lakes, Hansa Yellow, and Dairylide Yellows.

YELLOW LAKES — Produced from several dyes and pigments of different hues. They are useful when yellow must be printed over darker colors, but not hide or cover them. They are usually very transparent and have varying degrees of permanency and resistance to bleed. (Lake pigments are usually transparent coloring substances produced from organic dyes by depositing the colors on one of the transparent white materials discussed earlier. They might be considered as dyed transparent whites usually alumina hydrate.)

HANSA YELLOWS — Strong, permanent, and resistant to many chemicals. They are produced in a variety of hues and are used frequently for strengthening the color of Chrome Yellows and where good permanency is required.

DIARYLIDE YELLOWS — Usually are not so fast to light as Hansa Yellows, but are more transparent. They differ as to transparency, permanency, and strength, and are used frequently for toning Chrome Yellows where extreme fastness to light is not required.

ORANGES — Most commonly used in printing inks are Persian Orange, a transparent lake pigment, generally not very fast to light. There are a number of orange toners, marketed under various names, each having specific properties as to permanency, transparency, and bleeding.

REDS — Range in shade from orange to deep maroon, from "dirty" reds such as light and dark Para Red to the very clean, brilliant reds used for three- and four-color process work. Transparency and permanency to light and resistance to bleeding are available in many of the shades. Here are a few of the more common types: (a) Para Reds, (b) Toluidines, and (c) Fire Reds.[38]

These reds are generally quite dirty in color or "undertone," but are fairly fast to light, semitransparent and find wide use in poster and label inks.

LITHOL REDS — Available in a variety of shades, from light lithol, almost an orange in color, to the very deep lithol maroon. In between these extremes are some very brilliant and deep shades that are used extensively in many kinds of inks where extreme permanency to light is not important.

PHLOXINE or EOSINE LAKES — Clean, brilliant reds with "purplish" or "bluish" undertones, not fast to light. Extensively used in the letterpress process for the printing of newspapers, magazines, folders, and books that are not normally exposed to light for long periods. They are seldom used with lithographic inks because they bleed in water.

RHODAMINE REDS — Have good light fastness, do not bleed in water, and are quite suitable for offset and letterpress process inks where permanency to light is required. They are more costly and are used only where their unusual color and other properties are required.

LAKE RED "C" — Often used for making the very brilliant orange shades or "warm reds," as the offset printer calls them. It is a most useful pigment, reasonably fast to light and quite transparent.

MADDER LAKES — Relatively "dirty" in color, but have unusual resistance to bleeding and good permanency to light.

It is interesting to note that the cleanest and most brilliant reds are not necessarily the most permanent. The cleaner the color and the more permanent the color, the more expensive it is.[39]

Blues are available in a wide variety of hues and properties:[40]

PEACOCK BLUE — Available in both "fugitive" and permanent varieties. The fugitive types have very poor permanency and often bleed in water. However, they are relatively inexpensive and are clean, brilliant, greenish shades of blue.

PHTHALOCYANINE BLUES — Possibly the most useful of the light blues or "greenish" shades, since they have excellent light fastness, are nonbleeding in almost all solvents, and have very good resistance to most chemicals. They are very clean, brilliant shades, available in a variety of hues; and, while very expensive per pound, their extreme color strength makes them economical for a wide range of uses.

Both the Peacock and Phthalocyanine blues are used as bases for color process work.[41]

VICTORIA BLUE — A clean "Royal Blue," fairly fast to light.

ALKALI BLUE — These are less permanent and not as brilliant as the Victoria Blues, but have generally greater tinctorial strength and are less expensive. They are especially useful for "toning" blacks, where high color strength and dark top-tone add density and strength to carbon blacks. Their blue color neutralizes the natural brown tone of most black pigments and actually adds "blackness."

PURPLES — Varying degrees of permanency. The most permanent colors are generally the most expensive. In this group are the magenta and cerise types, ranging between the process red shades and the true purples.

GREENS — "Fugitive"-type green lakes and permanent green toners are used to produce clean, brilliant shades of green. (A very useful green toner is the Phthalocyanine Green, which has all the good properties described for Phthalocyanine Blue.)

Most of the transparent organic pigments discussed at this point are made by long and complex chemical procedures from raw materials obtained from coal tar. They are often referred to as "Coal Tar Colors."[42]

Fluorescent Pigment Colors

Used in gravure, flexographic, letterpress, offset, and silk screen inks, they are much more expensive, are more difficult to handle, and require heavy films of ink or multiple impressions in order to be effective. Fluorescent pigments are available in a limited number of colors and cannot be mixed to produce intermediate shades without sacrificing brilliance. These inks are not very light-fast.[43]

Flushed Colors

In the normal course of pigment manufacture, the color is filtered from its suspension and then dried. However, many colors today are sold as "flushed colors."[44]

When a color is manufactured as a flushed color, the pigment is not dried after being filtered. The "press cake," as the pigment is called at this stage of its manufacture, contains from 30 to 80 percent water.[45] The press cake is mixed by kneading action with oil or varnish. The last traces of moisture are removed by vacuum and/or heat.

Flushed colors find their greatest use where the drying of the pigment results in the formation of hard and difficult-to-grind particles. In some cases, production is increased and manufacturing simplified by the use of flushed colors. Pigments are flushed in a wide range of vehicles, from mineral oil for news ink use, to litho oils and gloss ink varnishes.

Dyes

Dyes are used in printing inks because of their optical properties, i.e. transparency, high purity, and color strength.[46] Dyes are distinguished from pigments by their solubility in printing ink vehicles. They are used primarily as "toners." One example is Methyl Violet, which is frequently employed in publication black and news inks.

Addition Agents (Additives)

To impart unique characteristics to these inks, ingredients such as surface active agents, driers, starches, waxes, reducing oils, antioxidants, gums, and lubricants are utilized.[47]

Additives must be used with extreme caution in the pressroom. Compatibility of materials with that of the intended additive is absolutely essential. The following is a partial listing of the major usage of additives in the printing ink industry.[48]

SURFACE ACTIVE AGENTS — Used to assist the dispersion of pigments and better wetting. Their use must be carefully controlled, since each pigment-vehicle combination will behave differently — what is effective in one case may be harmful in another.

DRIERS — Driers act as catalysts to speed the oxidation and drying of the varnish. They are usually derivatives of cobalt, manganese, and lead. Compounds of zirconium, zinc, copper, and calcium may be used as well. In formulating printing inks, great care must be exercised in the selection of the type of drier and in the determination of the amount to be used. Each vehicle has its own drying characteristics.

STARCHES — Corn starch, for example, and other dry powders such as dry magnesia are used to prevent setoff and to "body up" an ink. Too much will cause fillup, piling, and/or caking.

WAXES — Waxes are used primarily to prevent setoff and sheet-sticking and to improve scuff resistance. The most commonly used waxes are beeswax, carnauba wax, microcrystalline, paraffin wax, ozokerite, and polyethylene.

The waxes will "shorten" an ink. Compounds are used to reduce the tack of an ink.

REDUCING OILS — Used to aid penetration and rapid setting. Often used much in the same way as the greases.

ANTIOXIDANTS OR ANTISKINNING AGENTS — Sometimes used to reduce skinning on the press, as well as to reduce excessive drying. Excess amounts will retard the ink from drying on the paper after printing.

Gums — These ingredients (Body Gum and Binding Varnish) assist in adding viscosity to an ink. They "pull" the ink together and help it to print sharply.

Lubricants — Petroleum jelly, cup grease, tallow, and wool-grease will reduce the tack of an ink and cause it to set quickly. They also assist in lubricating the ink so that it will distribute and transfer properly.

FORENSIC METHODS OF EXAMINATION OF PRINTING INKS

While addressing the 1979 INTERPOL meeting held in St. Cloud, France, BATF chemists concluded their presentation with some observations regarding the subject of printing inks.[49] At that time printing inks were acknowledged the least forensically known of the industrial inks. Unlike their counterparts in the writing ink industry, the printing inks industry was considered the most "flexible" when it concerned the following of rigid batch formulations.[50] Also, these printing inks relied upon the use of pigments as opposed to dyes, which are the mainstay of the other inks discussed in this textbook.

Printing inks and the paper surface on which they are printed lend themselves to trace elemental analysis for characterization; N. A. A. has made some positive contributions directed towards that end. A comprehensive report covering a six-year period through the early to late 1960s, funded by the Atomic Energy Commission,[51] found a wide variety of evidence materials through neutron activation analysis. Ink pigments and paper that was heavily inked (i.e. currency supplied by the United States Department of the Treasury) were subjected to N. A. A. methodology. The results of these studies indicated that certain key elements could be observed in pigments and papers, but not in sufficient quantities to discriminate between the papers and the inks utilized.[52]

The application of Energy Dispersive XRF, in an attempt to distinguish counterfeit inks in currency from authentic inks in use by the Bureau of Engraving and Printing, has demonstrated its inability to detect the trace metals found in that currency.[53]

Pyrolysis G. C. has demonstrated limited ability with printing inks; unfortunately the printing inks in question cannot be placed on the paper's surface for more than a period of twenty-four hours for the method to be effective.[54] On the other hand, Pyrolysis G. C. has worked reasonably well in the analysis of paper, as demonstrated by Browning.[55]

The application of High Performance Liquid Chromatography to the forensic characterization of offset printing inks is the most recent approach to the question of the identification of these inks. BATF chemist R. O. Keto recently applied H. P. L. C. techniques in an attempt to differentiate between soluble pigment components commonly found in black and green offset inks.[56] Although more research needs to be conducted in this area, results, at present, appear promising.

BATF is currently exploring a number of analytical techniques (AA, XRF, AE, etc.) in an attempt to shed additional light on the subject of the identification of printing inks.

A GLOSSARY OF GRAPHIC ART TERMS

The authors felt the necessity of including a limited glossary of graphic art terms aimed at those individuals who desire a better understanding of the terminology utilized within the printing ink industry. This glossary is, by no means, complete.

Acetone — A very active solvent used mainly in gravure inks. The fastest drying solvent in the ketone family.

Adhesion — The attachment of a material such as printing ink film to a solid surface.

Adsorption — The concentration of molecules of a particular kind at the interface between two phases such as the pigment and vehicle in printing inks. Adsorption can effectively remove a component such as the drier from an ink vehicle.

Alcohols — A family of organic solvents containing the grouping C-OH, used in flexographic and gravure inks. The most common members of this group are: Methyl (wood) alcohol, Ethyl (grain) alcohol, Propyl and Isopropyl alcohol.

Ambient Conditions — A term used to denote the temperature, pressure, etc., of the surrounding air.

Aniline Dye — Any of numerous organic dyes prepared from coal tar or its derivatives.

Antioxidants — Agents that retard the action of oxygen in drying oils and other substances subject to oxidation.

Antiskinning Agents — Chemical substances that retard the skin formation on the surface of an oxidizable oil or ink. They are frequently called **Antioxidants**.

Ball Mill — A type of dispersion equipment used in the production of certain types of printing ink. It consists of a rotating cylinder containing balls that cascade and disperse the pigment by impact and attrition as the cylinder revolves.

Base — A dispersion containing usually only one coloring matter, pigment, or dye, properly dispersed in a vehicle. This is subsequently used for mixing to produce the desired end product.

Binder — The components in an ink film that hold the pigment to the printed surface.

Bleach — Refers to the method of measuring the tinctorial strength of an ink or toner. Usually accomplished by mixing a small portion of the ink (or toner) with a large amount of white base and evaluating the tinctorial strength of the ink versus a control standard.

Bleed — **1.** The spreading or migration of an ink component into an unwanted area. **2.** The spreading or running of a pigment color by the action of a solvent.

Blister — Small raised area, caused by expansion of trapped gas or liquid beneath the surface.

Blushing — A milky or foggy appearance in a transparent ink or coating, due to precipitation or incompatibility of one of the ingredients. This effect is commonly caused by excessive moisture condensation and is most frequent in periods of high humidity.

Body — **1.** A general term referring to viscosity, consistency, and flow of a vehicle or ink. **2.** Used also to describe the increase in viscosity by polymerization of drying oils at high temperatures.

Capillary Action — A phenomenon associated with surface tension and contact angle. Examples are the rise of liquids in capillary tubes and the action of blotting paper and wicks.

Carbon Black — An intensely black, finely divided pigment obtained by burning natural gas or oil with a restricted air supply.

Casein — A protein usually obtained from milk. Used to make sizings, adhesive solutions, and coatings. Used as a binder in aqueous dispersions of pigments.

Centipoise — A unit of measure of viscosity. One hundred centipoises equal one poise.

Chalking — A condition of a printing ink in which the pigment is not properly bound to the paper and can be easily rubbed off as a powder.

Channel Black — Carbon black produced by impinging a natural gas flame against a metal surface. Because of air pollution control requirements, this type of black has been almost completely replaced by **Furnace Black** in the United States.

Cohesion — That form of attraction which causes the particles of a substance to become or be united throughout its mass.

Colorant — The color portion of an ink that may be a pigment or a dye or a combination of the two.

Color Strength — In printing ink, the effective concentration of coloring material per unit of volume.

Crocking — Smudging, or rubbing off, of ink.

Deflocculation — The dispersion of pigment clusters to smaller units in an ink.

This is the reverse of flocculation.

Densitometer — An instrument that measures the light reflected from a surface. It is used as a control instrument to check the uniformity of print color.

Diluent — A solvent that is added to reduce the viscosity. It need not always be a true solvent for the binder in the vehicle, but is effective in certain mixtures with a true solvent.

Dispersion — A uniform distribution of solid particles in a vehicle, generally obtained by mixing or milling.

Doubletone Ink — A type of printing ink that produces the effect of two-color printing with a single impression. These inks contain a soluble toner that bleeds out to produce a secondary color.

Driers — Substances added to inks to hasten their drying. They consist mainly of metallic salts, which exert a catalytic effect on the oxidation and polymerization of the oil vehicles employed.

Drying of Ink — The conversion of an ink film to a solid state. This can be accomplished by any of the following means, either singly or in combination: oxidation, evaporation, polymerization, penetration, gelation, precipitation.

Dyes — Coloring materials that are soluble in a vehicle or solvent as opposed to pigments that are insoluble.

Dye-pigments — Dyes that by nature are insoluble in water and can be used directly as pigments without any chemical transformation.

Emulsion — A mixture of two mutually insoluble liquids in which one liquid is finely distributed as droplets in the other.

Eosine — A fugitive organic dyestuff used to produce a brilliant red pigment for printing ink.

Extender — A transparent or semitransparent white pigment or a varnish that is used to alter the color strength and working properties of an ink, without affecting its hue.

Fading — The change of strength of color on exposure to light, heat, or other influences.

Feathering — A ragged or feather edge that shows at the edge of type or cuts. It may be caused by poor ink distribution, bad impression, excessive ink, or an ink not suitable for the paper.

Filler — Inert substance in a composition to increase the bulk and strength and/ or lower the cost.

Flash Point — The temperature at which the vapors of a solvent, oil, or vehicle will ignite or explode after applying a flame.

Flow — The property of ink causing it to level out as would a true liquid. Inks of poor flow are classed as short or buttery in body, while inks of good flow are said to be long.

Flushing — A method of transferring pigments from dispersions in oil by displacement of the water by oil. The resulting dispersions are known as flushed colors.

Fugitive Colors — Inks made from pigments or dyes that are not permanent and that change or lose color rapidly when exposed to light, heat, moisture, or other conditions.

Furnace Black — A form of carbon black obtained by decomposing natural gas and/or petroleum oil under controlled conditions in a furnace and precipitating the pigment in special chambers.

Ghosting — Presence of a faint image of a design, appearing in areas that are not intended to receive that portion of the image.

Gum — 1. In lithography, a water-soluble colloid such as gum arabic, cellulose gum, etc., used for coating a lithographic plate to make the nonimage areas ink-repellent and to preserve the plate for future use. 2. A general term referring to the resinous binders (usually of natural origin) that are used in the formulation of inks and varnishes.

Halo Effect — Piling up of ink at the edges of printed letters and dots. Also colored or sometimes uncolored areas adjacent to them, caused by the spread of colored or uncolored vehicles.

Hue — One of the attributes of color, which is determined by its dominant wavelength; more commonly referred to as shade.

Indelible Ink — An ink used on cloth to withstand laundering.

Inks, Cover — Cover inks are generally opaque and heavy bodied and have high pigment concentration.

Inks, Dull — Inks that dry with a dull or matte finish.

Inks, Halftone — Inks formulated for good reproduction of fine detail, such as half-tone dots on coated stock. They generally have high tinctorial strength and are finely dispersed.

Inks, Job — Heavy-bodied inks formulated to print on uncoated stock using small sheet-fed presses.

Ink Receptivity — That property of a sheet of paper (or other material) which causes it to accept and/or absorb ink.

Jet — Term used to describe the blackness or intensity of the masstone of black or near black surfaces.

Lampblack — A carbon black pigment prepared by the incomplete combustion of vegetable oils, petroleum, or asphalt materials. Used to achieve a dull, black ink.

Length — The property of an ink whereby it can be stretched out into a long thread without breaking. Long inks have good flow in the fountain.

Lithographic Inks — Inks used in the lithographic process. The principal characteristic of a good lithographic ink is its ability to resist excessive emulsification by the fountain solution.

Livering — An irreversible increase in the body of inks as a result of gelation or chemical change during storage.

Magnetic Inks — Inks made with pigments that can be magnetized after printing and the printed characters later recognized by electronic reading equipment.

Masstone — The reflected color of a bulk ink.

Metallic Inks — Inks composed of aluminum or bronze powders in varnish to produce gold or silver color effects.

Metamerism — A condition when colors match under one light source, but do not match under another light source.

Mileage — The surface area covered by a given quantity of ink or coating material.

Mineral Oil — Oils of petroleum origin consisting of high molecular weight hydrocarbons.

Moisture-set Inks — Inks that dry or set principally by precipitation. The vehicle consists of a water insoluble resin dissolved in a hygroscopic solvent. Drying occurs when the hygroscopic solvent has absorbed sufficient moisture either from the atmosphere, substrate, or external application to precipate the binder. An important characteristic of these inks is their low odor.

Nigrosine — Deep blue or black coal-tar dyestuff.

Non-scratch Inks — Inks that have high abrasion and mar-resistance when dry.

Ochre — Naturally occurring yellow iron oxide pigment.

Opacity — The ability of an ink to obliterate or hide the underlying surface by preventing the transmission of light or color through the ink film.

Optical Character Recognition Ink (OCR Inks) — Inks composed of lowest reflectant pigments, such as carbon black, read by optical scanners (OCR readers). Nonreadable inks, though visible to the human eye, cannot be read by OCR readers, because they present no reflectance contrast to the machine.

Overprint — The printing of one impression over another.

Penetration — The ability of a liquid (ink, varnish, or solvent) to be absorbed into the paper or other printing substrate.

Perfumed Ink — Regular printing ink to which a small percentage of concentrated perfume or scent has been added to impart a desired aroma or fragrance to the printed sheet.

Permanent Inks — Inks that do not readily fade or change color when exposed to light and weather.

Pigment — The fine solid particles used to give color to printing inks. They are substantially insoluble in the vehicle and in water.

Pinholing — Failure of a printed ink to form a completely continuous film. Visible in the form of small holes or voids in the printed area.

Pitch — A solid or semisolid material of an asphaltic nature used in ink to add flow or length.

Plasticizers — Liquid or solid additives used to improve flexibility.

Polar Solvents — Solvents with oxygen in their molecule, examples are water, alcohols, esters, ketones. They all posess a degree of conductivity that inhibits the static buildup characteristic of nonpolar solvents such as tolvol, xylol, and napthas.

Printing Ink — Any fluid or viscous composition of materials, used in printing, impressing, stamping, or transferring on paper or paperlike substances, wood, fabrics, plastics, films or metals, by the recognized mechanical reproductive processes employed in printing, publishing, and related services.

Process Inks — Process inks are those used in the modern method of reproducing illustrations by the halftone color separation process. The colors used are yellow, magenta (red), and cyan (blue); they are used with or without black.

Reducers — Varnishes, solvents, oils, or waxy or greasy compounds that are employed to reduce tack or consistency of the ink for use on the press.

Resin — A solid or semisolid organic substance used as a binder in printing ink vehicles.

Rosin — An oil obtained from the destructive distillation of rosin.

Safety Inks — Printing inks that will change color or bleed when ink eradicator or water is applied to prints. Also inks that will erase easily.

Shelf Life — The resistance to deterioration by oxygen and ozone in the air, by heat and light, or by internal chemical action.

Shortness — That property of a printing ink characterized by a lack of flow. Opposite of length.

Silk Screen Ink — Quick drying, full-bodied, volatile inks used in the silk screen printing process.

Silver Ink — A printing ink whose principal pigment consists of aluminum powder.

Size — **1.** The formation of a dried layer or the film so formed on the surface of a mass. **2.** An ink that dries with a sticky surface that will hold metallic or other powders.

Solvent — A material, usually a liquid, capable of dissolving another substance, usually a solid, to form a solution.

Stringiness — The property of an ink that causes it to draw into filaments or threads.

Substrate — The base material that is coated or printed.

Sympathetic Ink — A novelty ink that becomes visible only after one special treatment.

Tack — Tack is a relative measurement of the cohesion of an ink film responsible for its resistance to splitting between two rapidly separating surfaces.

Tensiometer — An instrument used to measure surface and interfacial tensions of liquids.

Thermosetting Ink — A thermosetting ink is one that polymerizes to a permanently solid and infusible state upon the application of heat.

Thixotropy — The property of a liquid or plastic material that involves a reversible decrease of viscosity as the material is agitated or worked. It is generally attributed to a loose structure of the dispersed solid particles, which breaks down under agitation. Also referred to as a shear thinning.

Tint — A very slight shade made by adding a small amount of color to an extender.

Toner — A highly concentrated pigment and/or dye, used to modify the hue or color strength of an ink.

Transparent Inks — Inks that lack hiding power and permit transmission of light, thus allowing previous printing or substrates to show through.

Undertone — The color of a thin film of ink as seen on a white background. The appearance of an ink when viewed by light transmitted through the film.

Vehicle — The liquid portion of an ink that holds and carries the pigment, provides workability and drying properties, and binds the pigment to the substrate after the ink has dried.

Viscometer — An instrument used to measure the viscosities of fluids.

Viscosity — That property of a material by virtue of which it tends to resist deformation or flow.

Washout Inks — Inks used on textiles that are easily removed by washing.

Water-based Inks — Inks containing a vehicle whose binder is water soluble or water dispersible.

Wax Set Ink — A printing ink designed to set and dry instantly upon immersion of the print in a bath of molten wax.

Wetting — Surrounding the pigment particles with varnish during the ink-making process. Pigments that wet out easily form better ink bodies and result in a finer dispersion.

Yield Value — A term describing the flow properties of a printing ink. The minimum force required to produce flow.

NOTES

1. C. Ellis, *Printing Inks: Their Chemistry and Technology* (New York, Reinhold Pub. Corp., 1940), p. 37.

2. *Encyclopedia Britannica* (London, E. B., Inc., W. Benton, Pub., 1967), Vol. 19, pp. 541-542.

3. F. B. Wiborg, *Printing Ink, A History* (New York and London, Harper Bros., 1926), p. 25.

4. See note 2 above.

5. See note 2 above, p. 30.

6. See note 2 above, p. 87.

7. See note 2 above, p. 88.

8. See note 2 above, p. 88.

9. *The Encyclopedia Americana*, International Ed. (New York, Americana Corp., 1972), Vol. 22, p. 591.

10. *Printing Ink Handbook,* 3rd ed. (New York, National Association of Printing Ink Manufacturers, Inc., 1976), pp. 5-8.

11. See note 10 above, pp. 9-10.

12. See note 10 above, pp. 21-23.

13. See note 10 above, pp. 21-23.

14. H. J. Wolfe, *Printing and Litho Inks,* 6th ed. (New York, MacNair-Donald Co., 1967), pp. 299-316.

15. See note 14 above, pp. 305-311.

16. See note 10 above, pp. 25-29.

17. See note 10 above, pp. 25-29.

18. See note 14 above, pp. 36, 337-344.

19. See note 14 above, pp. 36, 337-344.

20. See note 1 above, pp. 270-285.

21. See note 1 above, pp. 270-285.

22. See note 10 above, pp. 11-16.

23. See note 10 above, pp. 11-16.

24. See note 10 above, pp. 11-16.

25. See note 10 above, pp. 11-16.

26. C. A. Mitchell, *Inks: Their Composition and Manufacture,* 4th ed. (London, Chas. Griffin & Co., Lim., 1937), pp. 245-265.

27. See note 10 above, pp. 11-16.

28. See note 14 above, p. 187.

29. See note 10 above, pp. 12-16.

30. See note 1 above, pp. 145-453.

31. See note 10 above, p. 13.

32. See note 10 above, p. 13.

33. See note 14 above, pp. 101-132.

34. See note 10 above, pp. 13-14.

35. See note 14 above, pp. 133-185.

36. See note 10 above, pp. 14-16.

37. See note 10 above, pp. 14-16.

38. See note 10 above, pp. 14-16.

39. See note 10 above, pp. 14-16.

40. See note 10 above, pp. 14-16.

41. See note 10 above, pp. 14-16.

42. See note 10 above, pp. 14-16.

43. See note 10 above, pp. 14-16.

44. See note 10 above, pp. 14-16.

45. See note 10 above, pp. 14-16.

46. E. N. Abrahart, *Dyes and Their Intermediates,* 2nd ed. (London, E. Arnold Publ., Ltd.,

1977), pp. 210-228.

47. See note 14 above, pp. 251-257.

48. See note 10 above, p. 16.

49. R. L. Brunelle, A. A. Cantu, and A. H. Lyter, *Current Status of Ink Analysis.* Read before the INTERPOL Conference, St. Cloud, France, 1979, pp. 1-7.

50. See note 49 above.

51. U. S. Atomic Energy Commission and L.E.A.A. (U.S. Dept. of Justice), *Applications of Neutron Activation Analysis* (Oak Ridge, TN, U.S.A.E.C., 1970), 263 pages.

52. V. P. Guinn, "Applications of Neutron Activation Analysis in Scientific Crime Detection," U.S.A.E.C. Report GA — 7041 (General Dynamics Corp., 1963-64).

53. Private communication with L. A. Wolfe, U.S. Bureau of Engraving & Printing, Washington, D.C., 1981.

54. Private communication with A. A. Cantu, U.S. Bureau of Alcohol, Tobacco and Firearms, Rockville, MD, 1981.

55. B. L. Browning, *Analysis of Paper* (New York, Marcel Dekker, Inc., 1969), pp. 206-207.

56. R. O. Keyto, "Forensic Characterization of Printing Ink Pigments by High Pressure Liquid Chromatography." M.A. thesis, Antioch School of Law, Washington, D.C., 1981.

Suggested Readings and Resources

Apps, E. A.: *Printing Ink Technology.* New York, Chemical Pub. Co., Inc., 1959.

Apps, E. A.: *Ink Technology for Printers and Students.* London, Grampian Press Ltd., 1966.

Larsen, L. M.: *Industrial Printing Inks.* New York, Reinhold Pub. Co., 1962. The Printing Ink Research Institute, Lehigh University, Bethlehem, PA.

CHAPTER 6

TYPEWRITER RIBBON INKS

HISTORY

THE role of the typewriter as an instrument of immense importance to both commerce and correspondence cannot be overemphasized. The first recorded patent for a typewriter was granted to Henry Mill, a London engineer, in 1714. Mill's machine was, at best, very crude and cumbersome to use.[1]

The first United States patent for a typewriting machine was granted to W. A. Burt of Detroit, Michigan.[2] The most famous of the early patents was issued in 1868 to C. L. Sholes, C. Glidden, and S. W. Soule for a machine with understrike type bars that registered an impression beneath the platen. This was the forerunner of the so-called blind typewriter. An improved Sholes machine (1872) was promoted by James Densmore, who in 1873 negotiated a contract with Philo Remington of Ilion, N. Y., to manufacture it. The first Remington typewriter was offered to the public in 1874. The Remington machine was the first to feature the modern standard arrangement of keyboard characters.[3]

In spite of the fact that the famous American inventor Thomas Edison obtained the first patent for an electric typewriter (1872), it was the Blickensderfer typewriter company who introduced the first electrically operated model in the year 1908.[4]

The history of this machine has been the subject of boundless interest to countless students of varying disciplines. With the commercial success of the typewriter, document examiners began to view this instrument with mixed emotions. W. E. Hagan, in his work entitled, "A Treatise On Disputed Handwriting and The Determination of Genuine From Forged Signatures," comments on the role of the document examiner and that of typewriter identification.[5] Hagan's treatise, penned in 1894, is the first work of merit regarding the fields of questioned document examination and that of typewriter identification. Perhaps Hagan derived his ideas from Sir Arthur Conan Doyles' "A Case of Identity," which had graced the pages of the *Strand Magazine* some three years prior. The famous Baker Street consulting detective encountered the potential use of typewriting evidence: "I think of writing another little monograph some of these days on the typewriter and its relation to crime. It is a subject to which I have devoted some little attention. . . ."[6] It is interesting to note that Holmes/Doyle went on to observe: "It is a curious thing," remarked Holmes, "that a typewriter has really quite as much individuality as a man's handwriting. Unless they are quite new, no two of them write exactly alike. Some letters get more worn than others, and some wear only on one side. Now, you remark in this note of yours . . . that in every case there is some little slurring over the 'e,' and a slight defect in the tail of the 'r.' There are fourteen other characteristics, but those are the more obvious."[7]

After that brief, but necessary, regression to the history of the machine, let us direct our attention to the inks that impart the message from the keys to the page.

EARLY TYPEWRITER INKS

The subject of typewriter ribbon inks was given its first serious consideration by C. A. Mitchell: "The earliest inks used for typewriters were strong solutions of aniline dyestuffs in spirit or water, with an addition of glycerine to prevent the ink from drying too rapidly, and inks of this type are still on the market. . . . Glycerine also causes the ribbons to absorb moisture from the air, and thus alters the composition of the ink. To remedy this fault hot oleic acid is used as the solvent, and the ink diluted to require consistence with a mineral oil."[8]

Mitchell went on to comment "The tendency of the modern inks for typewriters is to approach more nearly to the type of printing inks — that is to say, insoluble pigments are used to a large extent. . . . The black pigments used are lamp-black and carbon blacks, whilst the mineral pigments used include Prussian blue for blue inks and antimony cinnabar (made by heating antimony sulphide in a current of air and steam) for red inks, since vermilion is too expensive."[9]

On the subject of typewriter ribbons, Mitchell observed the following:

> The fabrics used for the manufacture of typewriter ribbons were formerly made of silk, but are now composed of a fine-meshed cotton woven for the purpose and in such a way that the edges are not displaced by the blows of the type. . . . The principle used in the more modern processes is to attach a layer of the ink to each side of the ribbon. The apparatus used for the purpose comprises a series of rollers, through which the ribbons are made to pass in a continuous length. One of these rollers is coated with a film of the ink paste, which pressure of the second roller causes to adhere to one side of the ribbon, after which the other side is similarly coated with the ink.[10]

Harrison[11] observed that typewriter ribbons were made of varying combinations of silk, cotton, or rayon cloth, that had been impregnated with an ink. Harrison went on to note

An ink which is commonly employed consists of a slow-drying oil such as castor oil mixed with olein and an oil-soluble dyestuff. The choice of dyestuffs is limited and the light-resisting properties of the dyestuffs in common use leave a great deal to be desired. Where a greater degree of permanency is required, a "record" ribbon must be employed. This is loaded with carbon black and blue pigment whose function is to improve the rather brown tone of the carbon. Some of the carbon black-blue pigment mixture is transferred to the document from the ribbon and this gives a fair measure of permanency to the typescript. Blue record ribbon inks made use of Prussian Blue alone as to the colouring matter.[12]

MODERN METHODS OF ANALYSIS

Examiners of questioned or disputed documents are frequently asked to ascertain whether or not the text of a typewritten document has been altered by the use of either a different typewriter or the same typewriter at a later date. Analysis of the typewriter ribbon ink can (a) provide additional corroborative evidence that the questioned document is authentic, (b) provide that a different typewriter ribbon ink was used for subsequent alterations or additions, or (c) provide inconclusive results if the original typewritten entries and the questioned entries were made with the same type of ribbon, either on the same or a different typewriter.

No extensive research studies have been reported on the chemical analysis of typewriter inks; however, a few feasibility studies have been reported. Somerford reported that, by using a paper chromatographic technique, it was possible to analyze and compare the dyes in ribbon impressions.[13] Brown and Kirk described a reagent-type identification system used on fibers removed from the surface of the typewritten material.[14] They also experimented with horizontal, circular paper chromatography as well as electrophoresis for the comparison of typewriter ribbon inks. The *FBI Law Enforcement Bulletin* described a thin-layer chromatographic procedure for the comparison of typewriter ribbon inks; however, differentiation resulted in only 25 percent of the ribbons examined.[15] Tholl also experimented with thin-layer chromatographic technique and applied this procedure to the analysis of all major types of writing inks as well as typewriter inks.[16]

The year 1977 witnessed a study entitled, "Comparison of Typewriter Ribbon Inks by Thin-Layer Chromatography," conducted by the forensic chemists within the Scientific Services Division of the Bureau of Alcohol, Tobacco, and Firearms. Utilizing a procedure outlined earlier by Brunelle and Pro,[17] the typewritter ribbons were cut into 1 cm^2 pieces and placed into two-dram, screw-cap, disposable glass vials. Reagent-grade pyridine (3 ml) was added to each sample to extract the ink from the ribbons and allowed to remain for 30 min. to insure sufficient extraction.

One microlitre of the dissolved ink was spotted on a Merck precoated silica gel glass plate by using a $1\mu l$ disposable glass pipet. The ink spot was allowed to air-dry at room temperature for 15 min., and then each chromatographic plate was developed in covered glass tanks (8 by 8 by 3 in. or 20 by 20 by 8 cm) containing (A) ethyl acetate, ethanol, and water (70:35:30) and (B) *n*-butanol, ethanol, and water (50:10:15). The chromatographic plates were allowed to develop 30 min. in Solvent system A and 60 min. in Solvent B. After the plates were air-dried at room temperature, they were compared visually with ordinary white light and ultraviolet light.[18]

The thin-layer chromatography (TLC) procedure described is highly discriminatory for the various brands of typewriter ribbons. A wide variety of colors are available in typewriter ribbon inks, such as black, blue, red, green, purple, and brown. In most instances, typewriter ribbon inks of the same color produced by different manufacturers could be easily distinguished after running just one TLC with Solvent A. All inks of the same color from different manufacturers could be distinguished when two solvent systems were used. Either the inks have different dye and fluorescent components or the components are present in different concentrations. Chromatograms were run on different batches of the same formula ink produced by the same manufacturer. The results were inconsistent: some inks showed insignificant batch variations, while others showed dramatic differences from batch to batch.

An experiment was conducted to determine the effects of paper and ribbons on typewriter ink. Samples of the same pure liquid ink, ink dissolved from ribbons were analyzed by TLC and compared. Except for concentration differences, the results were the same. This finding indicates that paper and ribbons have no deterioration effect on the pure ink.

The results of this study reveal that TLC is a rapid, highly discriminatory technique for distinguishing typewriting inks. A meaningful comparison can be conducted with only one typewritten character and, in many instances, even less of a sample is required.

Excellent separation and resolution of dye components were achieved. More than 150 typewriter ribbon inks from several major manufacturers were analyzed and compared.* Typewriter inks manufactured by different companies could be readily distinguished by comparison of the dye components present or by the examination of the TLC plates under ultraviolet light. Also distinguishable were typewriter ribbon inks of different dye mixtures from the same manufacturer. It was not possible to identify the manufacturer of a typewriter ribbon ink. However, it was possible to prove that two or more typewritten entries contained different ink formulations.

If the inks are indistinguishable by TLC, then the typewriting was done with either the same ribbon or another ribbon that has the same ink formula-

---

*Allied Carbon and Ribbon Manufacturing Corp.; Phillips Process Co., Inc.; Curtis-Young Corp.; Burroughs Corp. (Fabric Ribbon Plant); Olivetti Corp.; Frye Copy Systems Inc.

tion. This study confirms that TLC analysis of typewriter ribbon inks provides an excellent investigative tool to the examiner of questioned documents.

NOTES

1. *Encyclopedia Americana* (Danbury, CN, Grolier Inc., 1981), Vol. 27, pp. 320-323.
2. See note 1 above.
3. See note 1 above.
4. See note 1 above.
5. D. A. Crown "Landmarks in Typewriting Identification," *Journal of Criminal Law, Criminology, and Police Science, 58*(1):107, 1967.
6. A. C. Doyle, *The Complete Adventures and Memoirs of Sherlock Holmes* (New York, Bramhall House, 1900), pp. 31-42.
7. See note 6 above.
8. C. A. Mitchell, *Inks: Their Composition and Manufacture* (London, C. Griffin & Co., 1937), pp. 346-349.
9. See note 8 above.
10. See note 8 above.
11. W. R. Harrison, *Suspect Documents — Their Scientific Examination* (London, Sweet & Maxwell Limited, 1966), p. 22.
12. See note 11 above.
13. A. W. Somerford, *Typewriter Ribbon Evidence.* Read before the 37th Annual Conference of the International Association for Identification. Havana, Cuba, Sept. 8-11, 1952.
14. C. L. Brown and P. L. Kirk, "Identification of Typewriter Ribbons," *Journal of Criminal Law, Criminology, and Police Science, 46*(6):882-885, 1956.
15. "A Scientific Look at Typewriter Ribbon Inks" (FBI Bulletin) (Washington, D.C., U.S. Govt Print Office, June 1965).
16. J. Tholl, "Applied Thin Layer Chromatograph In Document Examination," *Police, 1*:6-16, 1970.
17. R. L. Brunelle and M. J. Pro, "A Systematic Approach to Ink Identification," *Journal of the Association of Official Analytical Chemists, 55*:823-826, 1972.
18. R. L. Brunelle, J. F. Negri, A. A. Cantu, and A. H. Lyter, "Comparison of Typewriter Ribbon Inks by Thin-Layer Chromatography," *Journal of Forensic Sciences, 22*(4):807-814, 1977.

Suggested Readings

Adler, M. H.: *The Writing Machine — A History of the Typewriter.* Rowman, Co., 1973.
English, J. M.: Dye composition of typewriter inks as an indication of date of typing. *Journal of Police Science and Administration, 6*(1):74-76, 1978.
Hilton, O.: Identifying the typewriter ribbon used to write a letter — A case study employing new techniques. *Journal of Criminal Law, Criminology and Police Science, 63*(1):137-142, 1972.
Sang, J. L.: *A Classification System for Typewriter Ribbon Inks.* Presented at the 37th Annual Meeting of the American Society of Questioned Document Examiners, Rochester, New York, 1900.
Waters, C. E.: *Typewriter Ribbons and Carbon Papers.* (National Bureau of Standards, Circ. 431). Washington, D.C., U.S. Govt Print Office, 1941.

CHAPTER 7

ERASABLE INKS

HISTORY

THE conception of an erasable ink, developed for use in ball-point pens, is the most recent development in the history of that writing medium. Two giants in the writing instruments field; the Paper Mate Division of the Gillette Company and Scripto, Inc., found themselves in a battle for patent rights to this product. Gillette brought a civil suit against Scripto in attempt to enjoin Scripto from infringing the erasable ink patent held by their concerns and from marketing erasable ink pens, which Gillette believed involved the use of its trade secrets or confidential information.

Henry Pepper, chief chemist at the Paper Mate division of the Gillette Company, states that the idea of a rubber-based, erasable ink was conceived by himself in 1964. His idea of an erasable ink was scoffed at by the marketing specialists of that company; Pepper had been informed by these specialists, that if people wanted to erase what they wrote they would use a pencil.[1] Undaunted, Pepper was forced to wait twelve years to put his ideas of an erasable ink into practice.

The idea of an erasable ink proved to be an item of interest to another man. Doctor Phillip Daugherty, Director of Chemical Research of Anja Engineering Company (a subsidiary of Scripto, Inc.) formulated similar ideas regarding erasable inks. Doctor Daugherty has published in the field of the composition of various ball pen inks,[2] and he has gone on the record as stating that he conceived the idea of an erasable ink as early as 1963.[3]

The first United States Patent concerning this matter is dated 4/1/75 entitled, "ERASABLE WRITING MEDIUM SUITABLE FOR USE IN BALL POINT PENS." The inventors are listed as being Phillip M. Daugherty and Thomas E. Palmer, both affiliated with Scripto, Inc., of Atlanta, Georgia. This patent has been filed January 23, 1973.

The next patent pertaining to erasable inks is entitled, "BALLPOINT IN-

STRUMENTS WRITING WITH IMPROVED TRANSITORIALLY ERASABLE TRACE AND INK COMPOSITIONS THEREFOR," filed by Frank A. Muller and Henry Peper, Jr., both affiliated with the Gillette Company of Boston, Mass. The date in which this patent had been submitted is listed as 3/26/76.

The ensuing court struggle came to a climax in June of 1981. An agreement was reached by both companies on the settlement of their dispute. As part of the settlement, Gillette has granted a non-exclusive worldwide license under its erasable ink patents to Scripto and has taken an option for a non-exclusive, worldwide license under certain patents Scripto expects to obtain relating to erasable ink formulations.[4]

Doctor Phillip Daugherty, and Henry Peper have joined the ranks of those individuals who have made lasting marks in the continuing history of penmanship with their contributions of erasable inks. It should prove interesting to see what new wonders these two creative men will conceive in the future.

COMPOSITION

One of the novel concepts of this invention provides a ball-point instrument that combines the advantages of the extensively colored, easily visible, and permanent trace of ink with the erasability of a pencil trace for a limited time. Specific formulations are blended together to form the ink. The ink, due to its highly rubberish nature, is placed in a pressurized writing capsule. The pressurized gas (nitrogen) serves to push the ink onto the writing surface, partially volitized in such a way that the pigmented rubber cement is left sealed above the fibers on the paper.[5] It should be noted that this ink is approximately 100 times as thick as regular ball-point ink.[6] Pressurization of the capsule allows the mechanism to bypass atmospheric pressure thus permitting the instrument to write a consistent line regardless of the angle of approach.

The erasable ink pen comes equipped with a replaceable soft eraser on the top of the cap piece. The paper utilized by the writer determines the extent of the erasability of the ink. Surface finish or the porosity of the paper, the sizing and calendering, extent of the paper's cotton content are but a few of the variables that enhance or detract from this inks erasability. Generally speaking, the higher the cotton content, the better calendered, the less porous the paper is, the better the ink will live up to its expectancy. This is not to suggest that the ink will fail unless given ideal writing surfaces, but it will effect perfect erasability and the ink's permanence.[7]

It must be noted that this ink did not reach the marketplace until 1979. Therefore, any documents prior to that year that contain this ink would suggest fraud on the part of the individual in question.

PATENT INFORMATON

United States Patent #3,875,105

A U.S. Patent was issued to Daugherty et al., on April 1, 1975, entitled, "ERASABLE WRITING MEDIUM SUITABLE FOR USE IN BALL POINT PENS"; the assignee of this patent being Scripto, Inc., Atlanta, Ga.[8] The official abstract for the aforementioned patent number is as follows:

An erasable writing medium suitable for use in ball point pens comprising a discontinuous phase comprising a solid colorant and a homogeneous continuous phase including a matrix material having cohesive properties exceeding its property to adhere to the substratum being written upon, as well as various components for converting the phases into a writing medium. Upon being dispersed onto the writing surface, the matrix material precipitates from the continuous phase and entraps the colorant thereinto, thus preventing the colorant from penetrating the pores of the writing surface and also preventing the colorant from affixing itself to the solid members of the writing surface. A colored layer is thus formed on the writing surface which is easily removable without damage to the surface.

An example comprising both the components and the percentages involved with this "erasable writing medium" is also listed within the patent granted to Daugherty et al.

COMPONENT	%
Functional	
GANTREZ RESIN M556	28.0
Toluene	28.0
CYANBLUE BNF 55-3750 Pigment	11.3
Miscellaneous	
QUADROL	14.1
SARKOSYL "O"	3.6
Mineral Oil	3.6
DOWANOL EPH	11.4

United States Patent #4,097,290

On June 27, 1978, F. A. Muller and H. Pepper, were granted a patent entitled, "BALL-POINT INSTRUMENTS WRITING WITH IMPROVED TRANSITORIALLY ERASABLE TRACE AND INK COMPOSITIONS THEREFORE"; the assignee of this patent being the Gillette Company, Boston, Mass.[9] The official abstract for patent #4,097,290 is as follows:

The invention relates to a ball-point writing instrument capable of writing with an intense colored or black line which is easily visible and readable and as permanent and eventually non-erasable as the best customary ball-pen traces, but which, is easily erasable by mechanical means for an initial period of about two to four hours as a normal graphite pencil trace, without the use of bleaches or chemicals. These properties are attained by the provision of a novel ink composition containing stated rubbers and volatile solvents which control erasability.

An example of both the components and the preferred percentages involved with this patent is also listed within the patent granted to Muller et al.

COMPONENTS	%	Preferred %
Rubber Molecular weight 750,000	15-45	27
Low-boiling solvent (B.P. below ab. 180° C)	15-45	29
High-boiling solvent (B.P. above ab. 300° C)	15-35	22
Pigment (Dry basis)	12-30	18
Solid lubricant	2-8	4

The following tabulation presented typical formulations for erasable inks for use in writing instruments having a ball point:

	BLACK 839-41A	BLACK 814-96A	RED 814-92C	GREEN 839-41	BLUE 839-26C
Natural Rubber	22.5%	26.0%	29.0%	22.5%	22.5%
Aliphatic Diluent #6	23.5			23.5	23.5
Aliphatic Solvent 360-66		17.0			
V M & P Naphtha		14.9	29.0		
Terphenyl HB 40)	30.0	26.0			
DOP				33.5	27.0
Mineral Oil			27.0		
Pigment	20.0	17.0	15.0	16.5	23.0
Stearic #	4.0			4.0	4.0
Lauric Acid					
Erasability	Good	Good	Better	Better	Better

Explanatory:

Natural Pale Crepe Rubber Milled and Masticated to Average Mol. Weight of About 400,000 to 750,000

Aliphatic Diluent #6	Dist. Range	94° to 104° C = 100% Evap.	2.3 Min.
Solvent 360-66	Dist. Range	154° to 173° C = Evap. 42.1	
V M & P Naphtha	Dist. Range	121° to 139° C = Evap. 8.3	
Terphenyl (HB 40)	Boiling	345° to 396° C = Evap.	
DOP	Boiling Pt.	386.9° C	
Black	Pigment	839-41A Carbon Black	

			0.08. Micron
Black	"	814-96A	Graphite
			(2-5 Micron)
Green	"	839-41	Phthalocyanine Green
			0.015 Micron
Blue	"	829-26C	Phthalocyanine Blue
			0.015 Micron
			Victoria Blue 10.5%
			0.025 Micron
Red	"	814-92C	Organic Red 0.015
			Micron Suspended in Mineral Oil
			(35% Pigment Dry Basis)

FORENSIC METHODS OF IDENTIFICATION

Although classified as ball-point inks, the erasable inks do not readily lend themselves to standard laboratory procedures.

Ultraviolet examination has shown that the erasable inks do not fluoresce under either the long- or short-wave frequencies. When attempting to determine the relative transmittance or absorbance properties of this ink, by viewing through an infrared image conversion microscope (or equivalent), the examiner will note that this ink will not exhibit infrared fluorescence characteristics.

Standard TLC procedures, utilizing solvent system I (see Chapter 8), can give a separation of color(s) depending on the extracting solvents. Pyridine, according to the authors, gives a separation, while Flynn[10] claims it does not; Flynn asserts that acetone will provide an adequate separation. With pyridine extraction the authors see no thin layer chromatographic difference between the black and blue inks from Gillette and Scripto, but there is a discernible difference between the inks. Normal thin layer chromatographic dye separation will not always provide the necessary answers as to the nature of the ink; this is due, in part, to the coloring matter within the erasable ink. Another related consideration is the amount of pigment incorporated within each formula; United States Patent #4,097,290 describes the pigment content (dry basis) as ranging from 12 to 30 percent of each formula, with the "preferred" range being in the neighborhood of 18 percent. Flynn elected to attempt such analytical techniques as emission spectroscopy and pyrolysis gas chromatography on the basis of the aforementioned pigment content within erasable ink formulations; running blue and black inks in the emission spectrograph showed that these two inks had identical spectra . . . both showing spectral lines indicating the presence of copper and molybdenum in concentrations of about 3 to 1.

Characterized as being of a highly rubberish nature, this pigmented rubber cement lent itself to pyrolysis gas chromatography. P. G. C. has shown that these inks contain a complex polymer that did resemble pyrograms akin to some rubber cements.[11] To date, this area of forensic examination has been confined to a small number of examiners.[12,13]

In 1982, Fisher Pen Company introduced yet another erasable ball-point pen, known as the "Erase-It." This appears to be similar in writing and erasing characteristics to the previously mentioned ones. The TLC separations of both the blue and black ink are definitely different from the corresponding inks made by Scripto and Gillette. Basically pyridine does not extract the Fisher inks very well: what does extract does not separate readily in the case of the blue inks and not at all for the black inks.[14]

NOTES

1. M. C. Lynch, − − −, *The Wall Street Journal,* Sept. 29, 1980, p. 3.
2. P. M. Daugherty, "Composition of Ball Pen Inks" (Unpublished Manuscript, 1970).
3. Personal communication with P. M. Daugherty, Sept., 1981.
4. Writing Instrument Manufacturers Association, Incorporated, bulletin, June, 1981.
5. U.S. Patent No. 3,875, 105, granted to Daugherty et al., April 1, 1975.
6. See note 5 above.
7. J. C. Ransom, "The Erasable Ink Pen — History and Analysis" (Unpublished material, 1980).
8. See note 5 above.
9. U.S. Patent No. 4,097,290, granted to Muller et al., June 27, 1978.
10. W. J. Flynn, "Paper Mate's New Ink Pen" (Unpublished manuscript, 1979).
11. See note 10 above.
12. See note 7 above.
13. See note 10 above.
14. Personal communication with A. A. Cantu, Nov., 1982.

CHAPTER 8

THE FORENSIC EXAMINATION OF INKS

HISTORICAL DEVELOPMENT OF METHODS OF INK ANALYSIS

SINCE the beginning of the field of questioned document examination, document examiners have searched for new and better ways to detect fraudulent documents. Traditional methods such as handwriting analysis, watermark identification, typewriting and other business machine identification, obliterated and indented writing, deciphering and determination of the sequence of writings have often been successful for the detection of fraud. These techniques are used routinely for this purpose by the modern day examiner of questioned documents. New methods for detection of fraudulent documents developed slowly up to about 1950 because (a) document examiners traditionally would not consider any test that would alter the original condition of a document, (b) document examiners, with few exceptions, did not have the necessary scientific backgrounds to consider chemical and physical analysis of inks and paper, and (c) chemical and physical examination of inks and paper cause some, although slight, destruction to a questioned document.

Prior to 1950, inks on questioned documents were examined by observing the color under various wavelengths of light ranging from the ultraviolent to infrared. These techniques were sometimes supplemented with photography using selected filters. Occasionally, a courageous document examiner would conduct spot tests on inks to detect metals such as iron, copper, vanadium and chromium in fountain pen inks. These procedures were sometimes useful to distinguish among different types of inks; however, these tests did not provide individualizing information to characterize the various ink formulations.

By about 1950, document examiners gradually began to experiment with the examination of inks on questioned documents. In July 1951, Linton Godown[1] presented a paper at the annual meeting of the American Society of Questioned Document Examiners in which he first proposed the use of disk or thin layer chromatography for the examination of fluid inks. Subsequently, in

104

1952, Somerford and Souder[2] experimented with paper chromatography for the comparison of fluid ink. These works showed that only a micro quantity of ink was necessary for the examination and that destruction to the questioned document was minimal and insignificant. In 1952, Brackett and Bradford[3] also reported on the same topic.

By 1952 ball-pen inks began to appear on the market in large quantities. Brown and Kirk[4] showed that electrophoresis could be used to separate dye components of ball-pen inks and thereby provide a means for the comparison of different inks. They also compared electrophoresis with paper chromatography and reported that electrophoresis was more effective for the separation of many dye components in ink. Following these studies, many papers were reported that compared the relative effectiveness of paper chromatography and electrophoresis.

Crown et al.[5] reported in 1961 on a chemical spot testing procedure that could distinguish specific dyestuff constitutents in ball-pen inks. The studies of Godown,[6] Dick,[7] and Von Bremen[8] on IR luminescence, use of dichroic filters, and ultraviolet photographic techniques, respectively, also should be recognized for their developments in the field of ink comparisons.

Nakamura and Shimoda[9] reported in 1965 on the use of TLC on ball-point inks on a micro scale using TLC plates prepared from microscope slides. Using a solvent system of *n*-butanol, ethanol, and water (50:10:15 parts, respectively,) they were able to separate methyl violet into four separate spots, which represented the various isomers of pararosaniline.

In 1966, Tholl[10] applied thin layer chromatography to ink analysis and reported TLC could be used effectively for the separation of dyes as well as other components of inks. TLC was found to be well suited to the examination of very small quantities (micrograms) of ball-pen inks.

Prior to about 1966, ink examinations were limited to the development of new methods for the comparison of questioned and known ink samples. Very little attention was given to the determination of the origin of questioned inks or to determine the age of inks. The dating of inks was limited to the determination of periods of time when gross changes were made in the compositions of ink, such as the change from oil-based solvents to glycol bases in ball-pen inks. Knowledge of these changes provided a date prior to which the glycol ball-pen inks did not exist.

One of the earliest workers to identify inks for the purpose of dating was Werner Hofmann of the Zurich Cantonal Police, Zurich, Switzerland.[11] He collected ball-pen ink standards from a number of different manufacturers. These standards were used to match inks on questioned documents; the questioned inks were dated by referring to the first production dates of the specific matching standard formulations. Hofman used paper chromatography and TLC with various solvent systems, spectrophotometry, spot tests, and the usual nondestructive tests to aid in the comparison and matching of questioned and known inks.

In the mid 1960s, the Bureau of Alcohol, Tobacco and Firearms (ATF) Department of the Treasury, recognized the need for a more systematic approach to ink analysis and the dating of inks on questioned documents. This work was needed to supplement some of the existing methods of dating documents, such as dating watermarks and typewriter typeface designs.

The need for new and better methods to detect fraud has continuously been expressed by various agencies, primarily within the Treasury Department and the Criminal Tax Division of the Justice Department. For example, agents of the Intelligence Division of the Internal Revenue Service need to know not only who signed a particular document, but when the document was prepared or signed. It is not uncommon for dishonest taxpayers to backdate a receipt or series of records to substantiate tax claims on their income tax returns. Often documents are created or altered after an investigation begins in an attempt to conceal taxable income, which in some cases involves sizable sums.

Firearms records are often created or altered after the start of an investigation of a suspected firearms dealer. Since certain types of weapons, such as machine guns, grenades, and sawed-off shotguns, must be registered with ATF, proof of their legal registration must be presented.

The Justice Department has a need to detect fraud in many organized crime cases because it is often very difficult to associate a suspect with the particular offense except by the detection of fraud through document analysis. The Securities and Exchange Commission (SEC) is frequently concerned with fraud in the illegal manipulation of the stock market. Many of their cases involve the analysis of hundreds of documents, which may typically show the creation and dissolution of companies and the sale of unregistered stock for the financial gain of a few greedy people at the expense of the unknowing stockholders.

It is obvious that thousands of spurious documents are passed daily to government and other agencies and, after traditional methods fail to detect fraud, only the application of chemical and physical methods of analysis remain.

EVOLUTION OF THE BATF INK EXAMINATION PROGRAM

The ink examination and dating program originated in 1968 in the forensic laboratory when it was a section within the Internal Revenue Service (IRS) in Washington, D.C. The IRS expressed a strong need to be able to detect backdated documents submitted to auditors and tax investigators by taxpayers to support claims on tax returns. IRS investigators needed to know when these documents were prepared. Were the documents prepared prior to the investigation when they should have been? Or, were the documents prepared after the investigation commenced and then backdated?

Because determination of the date of preparation of a document was a very important problem to the IRS, Richard Brunelle, then forensic chemist in the IRS laboratory, decided to research the problem to explore ways to date documents.[12-15]

First, all traditional methods commonly used by document examiners were evaluated. There are basically three techniques that had been commonly used by document examiners to date the preparation of documents: (a) watermarks, (b) changes in typewriting styles, and (c) detection of a class of ink on a document at a time when the particular ink found did not exist.

All three of these classical methods are occasionally successful to detect backdated documents; however, these techniques are of limited value because (a) watermark designs do not change very often (except for coded watermarks), (b) typewriting typeface styles have become very similar from one manufacturer to another and often the changes are so minor they are difficult to detect, and (c) the ability to date documents by finding the presence of a particular type of ink is seldom useful because new classes of ink are not developed very often. For example, since the first century only about five classes of writing ink have been introduced; carbon, fountain, ball-point, fiber or porous tip, and rolling ball markers.

Because of the limitations of the above classical, nondestructive methods for dating documents, Brunelle explored the applications of ink analysis to the dating of documents. This approach had been used prior to 1968 by the Swiss on a limited basis. Werner Hofmann with the Zurich Cantonal Police Laboratory experimented with TLC and made comparisons of questioned inks with a limited collection of standards.

TLC proved effective for comparison and differentiation of inks; however, very little work had been accomplished in the dating of inks by TLC or any other method prior to 1965. Brunelle concluded from preliminary research that (a) inks manufactured by different companies could be readily distinguished using TLC, (b) quality control in the manufacture of inks was excellent and that there was very little variation in formulas from batch to batch, (c) ink manufacturers kept accurate records on their various formulations and dates of production, and (d) the ink manufacturing industry demonstrated a willingness to cooperate with ATF by supplying samples of standard ink formulations and their corresponding first dates of production.

As a result of this preliminary research, Brunelle decided to establish a standard ink reference file (Standard Ink Library) at ATF in 1968. Every writing ink manufacturer in the United States was requested to supply samples of every different ink formulation they made and also samples of older formulations made prior to 1968 that they had on hand. Also requested was the corresponding first date of production of each formulation.

The cooperation received from the ink industry was outstanding; and, within one year, the Standard Ink Library contained over 2,000 ink standards consisting of primarily ball-point, fountain pen, and fiber tip pen inks. The purpose of the Standard Ink Library was to date inks on questioned documents by matching questioned inks with standards having "known" first production dates. For example, if a questioned ink on a document dated 1975 matches a standard first manufactured in 1978, then it can be concluded that the ink entry was made some time in 1978 or after.

In this new and unique approach to the dating of writing inks, the identification of ink formulations on questioned documents depends on the maintenance of a complete up-to-date standard ink library. The actual identification is made by comparing the characteristics resulting from the analysis of questioned ink with the corresponding results obtained from known standard inks in the library. Clearly, the larger the number of characteristics that match, the higher the degree of certainty of the identification.

Knowledge of this new approach to the dating of inks quickly spread throughout the United States; and, by 1975, several hundred ink dating cases were examined at ATF for numerous government agencies. The demand for ink dating examinations in document fraud cases was growing at a rapid rate.

The ATF Standard Ink Library now consists of over 4,000 ink standards from ink manufacturers throughout the world. A systematic ink sampling program with the various ink manufacturers has been in effect since 1968, and new formulations have been submitted to ATF on a routine basis since that time (see Fig. 8-1).

Although the ink library approach has been and remains the primary method for the dating of inks, further research was performed at ATF between 1973 and 1975 by Brunelle and Antonio A. Cantu, forensic chemists employed by the Forensic Science Branch. This research led to the development and implementation of an ink tagging program in 1975. On a voluntary basis, ink manufacturers began adding tags to their inks during the manufacturing process. By changing the tag annually, it is possible to determine the exact year ink on a questioned document was manufactured by identification of the tag. Approximately, 40 percent of all writing inks manufactured in the United States now contain taggants.

The significance of this research was important because the tags provide a simulated formulation change every year, which greatly increases the chances of detecting an ink on a document that was not in existence at the time the document was dated. Without frequent formulation changes, the ink library method becomes less helpful in the detection of backdating fraud.

In 1979, another major breakthrough was made at ATF. Cantu developed a laboratory procedure to determine the relative age of inks on documents.[16] It was determined that there is a relationship between the age of ball-point pen ink and the rate at which the ink can be extracted from paper into an organic solvent. The longer an ink has been written on a document, the drier it becomes and the slower it will extract. Conversely, the newer the ink, the faster it extracts. By comparison of the extraction rates of questioned inks with ink of

Figure 8-1. The Bureau of Alcohol, Tobacco and Firearms' Standard Ink Library.

known dates, it is possible to determine which ink was written first. When sufficient inks with known dates on a document exist covering a span of years, it becomes possible to closely estimate how long the questioned entry has been written.

Research on the dating of inks at ATF is a continuing process and the lab is recognized internationally as the world's leader in this field.

BACKGROUND

The analysis of writing inks on questioned documents presents special problems that are not incurred during the analysis of bulk samples of liquid ink. The major problem is the limited amount of ink sample available for analysis on questioned documents. Sufficient quantity of ink must be removed from the document for examination; however, the samples removed must not destroy the legibility of the writing. For example, when the ink to be examined is limited to a person's signature, only approximately 0.5 μg of ink can be sampled without affecting the legibility of the writing. The number and types of examination performed is proportional to the amount of ink writing available. For the above reasons, physical, nondestructive tests are usually conducted prior to chemical examinations.

Forensic ink examinations are normally conducted for two reasons: (1) to compare two or more ink entries on questioned documents to determine whether the inks are the same or different (this would be done, for example, to determine whether a check, receipt, or ledger had been altered prior to or during an investigation; and (2) to determine the age of ink on a questioned document to predict when a particular entry was written. This type of examination has become routine in many types of fraud investigations such as medical malpractice, estate settlements, income tax evasion, and any time the date of preparation of a document or sample of writing is in question.

The examination of inks for comparison purposes is relatively straight forward and can be performed by anyone properly trained in techniques of analysis involved, knowledge of ink formulations, and interpretation of results obtained from the analyses. Dating of inks is much more complicated; and, for this reason, the dating of inks will be dealt with in-depth in the following chapter.

The following procedures are usually conducted in the order presented when the object of the examination is the comparison of inks to determine if the inks are the same or different. The purpose of these tests is to develop as many points of comparison as possible between questioned and known inks so that the conclusion reached at the completion of all examinations can be stated with a high degree of scientific certainty.

PHYSICAL EXAMINATION

Color

Make a close visual examination of the color of the inks being compared and classify according to shade (blue, blue-violet, dark blue, etc.).

Type of Ink

Examine the ink writing visually with and without the aid of magnification (10X to 100X). Determine the type of ink used (ball-point, porous tip, fountain, rolling ball marker, etc.).

Ball-point pen inks are relatively easy to recognize due to the frequent appearance of ink deposits (gooping) and striations caused by the ball of a ball-point pen.

Great caution must be exercised to identify the specific type of non-ball-point ink. The writing strokes of non-ball-point inks such as porous plastic tip pens, fountain pens and rolling ball marker inks are quite similar and considerable experience is required to distinguish among these and other non-ball-point inks.

The types of writing ink are generally classified as

1. Ball-point Inks (glycol or oil-based)
2. Fluid Inks
   a. water-based — i.e. fountain pen, rolling ball markers, fiber or felt tip, extruded plastic tip
   b. solvent-based — i.e., broad tip markers, laundry markers, glass or other nonporous surfacemarkers

Ultraviolet Examination

Observe the ink writing on the document using both long- and shortwave ultraviolet light and note both the fluorescence and color of the fluorescence. Except for a few fountain pen inks and some red-colored inks, most inks do not fluoresce under ultraviolet light.

Visual Infrared Examinations

TRANSMITTANCE OR ABSORBANCE — Determine the relative transmittance or absorbance properties of the ink by viewing through an infrared image conversion microscope or equivalent. Certain inks will transmit or absorb infrared light depending on the presence or absence of graphite, carbon, or pigmented dyes in the ink. If the ink absorbs infrared light, the ink entry will appear dark black when viewed under the infrared image conversion microscope, whereas an ink that transmits or reflects infrared light will essentially become invisible.

Infrared Luminescence

Determine the IR luminescence properties of the ink by viewing the ink with infrared light using a blue-green filter (copper sulfate). Inks that have luminescent properties will appear bright white, and inks that do not luminesce will appear black. *Caution*: Although, in general, inks with different luminescent properties can be said to be different inks, extreme caution must be exercised before reaching this conclusion. Ink from the same pen will occasionally show different luminescence properties due to (a) non-uniform paper, which causes localized diffusion of luminescent components, and (b) hand perspiration or other exogenous agents that can cause selective diffusion.

CHEMICAL EXAMINATION

Solubility Tests

Using a 5 μl disposable pipet, determine the relative solubility of the ink by treating a minute area of ink writing with pyridine, methanol, and ethanol-water mixture (1 + 1). (Use a portion of writing that won't interfere with the legibility of writing such as a beginning or end stroke.) Normally, all ball-point inks will dissolve in pyridine. Water-based fluid inks will dissolve in ethanol, methanol, or ethanol-water (1 + 1). Solvent-based fluid inks will generally dissolve in pyridine.

Ink Sampling Procedures

Chemical examination requires removal of small portions of ink from the questioned document. Four slightly different methods have been used for this purpose.

SCALPEL METHOD — Using a sharp, clean-bladed scalpel, cut along the ink line to obtain a total of about one-half inch of ink line. This method is generally used when the writing surface is hard or thick such as cardboard or book covers.

BLUNTED 16 to 20 GAUGE HYPODERMIC NEEDLE METHOD — Using a rubber pad as support to the document, carefully punch, but do not completely remove about eight to ten micro plugs of ink on paper. Turn the document over and pull out the plugs with fine needle-nose tweezers.

HOLLOW 16 to 20 GAUGE HYPODERMIC NEEDLE WITH PLUNGER METHOD — The point of the hypodermic needle is clipped using wire clippers, and a small file is used to turn the clipped point into a boring device similar to a micro cork borer. Take this boring device and press down on the ink writing using a hard cardboard type material as a support. A plug of ink and paper will move into the micro borer, which is removed simply by the hypodermic needle plunger.

This procedure provides the most uniform sample of ink and is considered to be the method of choice in terms of minimum destruction to the document and the overall neatness of the procedure. Eight to ten micro discs are removed for examination.

MICRO SAMPLING PROCEDURE — When it is necessary to only obtain one or two micro discs or plugs by the procedures described previously, because only a minimun amount of ink writing is available for examination (a single number or letter, for example), it is desirable to use a micro sampling procedure. Take one or two micro discs using the hollow needle method and place in a 1 dram V-shaped vial. Add 1 to 5 μl of extracting solvent using a 10 μl pipet, and suck and blow out the solvent into the vial with the pipet until all of the ink has dissolved from the fibers of the paper. Then suck up the remaining solvent into the 10μl pipet for spotting on a TLC plate. This procedure concentrates the small amount of ink in a minimum volume of solvent and allows for a TLC examination to be conducted with extremely small quantities of ink.

A similar procedure involves placing one micro disc of ink directly on a TLC plate and eluting the ink from the paper fibers directly at the origin of the TLC plate.

One important precaution must be taken regardless of the procedure used for removing samples of ink from the document for subsequent chemical examination. Caution must be taken to insure that only the ink of interest is removed. Occasionally ink writing appears on both sides of the document and if the examiner is not careful, the desired sample is removed with some other ink on the back side of the document. This can be prevented by turning the document over after removal of each microdisc of ink to be certain unwanted ink was not penetrated or removed by the micro boring device or other instrument used.

THIN LAYER CHROMATOGRAPHIC EXAMINATION (TLC)

TLC is a rapid technique for the separation of the organic components of ink and enables an easy comparison of the visual ingredients (dyes) in the various ink formulations. The distance that a compound travels in a given period of time using a particular solvent system and chromatographic medium relative to the distance the solvent front travels is defined as the Rf value. This value varies with the chemical properties of compounds and therefore is useful for identification of dyes and other organic ingredients in writing inks. If two or more inks contain dyes and other compounds with the same Rf values using two different solvent systems and separating media, then it is virtually certain the inks are the same formulation.

TLC is inexpensive to use, fast, requires very little sample, and highly discriminating, which makes this technique the one most commonly used for the comparison of inks. One TLC examination can be conducted in about fifteen minutes using approximately 0.1 μg of ink. The technique can distinguish quantitative as well as qualitative differences in inks, and less than $50.00 worth of equipment is required for the examination.

Depending on the amount of ink available for analysis, up to three different TLC examinations may be necessary to distinguish minute differences in similar ink formulations. Considerable experience is required for the interpretation of results of TLC examinations. Knowledge of the significance of small variations in TLC patterns, ink manufacturing practices, the extent of batch variations, reproducibility of chromatographic plates, the effect of ambient conditions on ink, and other factors have to be taken into consideration prior to reaching any conclusions regarding whether the inks being compared are the same or different formulations.

The following is a step-by-step procedure that has been used effectively by the Forensic Science Branch of the Bureau of Alcohol, Tobacco, and Firearms.

TLC Procedure for Comparison and Matching
Questioned and Standard Inks

Reagents and Equipment

1. Eastman chromogram sheets 8″ × 8″ (silica gel without flourescent indicator)
2. Merck precoated glass plates (silica gel without flourescent indicator)
3. Reagent grade pyridine, methanol, ethanol, ethyl acetate, *n*-butanol, and distilled water
4. 10 *µ*l disposable micropipets
5. 1 dram glass screw cap vials
6. TLC glass developing tank with air-tight cover to accommodate 8″ × 8″ chromatogram
7. U.V. — visible spectrophotometer (with attachment for scanning TLC plates)

Procedure

Using the ink sampling procedure previously determined appropriate for the amount of ink available, place eight to ten micro discs of ink from the written line into a 1 dram glass vial. Treat a control sample of paper from the questioned document in the same manner. Add one drop, or about 10 *µ*l, of the solvent found to be the most suitable to dissolve the ink (usually pyridine for ball-point ink). Allow fifteen minutes to completely dissolve.

Note and record the color of the ink in solution and then spot on an Eastman chromatograph sheet 15mm from one end of the sheet using a 10 *µ*l micropipet (see Fig. 8-2). Allow spot to dry before respotting. Fascilitate drying with a stream of hot air, but avoid prolonged exposure to extreme heat or light. Repeat spotting until all solution is exhausted. Up to ten different ink samples can be analyzed simultaneously on the same chromatogram by spotting each ink about three-fourths inches apart. After the spotted ink is dry, place the chromatogram in the developing tank which has been previously equilibrated for fifteen minutes with 100 ml of solvent system (see Fig. 8-3). Allow the chromatogram to develop thirty minutes, then remove from the tank and allow to dry. Record the Rf values as observed under visible and ultraviolet light. Account for any components that are contributed by the paper (usually flourescent). The length of time to leave the plate in the tank is not critical as long as maximum separation is achieved and all questioned and known samples are treated the same. Often only fifteen minutes is required (see Color Plate I-1 and I-2).

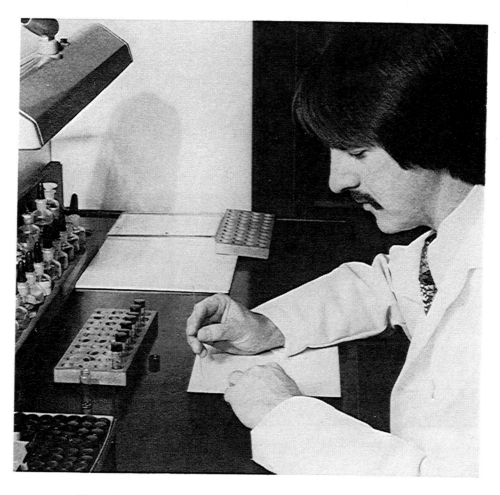

Figure 8-2. Spotting Ink Samples on a Thin Layer Chromatogram.

Compare the thin-layer chromatograms (TLC) of the questioned inks with TLC's of standard writing inks of the same type and color. Inks that have qualitatively different dye compositions can be readily distinguished.

To distinguish qualitatively similar inks, prepare additional TLC using Merck plates and solvent system I (see Color Plate I-3). It may be necessary to remove additional samples of ink from the document. Spot questioned and similar standard inks on the same chromatogram plate. Spots should be equal or nearly equal color intensity. Develop the spotted plate for about thirty minutes. Visually compare the separated color components, recording Rf values, color, and relative concentrations of the dye components. Examine the developed plates under ultraviolet light and record the presence, color, and Rf values of any detected flourescent components (see Color Plate I-4).

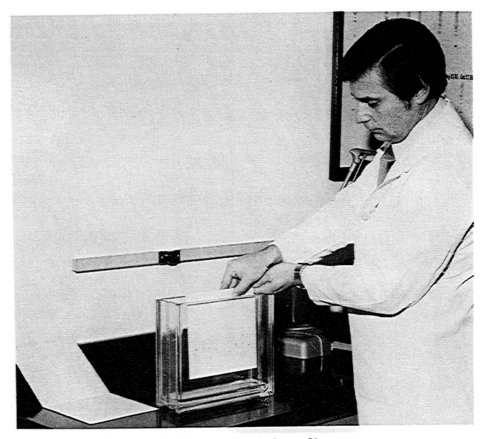

Figure 8-3. Development of Thin Layer Chromatogram.

Table 8-I

SOLVENT	PROPORTION
System I	
Ethyl acetate	70
Absolute ethanol	35
Distilled water	30
System II	
n-Butanol	50
Ethanol	10
Distilled water	15

If all but one standard ink has not been eliminated at this point, prepare one more TLC using Merck plates and solvent system II. Spot questioned and known inks on the same plate and repeat the foregoing procedure (see Color Plate I-5).

-1. TLC comparison of black ball-pen inks (East-nan Plate/Solvent System I).

I-2. TLC comparison of blue ball-pen inks (Eastman Plate/Solvent System I).

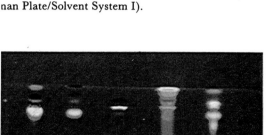

-3. TLC separated ultraviolet fluorescent compo-nents in ball-pen inks (Merck Plate/Solvent System).

I-4. TLC comparison of black ball-pen inks (Merck Plate/Solvent System I).

I-5. TLC comparison of black ball-pen inks (Merck Plate/Solvent System II).

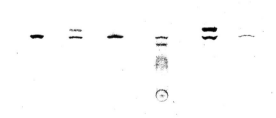

I-6. Comparison of TLC results for black ball-pen inks: *Left* — Merck Plate/Solvent System IV; *Right* — Merck Plate/Solvent System I.

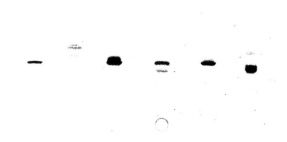

I-7. TLC comparison of blue and black porous-tip inks (Merck Plate/Solvent System I).

I-8. TLC comparison of blue and black fountain-pen inks (Merck Plate/Solvent System I).

SPECTROPHOTOMETRY

The procedures described previously are usually sufficient to eliminate all but one of the standard inks. If more information is needed to distinguish them, the Merck plates containing the separated dye components of the questioned and known inks are scanned on a spectrophotometer equipped with an attachment for scanning spots on TLC plates. This allows for a more accurate determination of the relative dye concentrations (see Fig. 8-4).

Each blue ink is usually scanned in the visible region at 550 mm, with a zenon light source. The percent transmission of light through each separate dye component is recorded and the relative amount of each dye present with respect to the other is calculated. The wave length chosen for scanning varies according to the color of the ink and depends on which dyes are present.

OTHER INK EXAMINATIONS

Whenever sufficient ink is available for examination further analysis can lead to the identification of a component that may provide further evidence that the questioned and known inks are the same. For example, there are a variety of fatty acids, resins, preservatives, and viscosity adjustors added to inks that sometimes can be detected by TLC, GLC, or HPLC when these components are present in adequate quantities. Also, amorphous carbon and graphite, which are common dispersion ingredients in ball-point inks can be distinguished using electron diffraction methods. Writing inks also frequently contain flourescent materials that enable these inks to be distinguished from each other and identified spectrophotoflourometrically. Recent research involves the use of high pressure liquid chromatography (HPLC).[17] Preliminary research indicates that this methodology is even more discriminating and sensitive than TLC, especially for invisible ink components (see Fig. 8-5).

SPECIAL PURPOSE SOLVENT SYSTEMS FOR TLC

Occasionally effective resolution of certain ink dye components requires the use of special solvent systems. For example, inks that contain low polarity dye components require less polar solvent systems. Otherwise all of the dyes travel together and end up at the solvent front. Solvent System III shown in Table 8-II has proven effective for the separation of low polarity dye components or components that travel to the solvent front using Solvent System I and II.

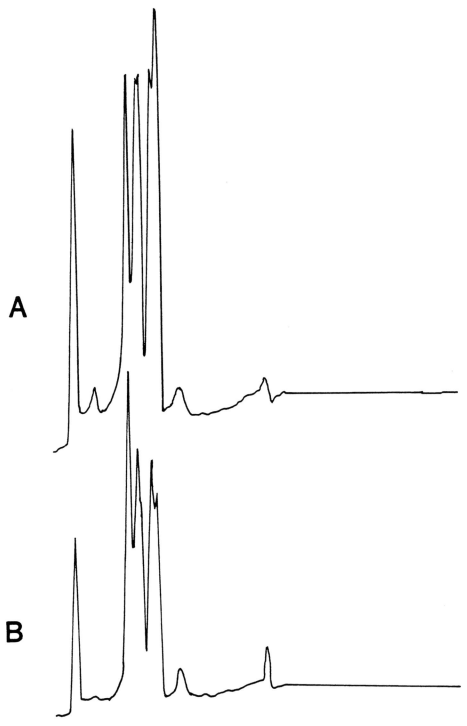

Figure 8-4. Densitometric Comparison of Ball-point Inks with Same Dye Components, but in Different Concentrations

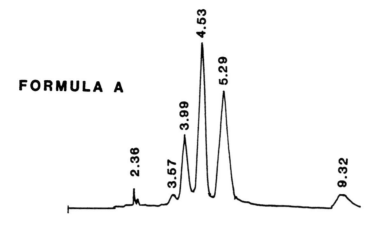

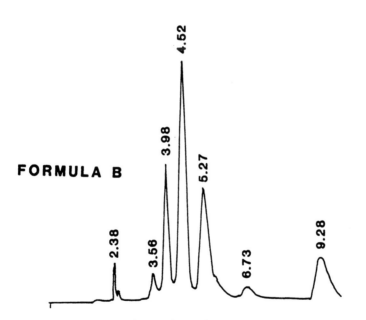

Figure 8-5. HPLC Comparison of Two Similar Ball-point Inks.

Nigrosine black ballpoint inks also frequently require the use of a solvent system different from Solvent System I, II, and III.

Solvent System IV (shown in Table 8-III) works effectively on inks containing nigrosine dyes (see Color Plate I-8).

Table 8-II

SOLVENT	PROPORTION
System III	
Cyclohexane	10
Chlorobenzene	2
Ethanol	1

Table 8-III

SOLVENT	PROPORTION
System IV	
Ethyl acetate	2
Ethanol	1
Chlorobenzene	10
Methanol	1

Another all purpose solvent system similar to Solvent Systems I and II developed by Jerry Kelly[18] can also be used for very effective resolution dye components in most inks. It is a 2 phase system and is made as shown in Table 8-IV.

Table 8-IV

SOLVENT	PROPORTION
System V	
Water	32
Acetic Acid	17
N-Butanol	41
Butyl Acetate	10

This mixture separates into two phases and the top phase is used as the solvent system.

COMPARISON OF TYPEWRITER CARBON AND INK IMPRESSIONS

Carbon paper is covered on one side with a thin coating of a mixture of waxes, oils, carbon, and dyes in various proportions. Even black colored carbon paper usually contains dyes in addition to carbon.

Carbon paper may be divided into two categories: (a) single-use carbons, consisting of one-time and book carbons, and (b) multiple-use carbons, which consist of typewriter carbons and pen/pencil carbons. Variations in the formulations are determined by the intended use for the carbon paper. For instance, pencil carbon waxes are much softer than typewriter waxes and react to a rubbing pressure rather than to the sharp blow of a typewriter.

These formulations may either be applied as a hot melt wax or in a solvent system. The hot melt wax is manufactured by taking a hot wax ink mixture and applying it in an even coat over various weights of kraft tissue. Solvent carbon is an innovation that provides increased life and greater legibility over the hot melt application. In this manufacturing process, several types of resins, solvents, and inks are combined to form a slurry. An extremely even layer of the slurry is coated on paper or a polymeric film, and the excess solvent is driven off. The spongelike surface acts as a liquid ink reservoir compared to the hot melt type where the surface is a solid wax. In the solvent-type carbon, as the carbon paper is used, the ink surface is gradually replenished by drawing liquid ink from the unused areas of the carbon. In the case of hot melt wax, as the carbon paper is used, a piece of the applied coating is transferred to the copy sheet and depleted. Solvent carbons are much cleaner than wax carbons because the coating remains with the paper or film backing.

Typewriter carbon paper and ribbon impressions contain dyes that are amenable to analysis by TLC. Studies show TLC to be very effective for the comparison of typewritten carbon[19] and ribbon impressions.[20] A successful comparison can be performed with as little as one typewritten lower-case letter.

Differentiation of these impressions can be used to detect altered typewritten documents and additions to previously typed material: impressions such as often found on wills, contracts, and corporate records.

NOTES

1. Godown, *Differentiation and Identification of Writing Inks by Chromatographic Analysis.* Read before the Annual Meeting of the American Society of Questioned Document Examiners, Rochester, New York, 1951.
2. A. W. Somerford and W. Souder, "Comparison of Writing Inks by Paper Chromatography," *Journal of Criminal Law, Criminology and Police Science, 43*(1):124-127, 1952.
3. J. W. Brackett and L. W. Bradford, "Comparison of Ink Writing on Documents by Means of Paper Chromatography," *Journal of Criminal Law, Criminology and Police Science, 43*(4):530-539, 1952.
4. C. Brown and P. L. Kirk, "Horizontal Paper Chromatography in the Identification of Ball Point Inks," *Journal of Criminal Law, Criminology and Police Science, 54*(3):334-339, 1954.
5. D. A. Crown, J. V. Conway and P. L. Kirk, "Differentiation of Blue Ballpoint Pen Inks," *Journal of Criminal Law, Criminology and Police Science, 52*(3):338-343, 1961.

6. L. Godown, "New Nondestructive Document Testing Methods," *Journal of Criminal Law, Criminology and Police Science, 55*(2):284-285, 1964.

7. R. M. Dick, "Application of Dichoric Filters to Ink Differentiation Problems," *Journal of Forensic Sciences, 15*(3):354-363, 1970.

8. U. Von Bremen, "Invisible Ultra-Violet Flourescence," *Journal of Forensic Sciences, 10*(3):368-375, 1965.

9. G. R. Nakamura and S. C. Shimoda, "Examination of Micro-Quantity of Ball Point Inks from Documents by Thin-Layer Chromatography," *Journal of Criminal Law, Criminology and Police Science, 56*(1):113-118, 1900.

10. J. Tholl, "Thin-Layer Chromatography Techniques Utilizing the Eastman Chromagram Sheet and Developing Apparatus," *Police Magazine, 2*(55):7-15, 1966.

11. W. Hofmann, *The Dating of Documents (with Particular Reference to Documents Written with Ballpoint pens* (Unpublished material, 1969).

12. R. L. Brunelle and M. J. Pro, "A Systematic Approach to Ink Identification," *Journal of the Association of Official Analytical Chemists, 55*:823-826, 1972.

13. R. L. Brunelle and A. A. Cantu, "Ink Analysis — A Weapon Against Crime by Detection of Fraud," American Chemical Society Symposium Series, *Forensic Science,* No. 13, 1975, pp. 134-141.

14. J. D. Kelly and A. A. Cantu, "Proposed Standard Methods for Ink Identification," *Journal of the Association of Official Analytical Chemists, 58*(1):122-125, 1975.

15. D. A. Crown, R. L. Brunelle and A. A. Cantu, "Parameters of Ballpen Ink Examination," *Journal of Forensic Sciences, 21*(4):917-922, 1976.

16. A. A. Cantu, *On the Relative Aging of Inks.* Read before the Eastern Analytical Symposium (1979), the American Academy of Forensic Sciences (1980), and the American Society of Questioned Document Examiners (1980).

17. A. H. Lyter, "Examination of Ball Pen Ink by High Pressure Liquid Chromatography (HPLC)." In I. Lurie, *Forensic Science* (in press).

18. See note 14 above.

19. R. L. Brunelle, J. F. Negri, A. A. Cantu, and A. H. Lyter, "Comparison of Typewriter Ribbon Inks by Thin-Layer Chromatography," *Journal of Forensic Sciences, 22*(4):807-814, 1977.

20. See note 19 above.

Suggested Readings

Bobbitt, J. M.: *Thin-Layer Chromatography.* New York, Reinhold Pub., Corp., 1963.

Coldwell, B. B. L. The comparison of inks & writings by paper chromatography. *Analyst, 80*:68-72, 1955.

Doud, D.: Chromatographic analysis of inks. *Journal of Forensic Sciences, 3*:486, 1958.

Godown, L.: *Report on Experiments on Examination of Ink by Electrophoresis.* Read before the American Society of Questioned Document Examiners, 1956.

Gordon, A. H., and Eastoe, J. R.: *Practical Chromatographic Techniques.* New York, Van Nostrand Co., Inc., 1964.

Gould, D. E., and MacCormack, T. A.: Ink for ball point pens. *American Ink Maker, 29*:37, 1951.

Hamman, B. L.: Nondestructive spectrophotometric identificaiton of inks and dyes on paper. *Journal of Forensic Sciences,* May:544-556, 1968.

Harrison, W. R.: *Suspect Documents — Their Scientific Examination.* London, Sweet and Maxwell, 1958.

Lederer, E.: *Chromatography.* New York, Reinhold Pub., Corp., 1957.

Lindsly, C. H., and Casey, R. S.: Behavior of ball point pens and inks as seen by a principal manufacturer. *Journal of the American Bar Association, 34*(5):376, 1948.

MacDonell, H. L.: Characterization of fountain pen inks by porous glass chromatography and electorphoresis. *Journal of Criminal Law, Criminology, and Police Science, 53*(4):507-521, 1962.

McBay, A. J.: Chromatographic methods of analysis applied to forensic problems. *Journal of Forensic Sciences, 3*:364-369, 1958.

Martin, E.: Chromatographic micro-analysis of dried ink. *International Criminology and Police Review, 81*:232-238, 1954.

Martin, E.: Identification of ballpoint pen inks. *International Criminology and Police Review, 114*:18, 1958.

Mathyer, J.: Comparison of inks by paper chromatography — Practical method. *International Criminology and Police Review, 148*:130-143, 1961.

Mitchell, C. A.: *Inks — Their Composition and Manufacture.* London, Chas. Griffin & Co., 1916.

Mitchell, C. A.: *Documents and Their Scientific Examination.* London, Chas. Griffin & Co., 1935.

Mitchell, C. A.: *Inks — Their Composition and Manufacture.* New York, Lippincott, 1937.

Packard, R. J.: Selective wavelength examination applied to ink differentiation problems. *Journal of Forensic Sciences, 9*(1):544-556, 1968.

Peifer, J. J.: Rapid and simplified method of analysis by thin-layer chromatography using microchromatoplates. *Microchemica Acta, 3*:529, 1962.

Pougheon, S., and Moloster, Z.: Identification of fluid and ballpen inks by paper chromatography. *Revue Internationale de Criminologie et Police Technique, 12*(3):207, 1958.

Raja, P. S., Banerjee, R. C., and Iyengar, N. K.: *Comparison of Inks by Paper Chromatography.* Read before the Annual Meeting of the American Academy of Forensic Sciences, Chicago, IL, Feb. 27-29, 1964, pp. 268-285.

Sannie, C., and Moloster, Z.: Research on the analysis of the ink of manuscript documents. *Revue de Criminologie et Police Technique, 6*(2):1-17, 1952.

Souder, W.: Composition, properties and behavior of ball pens and inks. *Journal of Criminal Law, Criminology and Police Science, 45*(6):743, 1956.

Stahl, E.: *Thin-Layer Chromatography.* New York and London, Academic Press, Inc., 1965.

Stein, E. W., and Hilton, O.: Questions raised by examiners of signatures and documents. *Journal of the American Bar Association, 34*(5):373-76, 1948.

Thompson, J. W.: The identification of inks by electrophoresis. *Journal of Forensic Sciences,* —:194-203, 1967.

Truter, E. V.: *Thin-Film Chromatography.* New York, Interscience Pub., J. E. Wiley & Sons, 1963.

Waters, C. E.: *Inks,* National Bureau of Standards circ. C 426. Washington, D.C., U.S. Govt Print Office, 1940.

Witte, A. H.: The examination and identification of inks. In *Methods of Forensic Science,* Vol. II. New York, Interscience Pub., 1963, pp. 35-75.

CHAPTER 9

THE DATING OF INKS

INTRODUCTION

DATING ink in a precise sense is not possible in that there is no way to determine exactly when a particular ink entry was written. It is possible, however, using the previously described comparative analysis procedures (Chapter 8) to determine the date the ink was first manufactured. Once a questioned ink can be matched with one and only one standard ink from a standard ink library, then all that is required is to determine from company records the date that particular ink was first manufactured. The reliability of this determination depends on the completeness of the ink reference standards, the accuracy of ink company records and the discrimination/capability of the analytical technique.

An improvement was made to this method of dating inks between 1971 and 1978 when several ink manufacturers began voluntarily tagging their inks during the manufacturing process. Research on the development of suitable tags and detection techniques was developed by chemists at the Bureau of Alcohol, Tobacco, and Firearms, and the tagging was begun at the request of BATF. This approach to the dating of inks has proven to be a valuable additional aid in the detection of fraudulent, back-dated documents. Since the development of these ink dating techniques, many federal agencies have made use of ATF's program.

Prior to the tagging program the success of proving back-dating fraud required the finding of an ink that was not in existence at the time the document was dated or allegedly prepared. The tagging program allows inks to be dated to the exact year of manufacture because the tags are changed annually. This process greatly improved the chances of proving fraud.

All attempts made by researchers to determine the actual date writing was made on a particular document have failed to be reliable. The reason for this is that any change that occurs in the ink on paper is related to the conditions under which the document is stored, since light, temperature, humidity, handling, and other factors all have an effect on the ink. Since the history of a questioned document can be rarely proven, the dating of ink by measurement of deterioration is impractical.

Recent research at the Bureau of Alcohol, Tobacco and Firearms has led to the development of a technique to determine the relative age of inks on a questioned document.[1] This method is based on the fact that the longer an ink has been on the surface of paper, the drier it becomes, and the slower it extracts into a solvent. The evaporation of low volatile components, the polymerization and/or oxidation of resins, and surface interactions all effect the "setting" of the ink and also the speed and extent at which an ink will dissolve in a chosen solvent.

For example, if two entries on the same document are written with the same formula ink but at different times, the ink written last will extract more and faster than the earlier entry. This is a valuable and reliable tool for the detection of altered documents. This method can be extended to estimate the absolute aging of inks by comparison of the extractibility of the questioned ink with standard inks of known age.

To measure the relative age of inks, solvents such as water, ethanol, pyridine, and methanol, in various proportions, are used to extract a small quantity of ink; and, ideally, measurements are made with a spectrophotometer at various times until complete extraction occurs. The optical density is ploted versus time to obtain the extraction versus time curve. Inks of the same formula but entered at different times on the same document will have different extraction curves.

The following sections of this chapter discuss the three basic approaches to the dating of inks on questioned documents.

DATING BY COMPARISON WITH STANDARDS

This method of ink dating requires complete cooperation from the ink manufacturing industry to obtain the ink standards and corresponding records of the first dates of manufacture of the various ink formulations. Brunelle et al., developed the world's largest collection of ink standards at the Bureau of ATF's Forensic Science Branch in Rockville, Maryland. (ATF Standard Ink Library). This library now contains over 4,000 different standards of ink obtained from both domestic and foreign manufacturers. These standards consist primarily of writing inks such as ball-point, porous tip, rolling ball markers, fountain pen ink, etc.

This method of dating has been used at BATF since 1968 and remains the primary method used for the detection of back-dated ink entries on questioned documents. Extensive research 2-5 and experience in the analysis of thousands of inks at ATF indicate (with few exceptions) that inks manufactured by different companies consist of different combinations of ingredients. The quality control is normally strictly controlled by the various manufacturers and their ink formulations change due to (a) changes in availability in raw materials, (b) the introduction of new writing tips, which may necessitate a new compatable ink, and (c) basic improvements of the ink's writing quality. Other reasons include economic and competative considerations.

The premise behind the ink standards approach to ink dating is that everytime a new formulation of ink is introduced commercially a date exists prior to which that particular formulation of ink did not exist. For example, an ink first manufactured in 1981 which appears on a document dated 1975 is evidence that the entry was back dated.

Standard Ink Library

The standard ink reference collection must be as complete as possible so that all pertinent standards are available for comparison with questioned inks. In addition to the standards, company records on the first production dates of each formulation must be obtained. As indicated earlier it is necessary to have the cooperation of the ink manufacturing industry to obtain the standards and first production dates.

An alternative to this method of establishing an Standard Ink Reference File is to systematically purchase inks from retail stores on a routine basis. This procedure is expensive and also requires that examiners detect any formulation changes by their own chemical anaylsis. Once the formulation change is detected, the first production date can then be confirmed with the appropriate ink manufacturer.

Once the Standard Ink Reference File is obtained, it is desirable to first categorize the inks according to their physical and nondestructive nature, color, type, and response to UV and IR examinations. Then Eastman TLC chromatograms should be prepared for each standard using solvent system I (given in the previous chapter). Once all of the standards have been examined by TLC, the chromatograms can be further categorized according to similarity in formulations and dates of first production. Before examining any standard inks, the inks should be smeared or written on Whatman filter paper and allowed to dry so that questioned and known inks are both examined from paper in a dry state. Eastman chromatograms are used for the standard reference inks because they produce a less complicated chromatogram, which facilitates comparisons of questioned and known chromatograms. Once inks in the Standard Reference collection have been found that are similar to the questioned ink, then plates with better resolving power (such as Merck plates) are used until only one standard matches the questioned ink.

The value of the Standard Ink Reference File method for dating inks is proportional to the frequency that ink formulations change. For example, if an ink company first produced an ink formulation in 1962 and this formulation did not change until 1980, then if this ink was found on a questioned document dated 1978, all you could determine is that the entry could have written any-time between 1962 and 1980. Fortunately, in most cases, changes are made more frequently than this because of changes in sources of raw materials and the other reasons previously mentioned.

Procedures for Dating Using Standard Ink Reference File

Basically the same procedure is used as described in Chapter 8 for the com-parison of inks. Once all of the physical and nondestructive tests are per-formed, questioned ink samples are removed from the document, dissolved, and prepared for TLC, as described in Chapter 8.

Develop TLC chromatograms in the sequence shown in Table 9-I or until the questioned ink matches only one standard ink.

Table 9-I

SEQUENCE OF TLC EXAMINATIONS

1. Eastman plate	Solvent system I
*2. Eastman plate	Solvent system I
*3. Merck plate	Solven system I
*4. Merck plate	Solvent system II
*5. Merck plate	Specialty systems

*Questioned and known inks on the same plate.

STEP 1 — The first TLC using the Eastman plate and solvent system I will serve to eliminate all but a few (3-9) standards in most instances. In a few in-stances where the questioned ink is a very unique formula, there may only be one or two possibilities of match at this stage of analysis.

STEP 2 — The questioned ink is spotted together with all of the similar stan-dards and developed again using solvent system I and Eastman TLC plates.

STEP 3 — Spot the questioned ink and all similar standards on a Merck plate and develop using solvent system I. This step will usually eliminate all but two or three standards because the Merck plates produce excellent resolution of the visible and invisible organic components.

STEP 4 — Spot the questioned ink and all remaining similar standards on a Merck plate and develop using solvent system II. Usually all but one standard ink will be eliminated at this stage of examination.

STEP 5 — If the questioned ink is one that contains nigrosine dyes, or causes many of the dyes to travel to the solvent front, then run another TLC using

Merck plates and solvent system III or IV.

STEP 6 — If two or more similar standards cannot be eliminated by steps 1 through 5 (this is very rare), then determine the relative concentrations of the dye components on the TLC plates using a densitometer equipped to scan TLC plates. This procedure will detect minor concentration variations in the dye components.

STEP 7 — If the questioned ink contains ultraviolet fluorescent components, these can be compared with the fluorescent components in the standard inks using spectrophotofluorimetry and measuring the excitation and emmission wavelengths.

The steps 1 through 7 can be performed with as little as ten to twenty micro discs removed from the questioned document.

Interpretation of Match Between Questioned and Standard Ink

Once all but one standard has been eliminated, it can be concluded with a high degree of scientific certainty that the questioned ink is the same formula ink as the standard it matched. This conclusion is based on the fact that research and experience has demonstrated that manufacturers either have seldom attempted to or have seldom tried to exactly duplicate each others formulas. In fourteen years of experience, BATF has found but a few inks produced by different manufacturers to be identical.

The only time a perfect match is not possible is if the standard is missing from the Standard Reference Collection or another formula produced by the same manufacturer is so similar it cannot be distinguished. An example would be a slight change in the amount of a resin present in the formulation. Also, if the questioned ink has experienced extensive fading, it may not be possible to match it with a standard.

It is not possible to determine whether two or more ink entries were written with the same pen, because many different pens can contain the same formula of ink. Pens with different brand names can contain the same ink formula because some ink manufacturers sell ink to pen companies all over the world. All that is being matched by this entire procedure is the formula of ink; however, this is sufficient to determine the date a particular ink could have been available to write on a document. No determination regarding when the writing was made is possible, only the date prior to which the entry could not have been made.

DATING BY DETECTION OF TAGS

Beginning in 1975 several ink manufacturers volunteered to assist the ATF Ink Dating Program by adding chemical tags to the inks during the manufacturing process. The tags are changed annually; as a result, this procedure allows the exact year of production of the ink to be determined.

Although the tagging code is confidential information, the tags consist primarily of rare earth compounds in various combinations. The tags are treated chemically with a host material to form a phosphor that can be analyzed and identified using an X-ray excited optical fluorescence spectrometer (XREOF) (see Fig. 9-1).

XREOF is a very sensitive technique for the detection and quantitative determination of rare earth materials. X-rays are used to excite the host molecules of the phosphor. There follows a transfer of energy, to rare earth ions that have highly selective line emissions.[6] In actual practice for the detection of

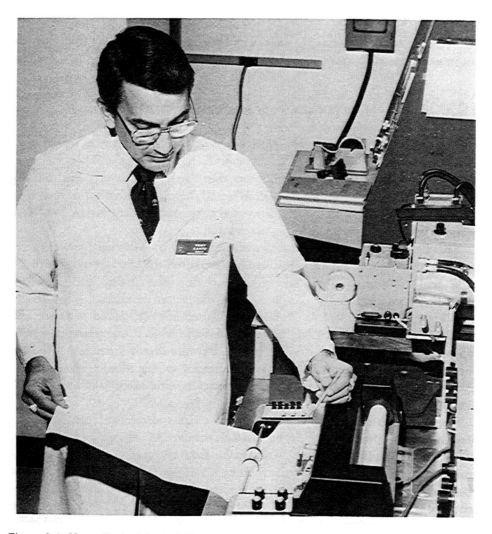

Figure 9-1. X-ray Excited Optical Fluorescence Spectrometer Used to Detect Tags in Inks.

rare earth tags in inks, approximately a total of one inch of ink line is removed from the document. Then the ink is extracted from the paper, mixed with a suitable host material such as strontium tungstate and heated in a muffle furnace at 1200°C for one hour to form the rare earth phosphor. This created phosphor is then analyzed by XREOF to detect and identify the corresponding rare earth tag in the ink.

Since each rare earth phosphor fluoresces at specific wavelengths, the tag can be positively identified and the technique is sufficiently sensitive to detect rare earths at the picogram concentration level.

Approximately 40 percent of the inks manufactured in the United States are tagged, and this tagging program has significantly increased the chances of detecting back-dated ink writing on questioned documents. In effect, those inks that contain tags have a change in formulation every year; and, the more frequent the formulations change, the better the odds of detecting an ink that was not in existence at the time the document was dated.

DATING INK BY RELATIVE AGING

The ability to determine the relative age of ball-point inks on questioned documents was developed in 1979 by Doctor A. A. Cantu at the BATF Laboratory.[7] The procedure is based on the fact that the longer a ball-point ink has been written on paper, the drier it becomes and the more difficult it is to extract into solvents or solvent mixtures. Conversely, the more recent an ink has been written, the more and the faster it will extract.

This basic theory had been previously expressed by Mitchell;[8] however, he experimented with fountain pen inks and measured the extractability into an *oxalic* acid solution. Kikuchi also researched this idea further and provided some developments into the absolute aging of fountain pen inks.[9]

When ball-point inks are contained in a cartridge (a closed system), the changes that may occur are negligible compared to when it is exposed on paper (open system) where the ink begins to dry at a rate that is formula and paper dependent. Even though ball-point ink appears to dry almost immediately when applied to paper, some of the components in some of the inks do not completely "set" or "dry" for several years.

The ability to determine the relative age of inks on a document or, to express this in another way, to determine the sequence of ink entries has proven to be another landmark development in the field of questioned document examination. The technique does not require a standard ink reference file, and it does not require sophistocated instrumentation to detect tags in the ink. It only requires at this stage of research that the inks being compared for relative age consist of the same formula ink on the same type of paper. Future research may even eliminate this restriction as well.

At this stage of research, the relative aging technique is very effective and useful when a questioned ball-point ink appears on the document with one or more known dated inks of the same formula as the questioned ink. This situation occurs, for example, in expense and income records, diaries, and other business records. When these conditions exist, variability, due to storage conditions of the document, and the effects of paper are eliminated, and any difference in extractability rates must be attributable to the relative age of the inks.

Parameters Involved With Relative Aging

The following are the principal parameters for ink placed on a surface:

1. $f =$ **formula of ink.** This is a careful and unique mixture of dyes, resins, oils, organic and inorganic solvents, humectants, corrosion inhibitors, etc. When the ink is in a "closed system," such as a pen, the changes that may occur are negligible compared to those which occur when the ink becomes exposed to an "open system." In the latter case, "drying" (fast or slow) is the major process for change.

The quality control in ink making involves the assurance that each batch of ink meets a given set of measurable standards. All experimental work to date demonstrates that quality control standards suffice to assure that each batch undergoes the same "drying" process when its ink is exposed to air from a cartridge.

2. $p =$ **surface,** such as paper, onto which an ink has been released from a pen.

3. $T =$ **time** evolved since an ink was exposed on a surface, i.e. T is the age of ink on a surface. This time or age may be in weeks, months or years.

As ink ages it becomes progressively "drier" and thus "harder" to extract into a solvent mixture. Initially, it is very extractable, but with time (T) it becomes more difficult. There will eventually be an age such that the extractability of an ink that old or older does not change. This "leveling off" age may be within months for "fast drying" non-ball-point inks and within years for "slow drying" ball-point inks. In ball-point-pen inks, interaction with surface (diffusion), as well as evaporation, polymerization, and/or oxidation of the low volatile, high molecular weight components (resins and oils) cause the "slow drying" effect.

4. $M =$ **mass of ink** removed from the surface for analysis, for extractability measurements. The total sample removed usually consists of an ink-on-surface combination; however, extractability only concerns the ink portion, or M. The microsamples removed usually contain about 0.1 to 5.0 micrograms of ink.

Ink looses its highly volatile components within minutes of exposure; after this, the "drying" process we are concerned with begins; this process involves little change in M since there only remain low volatile components. M will always refer to ink after the highly volatile components evaporate.

Extracting Parameters

In the extraction of an ink from samples obtained from an ink-on-surface specimen, the following parameters are the critical variables:

1. $S =$ **solvent mixture** made of one or more solvents. For ball-point inks, water (if it extracts) or ethanol fall into the weak extractor class while methanol or pyridine fall into the strong extractor class.

2. $V =$ **volume of S** used for extracting. This is usually between 5 to 10 microliters.

3. $t =$ **extracting time.** This usually ranges between 1 to 60 or 120 minutes depending on the ink parameters and the extracting parameters S and V.

Extractability Measurements

Before extractability measurements are carried out, it is essential to experiment to find a suitable extracting solvent. A solvent must be selected that will extract the ink at a rate that is measurable. A solvent that is too strong will extract all of the ink almost immediately and prevent accurate measurement: whereas a solvent that is too weak may never completely extract the ink. For this reason, it is very helpful to have access to standard inks of the same formula as the questioned ink to conduct these experiments without wasting questioned ink on the document.

If inks are relatively recently written, differences in weeks and months can be detected better with the use of gentle extraction solvents. Ethanol, methanol, and methanol or ethanol diluted with water have been effective in these situations. For older inks, stronger solvents such as pyridine or mixtures of pyridine and ethanol may be required.

The extractability of an ink is associated with the optical color density of the extracting solution, and this can be measured in several ways. Here color density is used in a broad sense in that it makes no reference to specific (or nonspecific) illuminating and observing wavelengths of light. Before discussing this further, it is necessary to provide additional definitions.

When an amount of ink M is placed in a volume V of solvent mixture S, extraction begins to take place of only those components that S can extract. If E represents the color density (in the broad sense) of the resulting solution after extracting for a time t, then E (which will simply be called extractability) is a function of the ink parameters (f, p, t, M) and the extracting parameters (S, V, T).

$$E = E(f, p, T, M; S, V, t) \qquad (1)\square$$

The following are some measurements of E:

1. The spectroscopic absorbitivity of the extracting solution at wavelength (λ) (usually 580 nm for blue or black inks; however, the maximum absorbance

should be checked for each ink)

$$A(\lambda; E) = K(\lambda)E \qquad (2)\square$$

were $K(\lambda)$ is a proportionality constant dependent on λ.

2. The optical density (not intensity) can be determined from an undeveloped spot produced by spotting $v < V$ microliters of the extracting solution on a TLC plate and illuminated with light of wavelength λ_i and observed at wavelength λ_o.

$$\rho = \rho\ (\lambda_i, \lambda_o, v; E) = K(\lambda_i, \lambda_o, \nu)E \qquad (3)\square$$

where $k(\lambda_i, \lambda_o, v)$ is a proportionally consistant dependent on λ_i, λ_o and v. This can be transmittance or reflectance TLC densitometry.

From the foregoing, it can be deduced that

1. E increases as mass M increases.
2. E decreases as age T increases.
3. E decreases as the porosity of p increases.
4. E decreases as the formula f of the ink becomes harder to evaporate.

Ratio of Extractability Measurements

By determining the ratio of extractability of the same ink at two different extraction times, it is possible to eliminate the problem of having it obtain equal amounts of questioned and known ink from the document, which is extremely difficult.

E increases as the mass M of ink increases. By Beer's law, in the range where it holds, E depends on M in a linear way. Thus,

$$E(M_1) = \frac{M_1 E(M_2)}{M_2}$$

where M_1 and M_2 are two different masses of ink.

If R_{21} is the ratio of two extractability measurements measured at two different times $(t_2 > t_1)$,

$$R_{21} = \frac{E(t_2)}{E(t_1)}$$

Then,

$$R_{21}\ (M_1 = R_{21}\ )M_2)$$

for any M_1 and M_2. Thus, R_{21} is independent of M.

Since R_{21} does not depend on M then it is an indirect measure of the *normalized (or equivalent) rate of extraction*. By normalized (or equivalent) we mean the following: consider two extracting curves that *differ only* in the mass of ink; by Beer's Law these curves are multiples of each other and thus become the same when each is normalized [divide by E $(t = oo)$]. We refer to these curves as having the same *normalized (or equivalent) rate of extraction*.

Analytical Procedure

Remove approximately 10 micro discs as described in Chapter 8 and place in a Knotes Microflex® tube (1.0 or 0.3 ml vial). Place a Microflex magnetic stirrer in the vial* and add 10 μl of the previously determined suitable extraction solvent. Start the magnetic stirrer immediately and, at specific time intervals (1.0 − 2 min − 5 min − 15 min), remove 1 microliter samples with a 1 microliter Dade *Volupette®* and spot on a TLC Merck silica gel 60 glass plate or other suitable plate. Once the sample is removed, immediately continue the magnetic stirring until all samples have been removed.† Since the procedure is a comparison technique where questioned and known samples are treated identically, no correction factor has to be applied for the reduction in solvent volume as samples are removed.

An *Aminco-Bowman®* spectrophotometer equipped with a TLC transmittance scanner is used to measure the optical density of the TLC spots − the peak area corresponds to the amount of ink extracted.

A spectrophotometer equipped with a micro cell accessory can also be used to measure the amount of ink extracted at the various time intervals. It may be necessary to adjust the amount of ink sample and volume of extraction solvent to accommodate the type of spectrophotometer used.

Determination of Relative Age

From the optical density measurements taken using the foregoing procedures, plot optical density (concentration of ink) vs. time for the questioned and known dated inks. The newest ink will show the highest extractions and fastest extraction rate, while the older inks will show the opposite.

To guard against the danger of not having removed the same amount of ink from each sample, take the ratio of a given pair of points.

CURRENT RESEARCH ON DATING OF INKS

The most recent documented research on the dating of inks was conducted by L. F. Stewart at the BATF Forensic Science Branch and involved the use of gas chromatography (G.C.) to measure the disappearance of the volatile components of inks with time.[10] These components, volatilized over a period of months while "drying" due to the "setting" process, can be measured for several months. This technique promises to be even more effective than the relative aging technique described in the previous section of this chapter, for inks writ-

---

*A long needle may be used to mechanically stir, provided the same degree or sequence of stirring is performed on all samples being compared.
†Recall, only two of these measurements are needed to determine R_{21}.

ten for six months or less. While this approach is based on the same premise, that inks dry on paper, the G.C. procedure does not rely on measurement of extraction rates. Rather, it relies on the total extraction of ink from the paper using strong solvents and then compares the relative concentrations of volatile components between the questioned and known inks. The older the ink, the lower the concentration of volatile components will be; conversely, the newer the ink, the more volatile components will be present.

The advantage of this G.C. procedure is that it eliminates any possible effect of paper because the ink is totally extracted with strong solvents, such as pyridine. This means that inks of the same formula can now be compared on different documents. Like the rate of extraction procedure, the results do not require removal of identical amounts of ink from the document, because only the relative concentrations of the volatile components are significant.

By comparison of the relative concentrations of the volatile components in the questioned ink with the volatile components found in known, dated inks, one can quite precisely determine the age of the questioned ink. The closeness with which it is possible to date the questioned ink depends on the number of known inks with the same formula with known dates on the documents of interest (see Fig. 9-2).

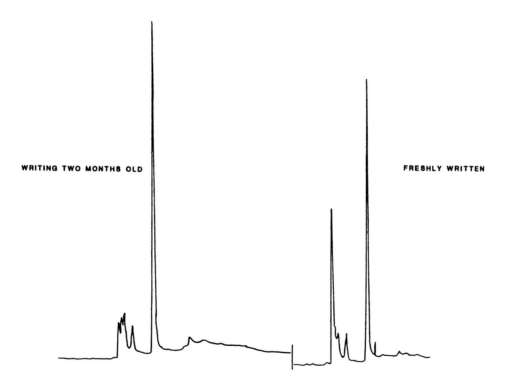

WRITING TWO MONTHS OLD   FRESHLY WRITTEN

Figure 9-2. GLC Comparison of Relative Age of the Same Ball-point Ink Formulation Written at Different Times.

FUTURE OF INK DATING

The progress that has been made over the past fourteen years at BATF in the dating of inks has contributed greatly to the field of questioned document examination and the ability to detect backdated documents. In the opinion of the authors, only the availability of time will effect the ability to determine the absolute age of inks in the future.

Since the start of this book, unpublished work has already been conducted independently by Howard Humecki[11] of Walter C. McCrone Associates, Chicago, Illinois, and John Strassburger[12] of Gillette Research Institute, Rockville, Maryland, utilizing Fourier transform infrared analysis (FTIR). Humecki's work involved spotting a thin film of ink (pyridine extract) on a KBr tablet and measuring the decrease of the carbonyl band and the increase in the methyl band of the FTIR spectra. This study showed that the ratio of these two peaks changed for some inks up to eighteen years old on paper.

Strassburger's work using FTIR was performed on erasable ink. His technique measured the diffusion of a setting agent (plasticizer) into paper and the oxidation of setting agents. Carbonyl and hydroxyl bands were found to decrease, while other bands increased with time.

FTIR may well provide the best approach to date for the relative aging of inks; however, considerable research must be done to evaluate this approach to the dating of inks. The Bureau of Alcohol, Tobacco, and Firearms is currently conducting such a study.

NOTES

1. A. A. Cantu, *On the Relative Aging of Inks*. Read before the Eastern Analytical Symposium (1979), the American Academy of Forensic Sciences (1980), and the American Society of Questioned Document Examiners (1980).
2. R. L. Brunelle and M. J. Pro, "A Systematic Approach to Ink Identification," *Journal of the Association of Official Analytical Chemists, 55*:823-826, 1972.
3. R. L. Brunelle and A. A. Cantu, "Ink Analysis — A Weapon Against Crime by Detection of Fraud," American Chemical Society Symposium Series, *Forensic Science*, No. 13, 1975, pp. 134-141.
4. J. D. Kelly and A. A. Cantu, "Proposed Standard Methods for Ink Identification," *Journal of the Association of Official Analytical Chemists, 58*(1):122-125, 1975.
5. D. A. Crown, R. L. Brunelle and A. A. Cantu, "Parameters of Ballpen Ink Examination," *Journal of Forensic Sciences, 21*(4):917-922, 1976.
6. V. A. Fassel et. al., "Trace Level Rare Earth Determination by X-ray Excited Optical Flourescence (XEOF) Spectroscopy," In *Analysis and Application of Rare Earth Materials* (Oslo-Bergen, Tromso, Universitets forlaget, 1973), pp. 110-111.
7. See note 6 above.
8. C. A. Mitchell, *Documents and Their Scientific Examination*, Chas. Griffen Co., 1935.
9. Y. Kikuchi, "Examination of the Age of the Writing in Blue Black Inks," *Police Science Laboratory Report, 12*:379, 1959.

10. L. F. Stewart, Determination of Relative Age of Inks by GLC. Read before the Annual Meeting of the American Academy of Forensic Sciences, 1982.

11. Unpublished communication, with H. Humecki, McCrone Research Institute, Chicago, Illinois.

12. Unpublished communication, with J. Strassburger, Gillette Research Institute, Rockville, Maryland.

CHAPTER 10

HISTORICAL DEVELOPMENT OF PAPER AND THE PAPER MANUFACTURING PROCESS

INTRODUCTION

THE study of the history of paper, papermaking, and the uses of paper is a fascinating one. Much has been written on these subjects, too much to attempt to condense into one small chapter. We have elected to present selected historical facts and present them in chronological order. This will serve as a form of stepping stone for those who wish to dig a little deeper into the intriguing and continuing story of paper, papermaking, and the many uses of paper.

The first attempt at such a chronology was accomplished by Joel Munsell. Munsells' *Chronology of the Origin and Progress of Paper and Papermaking*[1] was first printed in 1856. As Doctor Dard Hunter points out, Joel Munsell was the only American chronicler of the middle of the nineteenth century possessing sufficient vision and foresight to record the happenings in the field of papermaking that occurred during his own lifetime. Several flaws exist in Munsell's work; however, this is not to suggest that Munsell was in error. He printed the facts that were, to the best of his knowledge and at that time, accurate. Indeed, we are in debt to Mr. Munsell for all his efforts on this subject.

Much of this chronology belongs to the efforts of Doctor Dard Hunter, whose name is widely known throughout the papermaking industry. He, perhaps more than any other individual before him, rejoiced in the creation of one of humanities most remarkable achievements — paper.

Doctor Hunter has written extensively on the subject of paper and papermaking. The Library of Congress has, in its rare book preservation section, several of Doctor Hunter's efforts. One such effort is his *Papermaking through Eighteen Centuries*,[2] published in 1930, it remains today an excellent guide for those who wish a deeper understanding of mans' struggle to record this thoughts. In addition to that, Doctor Hunters' *Papermaking — The History and Technique of an Ancient Craft*[3] serves a similar purpose, for what is "missed" in the former work is "found" in the latter. Published in 1943, it has been reprinted several times and is, in the opinion of the authors, one of the finest books ever written on this subject.

It is not our intention to belittle or praise the efforts of a number of authors on this subject. We suggest that the reader consult our sources and formulate their own conclusions. This section starts with a statement whose author is unknown, but, it is believed to have been created sometime in the eighteenth century:

> RAGS Make Paper,
> PAPER Makes Money,
> MONEY Makes Banks,
> BANKS Make Beggars,
> BEGGARS Make
>   RAGS.

CHRONOLOGY OF PAPER, PAPERMAKING, AND RELATED SUBJECTS

BC

2700   Chinese characters conceived; Ts'ain Chieh credited with the invention.

2200   Prisse manuscript on papyrus, probably the oldest Egyptian document. The Great Harris Papyrus, in the British Museum, measuring 133 feet in length and 16³/₄ inches in breadth, is one of the largest in the world. It is dated in the 32nd year of Ramses III, Epiphi 6 (April 14). Papyrus is a built-up laminated material and should not be confused with true paper, which was not invented until about 105 AD.

1400- The earliest actual evidence of writing in China is the incised divina-
1300   tion bones discovered in Hunan Province in 1899, dating from the fifteenth and fourteenth centuries BC. These writings upon bones consist of short sentences addressed to the spirits. It was, no doubt, the long, narrow form of bones that influenced and suggested the method of Chinese calligraphy, vertical in form, from top to bottom.

900   True felt made by the Greeks, but not used as a "couching" material by papermakers until the introduction of papermaking in Europe.

500   During the life of Confucius (551-478 BC), China had no true ink and no true paper. Scholars wrote on strips of bamboo with a paintlike pigment held on the points of wooden sticks or reeds.

400-   Silk as a material for writing and books was used at this period,
300   perhaps even earlier. While silk was light in weight and could be rolled into scrolls, it was too expensive for general use, and strips of wood and bamboo remained in favor. In the official Han Catalogue,

compiled in the first century BC, more manuscripts and records on wood than silk are listed.

255   First mention of the use of seals for impressing in clay, without the use of ink.

250   Invention of camel's hair brush by Meng T'ien, eventually revolutionizing the writing of Chinese characters.

200   An improved method of refining parchment from sheepskin, thought to have been introduced by the King of Pergamum (197-158 BC). This led to the supposition that parchment was invented in Pergamum, from whence the name is derived.

AD

82   The Chinese philosopher Wang Ch'ung wrote: "Bamboo is cut into cylinders, which are split into tablets. When brush and ink marks are added we have writing — the classics being inscribed on long tablets, the historical records on shorter ones." The long bamboo tablets measured about twenty inches.

100   The Chinese dictionary, *Shuo-wen*, described books written upon narrow strips of wood held together by cords, in the manner of a Venetian blind. The third-century lexicon *Shih ming* likened the arrangements of the strips of wood to the teeth of a comb.

105   During the period of Chien-ch'u, Ts'ai Lun was made one of the Imperial Guards. Later Ho Ti (AD 89-15) appointed him privy councillor and it was during this reign that Ts'ai Lun, AD 105, announced the invention of papermaking to the Emperor. The paper was made from mulberry and other barks, fish nets, hemp, and rags.

142   According to a work compiled by Yu Shih-nan (AD 558-638), a scholar, Ts'ui Yuan, AD 142, wrote: "I send you the works of the Philosopher Hsu in ten scrolls — unable to afford a copy on silk I am obliged to send you one on paper." This would suggest that thirty-seven years after the invention of paper this substance was cheaper than silk, a substance previously used.

150   Papermaking improved by Tso Tzu-yi, after its invention by Ts'ai Lun.

Paper dating from this period found in the Great Wall of China; its' composition was that of rags.

175   Text of Chinese classics cut in stone, which later gave impetus to the stone rubbings, a form of printing.

250-300   Paper from this period found at Niya, Turkestan.

264   Earliest clearly dated paper. Found in Loulan Province.

300   According to Chinese records, it was about this period that paper began to be universally accepted as a substitute for wood, bamboo, and silk as a writing material.

390   A letter written by St. Augustine (AD 354-430) makes an apology for using papyrus instead of parchment, the papyrus being considered less formal and desirable.

400   Invention of true ink from lamp-black, used in China for brush writing and later for wood-block printing.

406   The commencement of the Tun-huang papers. These manuscripts date from AD 406-1035, all written upon paper. Ten thousand rolls were found in one cave on the border of Chinese Turkestan.

445   Fan Yeh, the first scholar to record the invention of papermaking by Ts'ai Lun, died.

450   General use of paper in Eastern Turkestan, replacing all other materials for calligraphy. The paper was made from rags and barks, with improvements in sizing with pastes made from grains.

470   The *History of the later Han Dynasty* (AD 25-221), written about AD 470, states: "From this time on it (paper) was used universally." Other references likewise attest that the making and use of paper spread rapidly throughout China.

610   Papermaking introduced into Japan from China, the country from which Japan received all of her cultural and artistic development.

627-   Between these dates, the earliest inscription extant was made from a
49   stone monument, found in 1901 at Tunhuang. This rubbing on paper dates from the period of T'ai Tsung of the T'ang Dynasty.

650   Chinese Buddist monks experimented with the duplication of images by the use of rubbings, charm blocks, stencils, and textile prints. These experiments were the forerunner of true block printing in the ninth century.

       Earliest use of paper in Samarkand, the paper imported from China, the world's most highly developed Empire.

674   A Chinese edict made it compulsory to use a toxic substance rendered from the berries of the Phellodendron amurense, commonly known as the Amoor cork tree, for the coloring of certain types of Chinese paper. Paper so treated was immune to the ravages of insects.

700   About this time a few papers began to be sized; first with gypsum, followed in succession with glue or gelatine made from lichen, then starch flour and other sizing agents rendered from grains.

751   In this year paper was made in Samarkand, the first place outside China to understand the secrets of the craft, revealed by Chinese prisoners of war.

770   The earliest instance of text printing upon paper, the million printed *Dharani* (prayers) of the Empress Shotoku. The paper was made from hemp, and the blocks used in the printing may have been of wood, metal, stone, or porcelain. A number of the *Dharani* are still in existence, but no printing block used in this work has ever been found. While the work was actually executed in Japan, it was accomplished under Chinese influence; therefore, this earliest of all text printing upon paper should be regarded as almost purely of Chinese origin.

793   Paper fabricated for the first time in Bagdad, introduced by Harun-al-Rashid (766?-809), who acquired skilled artisans from China for the purpose.

800   Earliest use of paper of Egypt, probably imported from Samarkand or Bagdad.
       Egyptian paper of the Erzherzog collection, Vienna, dating from AD 800-1388, examined in 1885 and found to contain rags. Until the discovery of Chinese rag paper in 1904, it was generally believed that the use of rags in papermaking was originated by the Arabs of Samarkand.

807   Paper made for the first time in Kyoto, the art center of Japan.

868   The earliest printed book, the *Diamond Sutra*, printed by Wang Chien. The book was found at Tun-huang Province. The roll, the original form of the true Chinese book, is sixteen feet in length. The *Diamond Sutra* was first printed in Japan in 1157.

875   Arab travellers in China report having seen toilet paper in use in that country during the ninth century.

883   An Egyptian letter of thanks dating between this year and 895 closes with these words: "Pardon the papyrus." Inasmuch as the letter is written on a handsome piece of papyrus, it is inferred that the apology was made for not making use of paper, this substance having but lately been introduced into Egypt.

900   True paper made in Egypt for the first time, the methods of the Chinese employed.

1035   The Persian traveller Nasiri Khosrau, on a visit to Cairo, was astonished to see "sellers of vegetables, spices, hardware, provided with paper in which all they sold was immediately wrapped up, if it were not so already." Probably the earliest recorded instance of "packaging," still in use today.

1100   Su Tung-p'o (AD 1036-1101) recorded that bamboo was used as a paper-making material in China.
       Earliest instance of papermaking in Morocco, having been introduced from Egypt.

First use of paper in Constantinople.

1102   Earliest use of true paper in Sicily.

1109   Earliest existing European manuscript on paper, a deed of King Roger, written in Arabic and Greek, Sicily.

1116   The Chinese made use of the first stitched books, printed on one side of the paper with "French fold," sewed with linen and cotton thread.

1140   A physician of Bagdad writes of the source of the wrapping paper used by the grocers: "The Bedouins and fellahs search the ancient cities of the dead to recover the cloth bands in which mummies were swathed, and when these cannot be used for their own clothes, they sell them to the mills, which make them paper destined for the food markets" (see 1855).

1147   According to legend, Jean Montgolfier on the Second Crusade was taken prisoner by Saracens and forced to labor in a Damascus paper mill. He is supposed to have returned to France and, in 1157, set up a papermaking establishment in Vidalon.

1150   El-Edrisi said of the Spanish City of Xativa (not Jativa or S. Felipe de Jativa): "Paper is there manufactured, such as cannot be found anywhere else in the civilized world, and is sent to the East and to the West."

1151   A stamping-mill for the maceration of rags for papermaking was put in operation in Xativa, Spain. This type mill was adopted from the Orient and was used in Europe until the intervention of the Hollander (see 1680).

1154   First use of paper in Italy, in the form of a register written by Giovanni Scriba, dated 1154 to 1166. It is thought that this particular paper has been imported from the East. No other specimens of paper are found in Italy until 1276, the date of the first mention of the Fabriano paper mills.

1189   The date usually given as the commencement of papermaking in France, in the town of Lodeve, in the department of Herault. This assertion is now considered an error and was based on an incorrect translation and mistaken date (see 1348).

1221   Emperor Frederick II (AD 1194-1250), King of Naples and Sicily, prohibited the use of paper for public documents, but the edict was not entirely effective.

1228   Earliest use of paper in Germany.

1276   First mention of the Fabriano, Italy, paper mills.

1282   Watermarks used in Europe for the first time. They consisted of simple crosses and circles (Italy).

1285   Earliest use of the fleur-de-lis as a watermark in paper. Shortly after this date, initials of the papermarkers appeared in watermarks.

1293   First paper mill in Bologna, Italy.

1298   After visiting China, Marco Polo wrote regarding the paper money he had seen in use in that country. Paper money was the first form of printing seen by European travelers, and at least eight pre-Renaissance European writers mentioned it. The description given by Marco Polo was the most comprehensive and most widely read.

1309   First use of paper in England.

1319-27   Earliest use of paper money in Japan. The Japanese notes were smaller than those of China, being about 2 by 6 inches. This paper money was secured by a gold or silver or other metallif reserve.

1322   First use of paper in Holland.

1337   Probably the earliest use in Europe of animal (gelatine) sizing for paper.

1348   Under this date it is recorded that a paper mill was established in the Saint-Julien region near Troyes, perhaps the earliest mill in France.

1390   The King of Korea ordered the establishment of a type-foundry.

First paper mill in Germany, established by Ulman Stromer, Nuremberg. (As a possible note of interest, the first recorded labor strike in the papermaking industry occurred at the Stromer mill).

1403   Movable type produced in the royal typefoundry, Korea. Specimens of this type are in the museum in Seoul.

1405   Paper is made for the first time in Flanders, at Huys.

1409   Earliest known book printed in Korea from movable type.

1423   The beginning of block printing in Europe, by use of the ancient Chinese technique. Image prints and playing cards were printed from wood-blocks and colored by hand.

1450-55   Johann Gutenberg's forty-two-line Bible produced. The beginning of book printing in Europe and the commencement of the use of paper on a comparatively large scale. The paper used in the printing of this Bible has never been excelled for durability and remains to this day a monument to the papermaking craft.

The earliest known use of an *ex libris*, a bookplate or label printed upon paper and pasted in the front of books to show ownership.

1465   Earliest mention of blotting paper in the English language.

1470   A bookseller's advertisement issued by Peter Schoffer is considered to be the first printed poster upon paper to be made in Europe.

1476   William Caxton established his printing office in Westminster and produced thirty books during the first three years. All of the paper used by Caxton was procured in the Low Countries.

1480   Anthony Koberger, printer of Nuremberg, distributed a printed circular to his customers, probably the first use of this form of advertising.

1482   Venetian papermakers separated the initials of the papermaker from the device or symbol of the watermark; introduced in France about 1567.

1486   The unknown schoolmaster printer of St. Albans issued the first English book printed on paper in which colored inks were used in the illustrations: *The Boks of Hauking and Huntyng*, by Juliana Berners.

1487   By this year almost every country of Europe had adopted printing, and large quantities of paper were consumed in the printing of books.

1495   First paper mill established in England, by John Tate, in Hewrtfordshire.

1508   Earliest use of paper in Scotland for book-printing, in Edinburgh.

1521   The earliest recorded use of rice straw in Chinese papermaking.

1535   The first complete Bible in English, Myles Coverdale's translation. In an examination of eleven copies of this Bible, ten different watermarks are found: seven forms of a large crown, one small crown, and two bull's heads, one with a snake and the other surmounted by a rose of bliss. The first Bible to be actually printed in England dates from 1537.

1540   The glazing or pressing-hammer introduced in Germany, taking the place of the old method of finishing the paper by hand in the Oriental manner.

1549   The Spanish missionary Diego de Landa, of the Monastery of Izamal, Yucatan, burned the library of the Mayas in Mani. According to Doctor Victor W. von Hagen (*The Aztec and Maya Papermakers*, New York, 1944), the Mayas were making a sort of bark paper as early as the ninth century of our era.

1550   Earliest use of "smalts" in coloring paper blue. Prussian blue was discovered by Diesbach in 1704; ultramarine has been made since 1790 and synthetic ultramarine was first made commercially by Guimet in 1828.

      Wallpaper introduced into Europe direct from China by Spanish and Dutch traders.

1570   About this time the earliest extrathin papers were introduced in Europe.

1575   The first paper mill in Mexico was established in Cilhuacan.

1580   First commercial pasteboard manufactured in Europe. In China and

Persia, board of this kind had been made centuries earlier.

1589   European printing introduced into China for the first time by Jesuit priests. In 1591, Japan received printing from the West for the first time.

1591   First paper mill in Scotland established at Dalry.

1597   Mitsumata (Edgeworthia papyrifera) first recorded use in Japan as a fiber for making paper.

1609   The earliest newspaper with regular publication dates, *Avisa Relation oder Zeitung*, published in Germany.

1622   The first English newspaper was issued in London.

1630   Paper cartridges first used by Gustavus Adolphus (1594-1632), King of Sweden.

1636   England visited by the first of her great plagues. It was thought, at the time, that the plague may have been brought into the country through the linen and cotton rags imported by the papermakers.

1638- First printing press set up in North America by Stephen Daye, at
39   Cambridge, Massachusetts. The first printing executed was a broadside on paper, *The Freeman's Oath*; first thing in book form, *Peirce's Almanack for 1639*; earliest existing specimen of Cambridge printing, John Eliot's *Bay Psalm Book*, dated 1640.

1661   First New Testament printed in America, John Eliot's translation into Algonquin, printed at Cambridge by Samuel Green and Marmaduke Johnson. The Old Testament was issued in 1663, the two making the first Bible printed in this country. The paper was of European manufacture.

1666   To save linen and cotton for the papermakers, a decree was issued in England prohibiting the use of these materials for the burial of the dead; only wool could be used for this purpose.

1679   The first "Dutch gilt" papers, originated in Germany, imported to the New World.

1680   The "Hollander," or beater, used in the maceration of materials for making into paper, invented in the Netherlands.

1687   Earliest use of orchres, umbers, and vermilion in the coloring of European papers.

1690   William Rittenhouse established the first paper mill in British America, near Germantown, Philadelphia, Pennsylvania.

1691   The first English patent pertaining to the coloring of paper.

1704   *The Boston News Letter* established in Boston by John Campbell, the earliest permanent newspaper in America.

1712   Peter the Great (1672-1725), Czar of Russia, visited Dresden and after seeing paper being made in the Schuchart mill procured workmen in Germany and returned to Moscow, where he established the first extensive paper mill in Russia.

1714   Invention and patent of a typewriter for "transcribing of letters, one after another, as in writing on paper." The patent was issued in England to Henry Mill.

1718   First colored printed (red and black) accomplished in America, by Andrew Bradford of Philadelphia.

1719   Establishment of *American Weekly Mercury*, Philadelphia, the first newspaper in Pennsylvania.

1720   Pressing-hammers gave way to wooden glazing-rolls for finishing paper with a smooth surface.

1728   The invention of the papier-mâché, or wet-mat, stereotyping process by the French printer Claude Genoux.

1733   The discovery of China clay by William Cookworthy, England. Clay was first used in "loading" paper about the year 1807; by 1870 this method of loading was a common practice.

1735   The original English patent for the fireproofing and waterproofing of paper, granted to Obadiah Wyld.

1740   The first papermaking moulds produced in the colonies, the work of Isaac Langle.

         French laws set down the sizes and weights, also the watermarks, of paper to be sold.

1741   Jean Guettard, French scientist, suggested the use of *conferva* (swamp moss) and other forms of vegetation as suitable material for papermaking.

1744   The date of the establishment of the first paper mill in the state of Virginia.

1750   First use of cloth-backed paper in Europe, used for maps, charts, etc.

1755   The earliest English printing of gold upon paper for the making of wall hangings. A patent was granted Joachim Bahre for his method of sizing paper to be printed upon in gold and silver.

1757   "Wove" paper used for the first time in European book printing.

1758   First forgery of English bank-notes.

1763   The first Bible to be printed in America in which American-made paper was extensively employed.

1764   A patent was granted to George Cummings for the coating of paper. The "coating" was composed of white lead, plaster of paris, and stone lime and mixed with water in such consistency "as to lay on with a brush." This method was first employed by the Chinese.

First paper mill in Rhode Island.

1767   First paper mill in Connecticut.

Earliest English patent pertaining to the decoration of playing cards.

1769   Earliest manufacture of paper in New York State.

1772   First use of paper in Europe for building coaches, sedan chairs, cabinets, bookcases, screens, etc.

*1773   An act was passed in England that decreed the death penalty for copying or imitating the watermarks in English bank-notes.

1774   The discovery of chlorine by Karl Scheele (1742-86), which was in later years used in the bleaching of paper stock.

1776   First paper mill in the state of Maryland.

By this year linen and cotton rags for papermaking had become so scarce and the need for paper in America so great that legislation obtained exemption from military service for all skilled papermakers. This same exemption prevailed in 1812.

1777   First paper mill established in North Carolina, near Hillsboro.

The earliest treatise on papermaking materials appeared in the *New World*, issued in Philadelphia.

1778   First spurious watermarks in imitation of English bank-notes made by John Mathieson.

1780   Earliest use of steel pens for writing upon paper; previous to this date quill pens were in use.

1782   First Bible printed in America in the English language, by Robert Aitken, Philadephia. The volume embraces more than 1400 unnumbered pages, the page size being 3½ by 6 inches.

1787   The beginning of papermaking in the state of Delaware.

1792   Papermaking introduced into the state of New Hampshire.

1793   Earliest English patent relating to the heating of papermaking vats by steam was granted to William Scott and George Gregory. This was an advanced step in papermaking technique, as previous to this intervention all vats had been heated by individual charcoal-burners.

1796   The first English patent granted for the embossing of paper, to John Gregory Hancock. The embossing was produced by placing paper upon an engraved die and subjecting it to pressure.

1797   A pamphlet was issued in London setting forth the use of jute as a papermaking material. The brochure was printed on paper made from this substance.

---

*Charles Price began the counterfeiting of Bank of England notes, which baffled the authorities; Price hung himself in the Bridewell prison.

Earliest use of yellows and brown (lead chromate) in dyeing European paper.

1798   The paper machine invented by Nicholas-Louis Robert, a Frenchman. The small, undeveloped machine was set up in the Essonnes paper mill and the French government granted Robert a fifteen-year patent and advanced money for the perfection of the machine. Aside from the models made by Robert, little was accomplished in France, and it was not until a number of years later that a really practical machine was built in England by John Gamble and Bryan Donkin (see section on papermaking history).

1800   Matthias Koops, living in London, began his experiments in the use of wood, straw, and the de-inking of paper. Three books were compiled by Koops using these materials for the paper upon which they were printed. The greater part of the present-day industry is founded upon the pioneer work of Koops.

The invention of rosin sizing for paper by Moritz F. Illig (1777-1845), but not mentioned by him until 1807.

1801   John Gamble received the earliest English patent pertaining to the paper machine. The title of this patent is: "An invention of making paper in single sheets without seams or joining, from one to twelve feet and upwards wide from one to forty-five feet and upward in length." The machine is described as follows: "a sheet of copper (screen) joined at both ends, passing round cylinders, forms an endless web, and this receives the pulp, which, travelling along, passes between the cylinders upon a wooden roller, which, when loaded, another is substituted in its place without stopping the machine."

1802   Probably the earliest use of bleached wood-pulp in English book production.

The mechanical agitator, or "hog," for the agitation of papermaking fiber in the vat was introduced in England.

1804   Aloys Senefelder (1771-1834), a Bavarian, accomplished the first successful lithography, thereby creating a demand for still greater quantities of paper.

1806   The name Fourdrinier appears for the first time in relation to the paper machine now bearing this well-known appellation (see section on history and section on paper making).

1807   A United States patent was procured by Francis Guy, Baltimore, for the manufacture of floor coverings composed of paper. It was claimed that the paper carpets were equal to the regulation product at about half the cost.

The date of the establishment of the earliest known paper mill in South Carolina.

1809   Samuel Green, New London, Connecticut, was given a United States patent for making paper from seaweed, and Francis Bailey, Salisbury, Pennsylvania, received a patent for the hot-press of paper.

John Dickinson, an English papermaker, invented and patented the cylinder paper-machine.

1810   It was probably this date before the Fourdrinier paper machine reached any degree of perfection, after patient work by John Gamble and Bryan Donkin.

In Europe and America, the Fatsia papyrifera pith "paper" of Formosa was seen for the first time when it was brought from China by sailing ship captains and sailors.

This date was the probable beginning of papermaking in the state of Georgia.

1812   In England between this year and 1818 there were circulated 131,221 pieces of forged bank paper. This abundant counterfeiting gave rise to the invention by Sir William Congreve (see 1819).

1814   The London Times for November 29 was the first newspaper to be printed on a cylinder press with the aid of papier-mâché matrices (stereotyping by the use of paper).

1816   Bishop records that the first steam paper mill in the United States was put into operation in Pittsburgh, Pennsylvania. The engine was of sixteen horse-power, and the mill employed forty workers.

1817   First paper machine erected in America, a cylinder machine operated in the mill of Thomas Gilpin, near Philadelphia.

1818   In England, to conserve paper, it was made a punishable offense to produce a newspaper exceeding 22 by 32 inches.

1819   Sir William Congreve (1772-1828) submitted his experiments in watermarking for bank-notes to the Bank of England and a few of his inventions were adopted and are still used.

1820   Thomas Bronsor Crompton granted a patent in England for drying cylinders for the paper machine. Previous to this time the semimoist paper was taken from the machine, cut into sheets, and dried in a loft as had long been the procedure with the handmade product.

1823   Gypsum (calcium sulphate) used for the first time in Europe as a loading material.

1824   The first machine for pasting sheets of paper together, forming cardboard. The patent was granted to John Dickinson, the inventor of the cylinder machine.

1825   John and Christopher Phipps were granted an English patent for what purports to be the original "dandy-roll" for watermarking paper. The specifications read in part: "the employment of a roller the cylinder part of which is formed of 'laid' wire . . . the effect produced by said roller passes and thus the paper so made has the appearance of 'laid' paper.

1826   First use in the Occident of the divided papermaking mould, making possible the formation of two sheets at one dipping of the mould into the vat. This type of mould had long since been used in China.

1827   First Fourdrinier paper-machine set up in America, built in England by Brian Donkin. The machine was put in operation at Saugerties, New York, in the mill of Henry Barclay.

On August 8, Nicholas-Louis Robert, the French inventor of the paper machine, died, a poorly paid school-teacher.

1829   First Fourdrinier papermaking machine to be built in America made in South Windham, Connecticut, and installed that same year.

1830   Commercially made sandpaper produced about this time, one side of the paper being brushed with glue, and sand, ground glass, or emery dusted upon paper. Previous to this date most workers made their own abrasives by coating ordinary canvas or heavy paper with glue and sprinkling sand upon the surface.

Bleach, invented by Scheele in 1774, first used by American papermakers in bleaching rags for making paper.

Paper first calendered in England.

1837   The first use of old manila rope as a papermaking fiber in the United States.

1839   Improved drying cylinders for the paper machine invented and patented by Robert Ranson.

1840   Watermarking used in postage stamps, the "penny black" of England. There were 240 small watermarked crowns on each sheet of handmade stamp paper. This was the first issue of adhesive postage stamps.

Between 1835 and 1849 the cylinder washer for attaching to the Hollander was invented and used successfully. The invention is attributed to the Breton brothers. This style of washer enabled papermakers to cleanse the surplus bleach from the rag stock more thoroughly than formerly.

1841   Charles Fenerty, a Nova Scotian, produced in Halifax the first ground-wood paper made in the Western Hemisphere.

1842   Will Egley, an English artist, produced the original Christmas card, an idea that was eventually to consume prodigious quantities of paper and cardboard in all countries where Christmas is celebrated.

1843   About this time the earliest "safety paper" was produced in England. The paper was printed on both sides in all-over patterns with special inks subject to erasure.

1844   The first commercial paper boxes made in America, by Andrew Dennison, a cobbler, at his home in Brunswick, Maine.

1847   First postage stamps used in the United States, founded on the George Plitt report on the "penny black" of England, used in 1840.

1848   About this time, W. H. Smith invented but did not patent light-and shaded watermarks, which enabled papermakers to produce portraits and other shaded pictures in watermarks. Before this date all watermarks were made of a single wire, sometimes with a "wove" background.

1850   First use of "ribbed" paper in printing postage stamps, Austria.
         Paper bags made for the first time, entirely by hand.

1851   First useful paper made from chemical wood fiber originated by Hugh Burgess and Charles Watt. The process was patented in the United States in 1854.

1855   About this time Egyptian mummies were imported to America, the wrappings and other fibers to be used in the making of wrapping paper for grocers, butchers, etc.

1856   Discovery of aniline dye (Perkin's mauve), used in coloring paper, inks, etc. By 1870, dyes of this type were in common usage.

         First English patent covering corrugated paper granted to Edward Healey and Edward Allan. The corrugating was accomplished by passing the paper between corrugated rollers or by pressing between corrugated dies.

1857   Experiments in the sulphite process for the preparation of wood fiber for papermaking begun in Paris by Benjamine C. and Richard Tilghman.

1860   About this time the original Jordan engine for refining paper stock was made by the Smith and Winchester Company for the Boswell Keene Company, East Hartford, Connecticut.

         As late as this date, rags formed 88 percent of the total papermaking material in the United States.

         Probably the first cigarette paper to be made from the fiber of the tobacco plant, the manufacturing taking place in Algiers.

1862   The earliest manufacture of tracing-paper as a definite commodity for professional use.

1863   The Boston Weekly Journal for January 14 printed on paper made from woodpulp.

1864   About this year the United States Government established a paper machine in the basement of the Treasury Building.

1867   The first ground-wood mill established in the United States.

1869   The original use of okra (Hibiscus esculentus or Abelmoschus esculentus) on a commerical scale in American papermaking.

1871   The earliest use in America of toliet paper in roll form, a United States patent issued to Seth Wheeler this year.

1875   First instance in the United States of coating paper on both sides.

1878   During this year, or early in 1879, the United States Bureau of Engraving set up machinery for the repulping of retired paper currency. This method of destroying old bills was abondoned in 1943; the retired currency is now destroyed by incineration or shredding.

1880   At this time there were about 350,000 tons of rags used yearly in the United States in the making of paper; of this amount, approximately 85,000 tons were imported from foreign countries. The rags brought from Egypt were considered the cleanest, as the rags were free from grease, owing to the limited meat diet of the Egyptians; on the other hand, the rags from England were the most filthy, containing the greatest amount of grease and impurities.

1882   Sulphite pulp first made in the United States on a commercial scale. The Ekman process was used.

1884   Sulphate pulp invented by Carl F. Dahl.

1885   The original manufacture and use in the United States of vegetable parchment, now universally employed in many branches of the food packing industry.

1887   John W. Mullen made the first paper tester, which was sold the same year to the Parsons Paper Company.

1891   Paper as insulation in telephone cables used by the Bell System; the paper was 0.0025 inch in thickness.

1894   A section of a Washington, D.C. street was paved with blocks made of paper, but the method used in manufacturing the blocks was undeveloped and the experiment did not have an opportunity to succeed.

        About this time automatic machines for the making of paper boxes were in general use, the beginning of the packaging era.

1896   Electricity used in papermaking for the first time in the United States in the mill of Cliff Paper Company, Niagara Falls, New York.

1903   First use of corrugated fiber containers, replacing wood boxes to a great extent.

1905   Glassine paper introduced into the United States.

1906   The first paper milk bottles made this year by G. W. Maxwell in San Francisco, California.

1907   By this date medicated papers were in universal use. These antiseptic papers included gout papers, Christy's chromegelatine for bandaging,

East India paper plaster for slight flesh wounds, mustard paper, Ricou's antiasthma paper, blister paper, Gautier's nascent iodine paper, hygenic paper handkerchiefs, towels, etc. Also, paper was used in the making of splints for fractures by treating mill-board with shellac, violin resin, pine, etc.

1909   First kraft paper manufactured in the United States.

1910   About this time the wrappings of bread in printed paper became universal in America. Also the wrapping of fruit in paper had its beginning.

1929   The Institute of Paper Chemistry established.

1939   Dard Hunter established the Dard Hunter Paper Museum.

1946   Plastics begin to challange paper in the marketplace; paper increases its markets through paper/plastics combinations.

1960s   Paper, through "disposables" enter traditional textile markets.

Paper industry experiences wave of intra- and interindustry mergers.

Industry's capital considerations seriously affected by environmental requirements, although some of these considerations had been regulated for seventy or more years.

Recycling becomes technology factor.

First fundamental design changes in paper machines since the early 1800s.

1968   World's first test-tube tree produced at the Institute of Paper Chemistry in research related to papermaking raw materials.

1973   Paper machines operating speeds surpass 5000 feet per minute for some paper grades. Widths reach 390 inches. Per capita United States paper consumption for 1972 reported at over 600 lbs. per capita.

THE HISTORY OF PAPER

Papyrus

Theophrastus[4] says that the papyrus books of the ancients were no other than rolls prepared in the following manner:

> Two leaves of the rush were plastered together, usually with the mud of the Nile, in such a fashion that the fibres of one leaf should cross the fibres of the other at right angles; the ends of each being then cut off, a square leaf was obtained, equally capable of resisting fracture when pulled or taken hold of in any direction. In this form these single leaves into the "scapi," or rolls of the ancients, about twenty were glued together end to end. The writing was then executed in parallel columns a few inches

wide, running transversely to the length of the scroll. To each end of the scrolls were attached round staves similar to those we use for maps. To these staves, strings known as "umbilici," were attached, to the ends of which bullas or weights were fixed. These books were rolled up, were bound up with these umbilici, and were generally kept in cylindrical boxes or capsae, a term from which the Medieval "capsula," or bookcover was derived.

Pliny the Elder, in his *Naturalis Historia*, describes another very early method of preparing sheets of papyrus for writing purposes.[5] His account was written in the first century AD. Pliny states that the stem of the papyrus reed, which was about two inches in diameter, was split lengthwise to form strips of varying width depending on whether they were taken from the middle or near the side of the reed. These strips were laid parallel to one another on a board and then covered with a second layer which ran at right angles to the first. By soaking in water the sheet which had been built up in this manner, the glutinous matter in the pulp was dissolved to cement the assembly into a coherent mass, which was pounded with hammers to form a thin, dense sheet. After drying, the papyrus was ready to use unless rough portions required polishing with ivory to improve the surface. Generally, the single sheets, ranging from six to ten inches in width, were pasted together to form a long sheet which might be rolled and conveniently handled.[6]

The accounts of Theophrastus and Pliny have provided invaluable insight into the development of early forms of paper. The oldest papyri known today are estimated to have been made about 2500 BC, although one document of uncertain date records events supposed to have occurred before 3500 BC[8]

The Greeks are known to have used papyrus in the fifth century BC, and the Romans employed it almost exclusively for correspondence and legal documents.[8]

Parchment and Vellum

The skins of animals were among the first substitutes to which man turned when he needed a convenient material on which to write. As a writing material, parchment and vellum were not a serious threat to the art of the manufacture of papyrus until around the third or fourth century AD. Pliny relates that parchment of good quality was first made in Pergamun, an ancient town in Asia Minor, about 150 BC, and that the artisans of that city were compelled to make excellent writing material from skins by their ruler. By attempting to assemble the largest library of his time, he had incurred the jealousy of the Ptolemies.[9] The Egyptians then prohibited the exportation of papyrus, which was almost exclusively made in Egypt at that time. This forced the king of Pergamun, Eumenes II, to promote the growth and utilization of parchment in order to fulfill his ambition.

The terms *parchment* and *vellum* are often used interchangeably because both have been used for writing material and both are manufactured in a similar fashion. The skin is first freed from the hair of the mammal to be followed by a good soaking in lime water, after which it is stretched and scraped. The unevenness that remains after the scraping is removed by rubbing the interior surface of the skin with pumice; this process is repeated until the desired surface is obtained.[10] Refinements in the preparation of parchment were made rapidly; by the fourth century AD, the sheets produced had a delicate texture and a smooth surface.

The relative sizes of parchment sheets in use at various times provides an interesting index of its popularity and corresponding scarcity. With increasing demand and consequently greater cost, it became usual to employ both sides, and about the thirteenth century, at the peak of its vogue, parchment was commonly used in the form of extremely small sheets three inches square or even smaller. During the Middle Ages, when parchment was almost unobtainable, it was common to scrub out the old ink from a previously written sheet and use it again. Manuscripts of this type are termed *palimpsests* and have been a source of irritation through the ages to scholars who have been able to recognize fragments of works of great antiquity beneath the relatively recent writings of some scrivener which are of little interest from either a historical or literary point of view.[11]

Palimpsests have been referred to as the link between classical times and the Middle Ages. A well-prepared leaf of parchment was so costly an article in the Middle Ages that the scribes employed by the monastic establishments in writing often availed themselves of some old manuscript, from which they scraped off the writing. This practice seems to have been followed long before this time, but not to so great an extent as during about the fourteenth and fifteenth centuries, when there were persons regularly employed as "parchment-restorers."[12] Sometimes the original writing, by a careful treatment of the parchment, has been so far restored as to be visible, and it is found to be paralled, diagonal, and sometimes at right angles to the writing afterwards introduced. In many cases the ancient writing recorded beneath is found to be infinitely more valuable than the monkish legends written afterwards. For example, Cicero's *De Republica* was rediscovered in the Vatican Library written under a commentary by Saint Augustine on the Psalms.[13]

True Paper Evolves

While their European counterparts were still writing on papyrus, a Chinese civil servant by the name of Ts'ai Lun quietly went about the business of inventing a new writing medium. Ts'ai Lun was born in a city of the Kwe-Chou Province in southern China. In 75 AD, he entered the service of the emperor. Ts'ai Lun was deeply given to study; whenever he was off duty, he would shut himself up for that purpose. Ts'ai Lun considered both silk and bamboo tablets, the writing materials for that period of Chinese history, to be too cumbersome and perishable. He conceived the idea of using bast fibers, hemp, and old rags like fishing nets for making various forms of paper. By 105 AD Ts'ai Lun had perfected his ideas in the form of a bark and rag paper.[14] He survived his invention for thirteen years, being ennobled as a marquis in 114 AD. During that same year, however, he could not find favor with the empress; he committed suicide by swallowing a dose of poison. We are indebted to Ts'ai Lun for one of the most far-reaching discoveries ever made in the annals of technology.

The Mould

The entire development of papermaking is so closely connected with mould construction that it is only through a study of moulds that the long history of paper is revealed.[15] The hand mould provided the first step from the transition of writing upon silk and cloth to that of paper. Ts'ai Lun, once again, is credited for the invention of the hand mould. He accomplished this end by the use of mortar and pestle, to provide the most elementary form of maceration.

Dard Hunter,[16] noted authority on paper and papermaking, gives us an account of Lun's discovery:

> In experimenting with waste cloth it was natural that the Chinese conceived the idea of first wetting and then beating the material until it was reduced to a fibre . . . the tangled and matted appearance of the beaten cloth fibres at once suggested the possibility of forming the myriad filaments into thin sheets . . . the difficult task was to devise an implement capable of picking up the matted fibres in an even, homogeneous sheet of paper. The need brought forth the invention of the papermaking mould, the implement that has remained throughout the centuries the most essential tool in forming paper by hand, and upon the principle of which the modern paper-machine is founded. To the papermaker the mould is as important as the loom is to the weaver.

As we have seen, the Ancients wrote on a host of differing mediums. Papyrus, parchment, vellum, and, in the Orient, a form of rag paper appear to have been the writing medium of choice by these Ancient civilizations. While Moses delivered the ten commandents upon pillars of stone this was not taken as a celestial sign regarding the writing materials utilized. The laws of Solon were reportedly inscribed on planks of wood; although this was a step in the right direction, it was entirely unacceptable. Tablets of ivory or metal were in common use by the Greeks and Romans; these were extremely difficult for the populus to ignore and even more difficult to misplace. Up through the Middle Ages people wrote upon any and everything that was available. During the Middle Ages, most of the Europeans who could read, and even greater percentage of those who could write, were ecclesiasties. They chose parchment and vellum to record the functions of the church, but the winds of change brought news from the East.

THE MIGRATION OF PAPER

We ask the reader to recall the works of Ts'ai Lun. His thoughts on the composition of rag and bark paper remained "state secrets" for in excess of five hundred years. The work *Nineteen Centuries of Pulp and Papermaking*,[17] touches on the migration of the papermaking secret to Japan. Moving westward caravan routes provided the method of transporting this Chinese "secret" to the Middle East; Samarkan in Turkestan being one of these known way-stations where some Chinese prisoners of war were "encouraged" to both teach and practice their trade. As a consequence of this "prompting" by Turkestani officials and because commerce was the primary objective of the caravan routes, it was not long afterward that bark and rag papermaking found its way to Bagdad. The next stop was to be Damascus; but, for some inexplicable reason, the migration of paper to this city took an additional two hundred years. With the dawning of the tenth century AD we find this art in Egypt. The methods by which papermaking found its way across the Mediterranean and into European hands appears to be twofold. Possibly travellers crossing the strait of Gibraltar carried this message from Morocco into Spain. The Spanish paper mills of Toledo were functioning as early as 1085.[18] The other possible route would have been that of crossing the Mediterranean from Egypt to Sicily. This is not to suggest to the reader that the Europeans were totally unaware of this new form of writing material. The bulls of the Popes of the eighth and ninth centuries were written on cotton card or cotton paper.[19] Interestingly enough, no writer from these   papal states called attention to these cards, or described it as a new material. A paperlike fabric made from the barks of trees was used for writing by the Lombards as early as the seventh century AD.[20] The art of compacting in a web of macerated fibers of plants appears to have been known and practiced, to some limited extent, in southern Europe long before the establishment of Moorish paper mills. How close to the ideas of Ts'ai Lun these paperlike materials came is a question for speculation.

The route of rag and bark papermaking into Europe belongs in the realm of the historian. Once again the law of supply and demand was responsible for the change of writing mediums. The fourteenth century witnessed a rebirth of learning. We see people thirsting for knowledge, hungering for wisdom that could only be satiated by materials that were plentiful. This demand for information by the masses spelled doom for the era of parchment and vellum. The more liberal use of paper at the beginning of the fifteenth century, by this newly-created class of book buyers and readers, marks the period of transition from the Dark Ages into the Renaissance. Paper was here to stay. The era of cloth and rag paper would be with us until one man, with a different interpretation of how paper should be made, came forth at the French Royal Academy.

NOTEWORTHY ACCOMPLISHMENTS

The Wasp as Paper Maker?

Cloth and rags would remain the main source of papermaking for centuries to come. Finally, the use of wood as a source of paper was suggested by the French naturalist and physicist Rene Antoine Ferchault de Reaumur (1683-1757).[21] As a naturalist Reaumur patiently observed the customs of the wasp. Through these observations, Reaumur concluded that the manner in which the wasps made their nests, especially the material that composed those nests, should strongly be considered by the papermaking industry. Reaumur suggested that the wasp seemed to invite us to make paper from wood. Ironically no record exists of Reaumur actually making paper from wood. Nonetheless Reaumur is given the credit as being the first scientist to make note of the fact that the wasp was actually the first professional papermaker.

The First Paper Machine

It should be noted that until the beginning of the nineteenth century all paper had been formed by hand. Increasing populations and the rising demand for education caused a minor panic among the papermakers. The demand for papermaking materials, rags and linen, exceeded the supply. These shortages encouraged scientists to come up with solutions to these problems. It was out of this necessity that Nicholas-Louis Robert invented and partially perfected the papermaking machine. As a possible note of interest, Robert, in later life, stated that he invented the machine for a different purpose. It was the undying strife and bickering among the handmade papermakers' guild that "forced" Robert toward his invention. In short, Robert invented his machine so that he might replace the large numbers of workers necessary for the production of paper by hand, thus ending a source of constant irritation to himself.

The principle of Robert's machine — the same principle of all modern papermaking machines — was to form the paper upon an endless woven-wire cloth that retained the matted fibers and at the same time suffered the superfluous water to drain through the meshes of the woven wire.[22] In forming paper in the hand mould the principle of the operation is identical; but, with the hand-mould, the sheet formed thereon is limited to the size of the mould; while, with the machine, the paper is formed in an endless length, the width being limited only by the width of the machine.[23]

Revolution was not only in the air in France during the last few years of the eighteenth century but in the streets as well. Robert, caught up in the fame of his invention, fell prey to the Revolution — in the sense that he felt compelled to sell his invention to a means to survive hard times. At the same time his partner wrote his brother-in-law, an English paper mill proprietor, suggesting that he raised money to construct a papermaking machine. Henry and Sealy Fourdrinier, London stationers, became interested in the development of a newer machine. Several additional patents were devised, and by 1803 the machine was capable of producing paper of good quality. The papermaking machine to this day bears the name of the Fourdrinier brothers, the only recognition they received for their part in the perfecting of the machine.[24] The Fourdrinier brothers lost a fortune as the result of perfecting the machine. There appeared a "flaw" in their patent; manufacturers took advantage of this flaw and built machines without being subjected to paying royalities.

The "Soda" Process

By the mid 1800s the papermaking industry still relied heavily upon the ground-wood process and handmade rag methods as the mainstay of making cheap paper in vast quantities. The industry was aware of a few methods of purification of wood fibers, but they were relatively untried, that is until Hugh Burgess and Charles Watt ushered in a new era in the production of paper. Burgess and Watt searched for a chemical method that would best eliminate the intercellular tissue from wood (lignin) while being essentially nondestructive to the wood cellulose. As Dard Hunter observed,

> The process, according to patent specifications, called for boiling the wood, after it had been cut in small chips or shavings, in a solution of caustic alkali, in a closed boiler, under high pressure of steam at a high temperature. After having been boiled to a fibrous mass, the pulp after having been washed was subjected to the action of chlorine or its compounds, with oxygen.[25]

Burgess and Watt were forced to emigrate to the United States due to a surprising lack of interest in their efforts by their native England. A plant was established at Gray's Ferry, near Philadelphia. After securing an American patent for this new process (soda), Burgess and Watt spent the remainder of their days experimenting with various papermaking materials deemed suitable for this new process. Like England, America proved somewhat stubborn against this soda process and it would take an additional decade before it was accepted into general practice.

The Sulphite Process

The year 1857 witnessed Benjamine and Richard Tilghman in Paris experimenting with fats immersed in a sulphurous acid. This solution was kept in wooden barrels, perforated with small holes a few inches apart and closed in with removable conical pegs made of soft wood. Benjamine Tilghman noted that the ends of these plugs, which were constantly wet by the solution in the barrel, became soft and fuzzy, but he failed to grasp the significance of his observations. Years later Benjamine Tilghman visited the paper mill of a friend to observe its pulping actions and his discovery of a few years prior suddenly took root.

Tilghman returned to his experiments with renewed vigor. He observed that a solution of sulphurous acid, kept at a high temperature and pressure, dissolved lignin but, unfortunately, left the remaining wood fibers red in color. His analysis found that the sulphurous acid converted partially into sulphuric acid and made the rational connection between that discovery and the reddish color of the remaining wood fibers. He began experimenting with various chemicals in an attempt to neutralize the sulphurous acid. Eventually he discovered that sulphite of lime would add that desired neutralization. As the result of his discovery the sulphite process of the pulping of paper was born. Unfortunately for both Benjamine and his brother Richard, they were unable to perfect the necessary additions to pulping machinery to make a commercial success of their discovery; dwindling financial resources forced these brothers to abandon their efforts regarding the sulphite process.[26]

The Sulphite Process Commercialized

Carl D. Ekman and George Fry carried on the work initated by the Tilghmans. Both men had undertaken considerable experimentation with this new sulphite process. Where they differed from the Tilghmans was in the neutralization process during the cooking of the pulp; Ekman and Fry utilized a solution prepared form bisulphite and magnesia, whereas the Tilghmans relied heavily upon that of lime.[27] Ekman succeeded in selling their ideas to American industrialists; by 1882, sulphite pulp was produced on a commercial scale.

NOTES

1. J. Munsell, *A Chronology of Paper and Paper-Making* (Albany, J. Munsell, 1856), 174 pages.
2. D. Hunter, *Papermaking through Eighteen Centuries* (New York, B. Franklin, 1971), 358 pages.
3. D. Hunter, *Papermaking — The History and Technique of an Ancient Craft*, 2nd ed. (New York, Dover Pub., 1978), 611 pages.
4. N. Humphreys, *Origin and Progress of the Art of Writing* (London, 1855).
5. Pliny the Elder, *Naturalis Historia*, pp. 13-20.
6. See note 5 above.
7. C. Ellis, *Printing Inks — Their Chemistry and Technology* (New York, Reinhold Pub. Corp., 1940), pp. 37-45.
8. See note 5 above.
9. See note 7 above.
10. See note 7 above.
11. See note 7 above.
12. D. N. Carvalho, *Forty Centuries of Ink* (— — —, Banks Law Pub. Co., 1904), pp. 280-295.
13. See note 13 above.
14. See note 3 above.
15. See note 3 above.

16. See note 3 above.
17. *Nineteen Centuries of Pulp and Papermaking* (Appleton, WI, Institute of Paper Chemistry, 1900).
18. See note 1 above, pp. 5-11.
19. See note 1 above, pp. 5-11.
20. See note 13 above, pp. 83-86.
21. See note 1 above, p. 22.
22. See note 3 above, pp. 341-400.
23. See note 3 above, pp. 341-400.
24. See note 3 above, pp. 341-400.
25. See note 3 above, pp. 341-400.
26. See note 3 above, pp. 341-400.
27. See note 3 above, pp. 341-400.

Suggested Readings

Clapperton, R. H.: *Paper: An Historical Account of Its Making by Hand from the Earliest Times Down to the Present Day.* Oxford, England, 1934. 158 pages.

Du Halde, P.: *The General History of China, Including an Exact and Particular Account of Their Customs, Manners, Ceremonies, Religion, Arts, and Sciences*, Vol. II. London, 1736, pp. 415-438.

Herring, R.: *Paper and Papermaking, Ancient and Modern.* London, 1855. 125 pages.

Hunter, D.: *Old Papermaking.* Chillicothe, Ohio, 1923. 112 pages.

Hunter, D.: *The Literature of Papermaking, 1390-1800.* Chillicothe, Ohio, 1925. 48 pages.

Kuniaski, J.: *Kamisuki Choho-Ki* (Papermakers' Treasury). Osaka, Japan, 1798. Wood-blocks by Tokei Niwa.

Von Hagen, V. W.: *The Aztec and Maya Papermakers.* New York, 1944. 120 pages.

Weeks, L. H.: *A History of Paper Manufacturing in the United States, 1690-1916.* New York, 1916. 352 pages.

CHAPTER 11

A PARTIAL COMPENDIUM OF
PAPER INDUSTRY TERMS

INTRODUCTION

THE examination of paper is a subject of interest to everyone who embraces any of the disciplines within the collective framework of the forensic sciences. This subject is of particular interest to those individuals in the fields of forensic chemistry, questioned document analysis, ballistics, and trace elemental analysis and to the members of those units whose function it is to collect and preserve evidence found at the scene of the crime.

It is with that end in mind that we sought to have in readiness a partial compendium of terms utilized within the paper industry. This partial compendium is, by no means, the final word in paper and paperboard products. Rather it is a restricted listing of those terms we have found to be of interest to those individuals whose daily work diet consists of a menu of ever changing paper evidence.

With the student in mind, it may serve as a ready guide for everything from ballistics (i.e. definitions of cartridge paper, basewad paper) and chemistry (i.e. definitions of the majority of paper in use today) to explosives (i.e. definitions of dynamite shell paper, firecracker paper). For questioned document examiners, a list has been included of all the known terms depicting defects in paper, from air bells through winder welts. In short, this is a guide for those individuals to consult first and then seek additional information regarding paper and paper products if necessary.

Terms have been extracted and abridged from *The Dictionary of Paper*, 3rd ed. (New York, American Paper and Pulp Association, 1965); The Institute of Paper Chemistry's *Paper Analysis for the Forensic Sciences* (Appleton, WI, Continuing Education Center, 1979); and *ASTM Standards* (American Society for Testing and Materials).

A PARTIAL COMPENDIUM OF PAPER INDUSTRY TERMS

Accessibility — The accessibility of a cellulose system represents that fraction of the system in which intermolecular cohesion is weak enough to permit a rapid participation in chemical reactions.

Acidity — The condition that results in an acid solution when the paper is treated or extracted with water. In testing paper for acidity, the specimen is extracted with water at room temperature or at 100° C, and the extract is tested to determine its pH or it is titrated to determine the total amount of acid extracted from the paper.

Adding-Machine Paper — Book-paper grade or a writing (tablet) in roll form used on tabulating and adding machines. Strength other than tensile strength is relatively unimportant. The surface of the paper should be free from lint or fuzz and the paper should not develop this defect under normal conditions. It has a medium finish and absorbency but is often sized for use of writing ink. Basic weight range: 16 to 18 pounds. Uniform caliper is an important characteristic.

Adhesive Felt — A heavy bogus paper, usually gray in color, which is used as a stiffener or backing in leather products, such as cap visors, pocketbooks, etc.

Air Dry — A term applied to pulp and paper. "Paper" is air dry when its moisture content (usually 3 to 9%) is in equilibrium with atmospheric conditions to which it is exposed (air-dry pulps are assumed to contain 10% moisture, according to trade custom). The method for calculating the % air-dry content is to take 1000 times the oven-dry sample weight divided by 9 times the wet sample weight equals the percent air-dry.

Air Knife — A thin, flat jet of air for removing the excess coating from a wet, freshly coated sheet.

Air-Mail Paper — A lightweight writing paper which is used for letters and circulars to be transported by airplanes. The basis weight is 5 to 9 lbs (17 = 22-500). Its light weight is its most significant property; opacity is also important.

Album Paper — A cover paper used principally for making photograph albums. It is made in solid colors, particularly in gray and black, in basis weights of 50, 65, and 80 lbs (20 = 26-500). A soft surface that will take paste without cockling is essential. It is free of impurities that can discolor the photographic print; the color should not rub off (Black album paper).

Alkaliproof Paper — A paper marked with a high degree of resistance to alkali, used in the packaging and wrapping of alkaline materials such as adhesives, soaps, etc. An important characteristic of this paper is its stability of color without appreciable discoloration when wet with 1% sodium hydroxide (caustic soda) or 40 degrees Baume sodium silicate. Made with a variety of pulp furnishes, primarily semibleached and fully bleached chemical wood pulps. Many book papers have this property, along with waxed and glassine papers.

Alum — Alum refers to compounds, in the true chemical sense, having a structure similar to that of a double salt $K_2SO_4 \cdot Al_2(SO_4)_3 \cdot 24H_2 \cdot$ Papermakers' alum is $Al_2(SO_4)_3 \cdot 14H_2O$, $Al_2(SO_4)_3 \cdot 18H_2O$, or a mixture of these hydrates.

Aluminum Paper — A base paper of ordinary wrapping weight coated with aluminum powder. It may be made by incorporating the powder in the paper at the beater or in a size press. In the manufacture of aluminum-coated paper, flake aluminum powder (not too coarse mesh) is incorporated with casein or other aqueous sizing vehicle or with lacquers in organic solution to form a coatable composition. In aqueous vehicles, it may be applied by a brush or other coating means; in organic vehicles, it is usually applied by a roll or air knife. After coating, the product may be calendered or embossed. It may be used for a variety of wrapping purposes, particularly for wrapping food products and tobacco.

Aniline Dyes — This term is used broadly to designate synthetic organic dyes and pigments (whether or not they are derived from aniline), as distinguished from animal and vegetable coloring materials (usually organic), natural earth pigment (usually organic) and artificial inorganic pigments. This term originally applied to dyes derived from aniline including the first synthetic dyestuffs known.

Antique Book Paper — A paper usually made in a cream-white color (frequently referred to as "natural" color) but which may also be made in other shades or colors. It is frequently used for novels where a specific bulk for a given weight is required. It is usually made of bleached chemical wood pulp with a preponderance of short-fibered pulp, although mechanical pulp may also be used.

Antitarnish Paper — The term was originated for a lightweight sheet or tissue made from rags and carefully bleached and washed, which was used for wrapping silverware, steel tools, cutlery, and other polished steel hardware. Later the term was applied to wrapping paper made from sulfite or sulfate pulp free from acid or sulfur compounds. Copper salts or other inhibitors, including vapor phase, are sometimes used in treating the paper when used for wrapping silverware or leaded glass. Todays uses include wrapping aluminum goods, leaded glass, hardware, razor blades, needles, and other tarnishable articles.

Apron — Originally an oilcloth attached to the headbox and extending over the Fourdrinier wire from the breast roll to the first slice. This combination forms an adjustable nozzle, in which the slice or slice lip is the adjustable upper portion, and the apron the bottom; it serves as a metering device which guides the stock from the headbox, over the apron, and onto the moving wire.

Asbestos Diaphragm Paper — **1.** An inorganic base paper made of specially processed white asbestos fibers in thicknesses of 0.003 to 0.009 inch; the paper may be treated with plastics and/or laminated to improve its mechanical properties. This paper is used for heat-resistant electrical insulations for the lighter temperature ranges. **2.** A paper made of specially processed white asbestos fibers combined with certain organic fillers to improve its mechanical strength in thickness of 0.005 to 0.015 inch. This paper is used primarily as a heat-resistant electrical insulation in combination with other dielectrics.

Asbestos Paper — A sheet of asbestos fibers, from 0.0015 to 0.0625 of an inch thick. For special purposes it may be laminated to greater thicknesses. The furnish consists mainly of asbestos fiber of varying qualities, depending upon the use to which the paper is to be put. The amount of sizing and filler may be as great as approximately 15 percent in papers for special uses. Asbestos paper is used as an insulating material where minumum thickness is required, principally as a protection against heat and as a fire retardant between floors, walls, and ceilings.

Ash — The inorganic residue obtained by igniting a specimen of pulp, paper, or other cellulosic material in such a way that the combustible and volatile compounds are removed. The "ash content" is the percentage of such residue based on the weight of the test specimen.

Autochrome Printing Paper — A coated paper suitable for multicolor printing.

Autotype Paper — A bond or writing paper similar to register paper, used for automatic registering machines or fanforms where multiple copies are required. It is made from cotton fiber and/or chemical wood pulps in basis weights of 9 to 16 pounds (17 = 22-500). A fairly smooth surface and good manifolding properties are important.

Bag — A flexible container made of foil, paper, or the like in one of four general types; square, satchel-bottom, flat, or automatic (self-opening); the term *duplex* is used when two layers of paper are employed; multiwall designates three or more walls.

Bagasse — The crushed stalks of the sugar cane after the sugar has been removed.

Baling — **1.** The operation of forming a bale of pulp, rags, waste papers, or other materials through compression in a bailing press. **2.** A method of packing paper, in which the paper is covered with burlap, baled up under pressure and protected on opposite sides by boards; iron bands are passed around the bale, thus keeping it solid. **3.** According to a JAN specification, bailing has the following connotation: a waterproof barrier utilized to prevent the entrance of water into the baled contents; usually, a plain or creped paper is placed around the bale, which is then overwrapped in the waterproof barrier.

Bamboo — A giant grass, often reaching a height of forty feet or more, found in the tropical regions of the eastern hemisphere. Bamboo has, in the past two decades, found a home in the semitropical regions of the Southern states. The fibers closely resemble those from straws in many of their characteristics. Its fibers have an average length of 2.4 mm, placing between softwood and hardwood fibers.

Barium Sulfate — A chemical compound ($BaSO_4$) obtained either from the natural mineral barytes or by chemical reaction and used as a filler, and as a coating pigment especially for photographic papers either as such or in combination with other pigments. The artificial product is called blanc fixe, fast white, pearl white, or permanent white.

Basewad Paper — A dense paper used in the base of a shotgun shell to help hold the paper tube to the brass wall of the shell. It is made in thicknesses of about 0.010 to 0.012 of an inch (see also *Wad Stock*).

Basic Size — A certain sheet size recognized by buyers and sellers as the one from which its basis weight is determined. Initially, it was that size which printed, folded, and trimmed most advantageously. Some of the specifications for basic sizes now in use are as follows:

	Dimensions in inches	Number of sheets in ream
Bible	25 × 38	500
Blanks	22 × 28	500
Blotting	19 × 24	500
Bond	17 × 22	500
Book	25 × 38	500
Box Cover	20 × 26	500
	24 × 36	500
	25 × 38	500
Cover	20 × 26	500
Glassine	24 × 36	500
Gummed	25 × 38	500
Hanging	24 × 36	480
Index bristol	25.5 × 30.5	500
Ledger	17 × 22	500
Manifold	17 × 22	500
Manuscript cover	18 × 31	500
Mill bristol	22.5 × 28.5	500
	25.5 × 35	500
Mimeograph	17 × 22	500

News	24 × 36	500
Offset	25 × 38	500
Postcard	22.5 × 28.5	500
Poster	24 × 36	500
Railroad manila	17 × 22	500
Tag	22.5 × 28.5	500
	24 × 36	500
Tissues	24 × 36	500
	20 × 30	480*
Tough check	22 × 28	500
Waxing	24 × 36	500
Waxing tissue	24 × 36	500
Wedding bristol	22.5 × 28.5	500
Wrapping	24 × 36	500
Wrapping tissues	24 × 36	480
Writing	17 × 22	500

*The weight of tissue is sometimes given for a ream of 480 sheets (20 × 30).

Basis weight — The weight in pounds of a ream of paper cut to its Basic size (q.v.).† The United States Government Printing Office uses a unit of 1000 sheets. This unit also appears in certain trade customs. For cultural papers, the basis weight of 500 sheets (17 × 22 inches) is sometimes called substance or substance number. In most foreign countries and in some domestic test procedures, the standard size is a square meter and the weight is expressed in grams per square meter. For paperboards, basis weight is expressed in pounds per 1000 square feet. The standard ream for boxboard is 500 sheets measuring 25 × 40 inches and is also used in reporting basis weight.

Bast Fiber — Fibers obtained from the phloem or inner bark of a woody plant but (unfortunately) also applied to fibers found in other outer portions of the plant, such as cortex and pericycle. Botanically, the term is superfluous, since the terms "phloem fiber," "cortical fiber," and "pericyclic fiber" are accurate and specific. Flax, hemp, jute, ramie, mitsumata, and gampi are typical bastfiber plants.

Beater — A machine consisting of a tank or "tub" containing a heavy roll revolving against a bedplate. Both roll and bedplate may contain horizontal metal bars set on edge. Pulp or waste papers are put into the tub and water added so that the mass may circulate and pass between roll and bedplate. This action frees the fibers (see also *Refiner*).

Beater Additive — Any nonfibrous material, such as a coloring or sizing agent, an adhesive, etc., that is added to the furnish to improve the processing and final properties of the paper.

---

†Usually 500, but sometimes 480 sheets.

Bible Paper — A lightweight opaque book paper used where low bulk is important, i.e. bibles, missals, encyclopedias, rate books, etc. Basis weights normally range from 14 to 30 pounds (25 × 38-500). Bible papers are made from bleached chemical wood pulps, cotton pulps or rag stock, flax straw pulp, linen rags, and combinations thereof and are usually heavily loaded with titanium dioxide or other pigments for maximum printing opacity. The most important properties, aside from printability, are sheet strength and reasonable permanence. The paper was first developed in England under the name of India Bible or India Oxford Bible Paper.

Blade Coating — A method of coating utilizing a flexible blade set at an adjustable angle against a web of paper or board supported by a soft, usually rubber-covered backing roll. Also called Trailing Blade Coating and Flexible Blade Coating.

Blanks — A term applied to a class of paperboard ranging in thickness from 0.012 to 0.078 of an inch, with corresponding basis weights of 120 to 775 pounds (22 × 28-500). They may be either single-ply Fourdrinier board, multi-ply cylinder board, or laminations of these. The liner may be made of deinked stock, clean shavings, bleached or unbleached groundwood, or chemical pulps. The surface may be either coated or uncoated, white or colored. Blanks are generally made to produce maximum stiffness and surface smoothness. They are used for various purposes where stiffness and good printing qualities are required as in streetcar signs, window displays, etc.

Bleaching — The process of chemically treating pulp to alter the coloring matter so that the pulp has a higher brightness. This is usually accompanied by partial removal of noncellulosic materials. The two classes of chemicals used are oxidizing agents (such as chlorine, hypochlorites, chlorine dioxide, and hydrogen peroxide) and reducing agents (such as sulfur dioxide and hydrosulfites). Bleaching may be carreid out in a single stage, but most processes use sequences of several stages.

Blister — **1.** A defect arising in paper when dried too suddenly on the drying cylinder or when the felts are not in good condition, leaving air between the felt and the sheet. **2.** A blister may also occur between two plies of a cylinder board owing to lack of ply adhesion. **3.** A defect in coated paper that results when it is subjected to a high temperature during the drying of ink on high-speed heat-set presses; this defect is generally caused by excessive moisture, use of excessive heat on the press, or coating through which moisture vapor will not readily pass. **4.** A rapid test for papers such as glassine or greaseproof made from highly hydrated pulps. These papers develop blisters when exposed to the flame of a match or candle just enough to char the sheet very slightly.

Blotting Paper — An unsized paper used generally to absorb excess ink from freshly written letters, manuscripts, and signatures. It is also where absorptivity is a required characteristic or where soft spongy paper is needed, even though the absorptivity is of secondary importance. It is made from rag, cotton linters, chemical or mechanical wood pulp, or mixtures of these. The paper is porous, bulky, of low finish, and possesses little strength. The normal basis weights range from 60 to 140 pounds (19 × 24-500). Blotting paper may also be embossed and used for desk blotters.

Bond Paper — A grade of writing or printing paper originally used where strength, durability, and permanence are essential requirements, as in government bonds and legal documents. Its use has extended into other fields, such as business letterheads and forms, where strength and permanence, though important properties, are not so essential; this accounts for the wide range of quality in this type of paper. These qualities are obtained through the use of cotton fiber pulp, bleached chemical wood pulps, and mixtures of these fibers in the manufacturing process. Bond paper must have good printing qualities as well as writing and erasing qualities, cleanliness, formation, finish, color, and freedom from fuzz. It is usually made in basis weights from 13 to 24 pounds (17 × 22-500).

Book Paper — **1.** A general term used to define class or a group of papers (exclusive of newsprint) having in common physical characteristics that, in general, are most suitable for the graphic arts. These physical characteristics are varied to meet the requirements of the type of impress employed and the objective use of the article produced. The basic materials used are mechanical and chemical wood pulps, grass (esparto), cotton fiber pulp, or selected reclaimed paper stock. Some of these pulps may be used alone, but usually the paper is made up of a mixture of two or three different types of pulps to which is added mineral filler, sizing, and coloring matter. The major portion of this paper is made on the conventional Fourdrinier machine and machine dried; however, some is made on cylinder molds and on hand molds. The paper may be surface sized or coated on the paper machine or as a separate operation. The principal finishes for uncoated book paper are antique, eggshell, machine, English, and supercalendered; for coated paper, dull, matte, or glossy. The basic size and count in the United States is 25 × 38-500. The usual weights range from 22 to 185 pounds with the majority of the tonnage in a range of weights from 30 to 70 pounds for uncoated, and 40 to 100 pounds for coated papers. The important characteristics are appearance and printability for the printing process selected. **2.** A generic term encompassing not only the printing grades made above but other grades of paper made by "book" mills such as tablet papers, envelope papers, gumming papers, etc.

Box-cover Paper — A paper used to cover paper boxes. It may be plain, antique, embossed, ink embossed, glazed, flint glazed, coated or printed to add to its usefulness or attractiveness. It is generally made of chemical wood pulps, although groundwood and rag pulps may be included in the finish. Strength requirements are nominal for setup box use but must be sufficient for scoring and 180 fold in folding cartons and boxes.

Breaker Stack — A method of coating with a flexible blade set at an adjustable angle against a web of paper or board supported by a soft backing roll. Also called trailing-blade and flexible-blade coating.

Breast Roll — A large diameter roll around which the Fourdrinier wire passes at the machine headbox just at or ahead of the point where the stock is admitted to the wire by the stock inlet. It is covered with corrosion-resistant metal or fiberglass and is usually driven by the wire.

Bundle — **1.** A unit of board measure weighing 50 pounds. The number of sheets varies with the size and the caliper. **2.** A shipping unit of paper, as well as a packing method (see *Count, Regular Number*).

Burst Factor — A numerical value obtained by dividing the bursting strength in grams per square centimeter by the basis weight of the sheet in grams per square meter.

Bursting Strength — A measure of the ability of a sheet to resist rupture when pressure is applied to one of its sides by a specified instrument, under specified conditions. It is largely determined by the tensile strength and extensibility of the paper or paperboard. Testing for bursting strength is very common, although its value, except for limited, specific purposes is questionable.

Calender — A set or "stack" of horizontal cast-iron rolls with chilled, hardened surfaces, resting one on the other in a vertical bank at end of the machine. The paper is passed between all or part of these rolls to increase the smoothness and gloss of its surface (see also *Supercalender*).

Carbon Paper — **1.** A coated paper used for making duplicate copies with pencil, pen, typewriter, or business machine, commonly known as carbon or duplicate copies. It may range in weight from 4 to 28 pounds (20 × 30-500) or, rarely, even higher. It may be coated on one side (semicoated) or both sides (full-coated) with a mixture of carbon black or some other oil-soluble substance according to the intended use. The application is generally made by means of a coating machine with heated rolls revolving in melted inks, or a rotary or rotogravure printing press only printing on certain sections of the paper. It may be supplied in different finishes such as intense writing, medium writing, or hard writing. Varieties include billing machine, pencil, adding machine, hectograph, typewriter, and lithograph transfer. **2.** In photography, a paper coated with gelatin and a pigment.

Cartridge Paper — **1.** A paper used to form the tube section of a shotgun shell. The furnish may consist of rag, flax, or chemical wood pulps, or high-grade reclaimed paper stock in various combinations. It is made on a cylinder machine, each ply being decked in about half an inch or so as to form a beveled edge on each side. It is from 0.008 to 0.012 of an inch in thickness, usually unsized and lightly calendered for pasting, and it is absorbent to facilitate waxing or other means of protection against dampness. The weight, caliper, density are uniform, the last near 190 grains per cubic inch. It may be colored or plain, and the color may be solid or duplex in nature. The size of the sheets varies with the shell gage, the width ranging from about 11 to 12 inches. Important properties include tensile strength, stretch, and stiffness (see also *Basewad Paper*. **2.** A groundwood, manila, or chemical wood pulp sheet used as a wrapper for stick dynamite.

Casein — The acid-coagulable protein of skim milk obtained as a by-product of the dairy industry. It is used in the sizing of paper and as an adhesive in the manufacture of coated papers.

Cash Register Paper — Base paper from which cash register rolls are made. Such paper is generally made of bleached chemical wood pulp alone or mixed with mechanical pulp and closely resembles unwatermarked bond, writing, or tablet paper. It is commonly produced in white and colors, and the weight is usually 16 pounds (17 × 22-500). It is converted into very narrow, small diameter rolls as required by cash registers. Such converted rolls are used in pairs — a "receipt roll," which is printed by the machine and handed to the customer, and a "detail roll" on which is printed total cash sales continuously for a complete check of a day's sales.

Chalking — **1.** A printing defect, in which ink pigment may be easily rubbed from the surface of paper. **2.** A condition encountered in some papers where fine particles of pigment leave the sheet during the finishing, converting, printing operation, or subsequent use.

Chromatographic Paper — A filter paper which has the properties of uniformity, texture, and porosity required for use in paper chromatography.

Cigarette Paper — A strong tissue paper of close, uniform texture, free from pinholes, used as a wrapper for tobacco in manufacture of cigarettes. It is generally made from flax pulp and contains no size. This paper may be either combustible or noncombustible. Combustible paper, also called free burning paper, contains from about 15 percent to about 30 percent of calcium carbonate filler. All cigarette paper is made from highly beaten stock, which contributes to its high strength and uniform formation but which, at the same time, necessitates the addition of large percentages of the filler to provide the desired porosity. The rate of burning of the cigarette is controlled largely by the porosity of the paper, which depends, among other factors, upon the percentage of filler in the sheet, and by the size and shape of the filler particles. The filler also contributes importantly to the whiteness and opacity of the paper. Noncombustible paper has little or no filler added. The normal weight of cigarette paper for consumption in the American industry is about 20 to 22 grams per square meter, and the calcium carbonate content is about 25 percent. Cigarette paper for roll-your-own cigarettes may weigh as little as 15 to 18 grams per square meter. Significant properties include strength, stretch, filler content, texture, color, opacity, and porosity.

Clothing — A term applied to paper-machine felts and Fourdrinier wires.

Conifer — A gymnosperm tree or shrub belonging to the order Coniferales, so called because the fruit of the tree is a cone, as in the pines and firs (see also *Softwood*).

Converter — A plant that manufactures paper products, such as papeteries, envelopes, bags, containers, coated paper, and gummed paper. Such operations are frequently carried out by primary paper and board manufacturers as well as by independent companies not engaged in primary manufacturing.

Cook — The operation of treating any cellulosic raw material (rags, pulpwood, straw, etc.) with chemicals, usually at a high pressure and temperature, for the purpose of removing impurities and producing a pulp suitable for papermaking.

Couch — To pick up, i.e. a couch roll on a machine is a transfer roll to pick up pulp from a wire or other cylinder. (Pronounced "cooch.")

Count — **1.** The actual number of sheets of paperboard of a given size, weight, and caliper required to make a bundle of 50 pounds. **2.** The number of sheets which make up a standard unit of a particular kind of paper. The weight, size, and count of book paper, e.g. 50 pounds (basis weight), 25 × 38 (size), and 500 (count), would usually be written as 50 pounds (25 × 38-500).

Cover Paper — A term applied to a great variety of papers used for the outside covers of catalogs, brochures, and booklets to enhance the appearance and to provide protection from handling, and for other printed matter in which substantial weight or bulk is important. Cover papers are made in white and usually in a wide range of colors. Most cover papers have plain edges, but some are available with deckle edges. Finishes range from antique through smooth to a wide variety of special finishes and coated surfaces. Cover papers are usually made from chemical wood pulp, sometimes in mixture with cotton fiber pulps. Common basis weights in pounds of uncoated cover papers are 50, 65, 80, and 2/65 (20 × 26-500); weights of coated cover papers are 60, 80, and 100 (20 × 26-500). The customary sizes are 20 × 26, 23 × 35, 26 × 40, and 35 × 46. Special characteristics of cover papers include dimensional stability, uniform printing surface, good folding qualities and durability.

Currency Paper — Paper used for printing paper currency, bonds, and other government securities. The paper for United States currency is manufactured on a Fourdrinier machine from new rag cuttings and flax pulp; it is tub sized with animal glue, loft dried, and plater finished. The basis weight is 24.16 pounds (12.75 × 16.38-1000). It may contain distinctive features to protect against counterfeiting. Significant properties are quick and uniform wettability, adaptability to printing by the intaglio process, high tensile strength and folding endurance, and resistance to wear. Also known as Banknote paper.

Cut Size — A term commonly used in the fine paper field to denote a guillotine or rotary trimmed sheet of paper having dimensions of 16 × 21 inches or less. Size 8½ × 11 inches is the most common cut size.

Cylinder Machine — One of the principal types of papermaking machines, characterized by the use of wire-covered cylinders or molds on which a web is formed. These cylinders are partially immersed and rotated in vats containing a dilute stock suspension. The pulp fibers are formed into a sheet on the mold as the water drains through and passes out at the end of the cylinders. The wet sheet is couched off the cylinder onto a felt, which is held against the cylinder by a couch roll. A cylinder machine may consist of one or several cylinders, each supplied with the same or different kinds of stock. In the case of a multicylinder machine, the webs are successively couched one upon the other before entering the press section. This permits wide variation in thickness or weight of the finished sheet, as well as a variation in the kind of stock used for the different layers of the sheet. The press section and the dry end of the machine are essentially the same as those of other types of machines.

Dandy — A skeleton roll, covered with wire cloth and supported above the Fourdrinier wire and riding on the wet web of paper at a point near the first suction box for the purpose of marking the sheet with a design (watermark) carried on the surface of the roll. Plain dandy rolls are used to level the surface and improve or assist in formation.

Deckle — On a Fourdrinier papermaking machine, the arrangements on the side of the wire that keep the stock suspension from flowing over the edges of the wire.

Deckle Edge — The untrimmed feather edge of a sheet of paper formed where the pulp flows against the deckle.

Deed Paper — Bond paper used in documents such as deeds. The usual finish is cotton fiber which may also be blended with bleached chemical wood pulps. The paper is generally surface sized. Permanence and durability are significant properties.

Defects in Paper — Air Bells, Back Mark (Pole Mark, Stick Mark), Baggy, Bark Specks, Blackening, Bleach Scale, Bleeding, *Blister* (Blow, Bubble), Blister Cut, Bronze, Burnt, Button Specks, Calender Crushed (Calender Backened), Calender Cuts, Calender Marked, Calender Scabs, Calender Scales, Calender Spots, Carbon Spots, Chain Lines, *Chalking*, Cinder Specks,

Clamp Marks, Clay Lump, Cockle, Cockle Cut, Color Spots, Couch Mark, Cracked Edge, Cracking (Flaking), Craters, Crocking, Curl, Cutter Dust, Damp Streaks, Dandy Mark (Dandy Pick), Dirt, *Drag Spots*, Drop Marks, Dusting, Fiber Cut, *Fish eyes*, Fluff, Foam Marks (Froth Spots), Foxed, *Fuzz*, Grainy Edges, *Grease Spots* (Oil Spots), Haircut, Iron Specks, *Knots, Lint, Moisture Welts, Motted Color*, Offsquare, Overdried, *Peeling, Pick, Picking, Pinholes, Pitch Spots*, Pucker, Ring Marks, *Rope Marks, Roping*, Rosin Specks, *Rubber Spots*, Scuffing, Shiner, Shive, Skipped Coating, *Slack Edges, Slime Hole, Slime Spots, Slitter Dust, Snailing, Speck, Suction Blanket Mark, Suction Box Marks, Suction Roll Mark, Turned Edge, Two-sidedness, Washboard Marks, Water Streaks, Wavy Edges, Welts, Winder Welts, Winder Wrinkles, Wire Hole, Wire Spot*, Wrinkle.*

Deflectors — Stationary elements placed beneath the Fourdrinier wire for the purpose of support of the wire and removal by scraping action of the water from the under surface of the moving wire. Deflectors have sharp leading edges and ordinarily have level top surfaces. They are positioned between table rolls to reduce the amount of water carried over from one table roll to another.

Deinking — The operation of reclaiming fiber from waste paper by removing ink, coloring materials, and fillers.

Digester — The vessel used to treat pulpwood, straw, rags, or other such cellulosic materials with chemicals to produce pulp for papermaking.

Direct Process Paper — A paper used for direct process reproduction (frequently known as the diaz process) that is made from bleached chemical wood pulps, although some may contain 25 to 50 percent cotton. The paper must have a very uniform formation, freedom from impurities (especially iron), extremely hard sizing, low pH (ca. 4.5), and a high finish. It must also have good fold, tear, opacity, and brightness. The paper is tub sized (with starch) and is calendered before and after sizing. A certain degree of wet strength is desirable, although the wet tensile strength and wet rub resistance are not as important as in blueprint papers.

Disk Refiner — A "refiner (q.v.)" whose working elements consist of one or more matched pairs of disks having a pattern of ribs machined into their faces and arranged so that one disk of the pair is rotated. The other disk is usually stationary, but may be driven in the opposite direction of rotation. Precision controls are provided for adjusting the clearance between the disk faces and applying pressure between them. The disks are enclosed in a case arranged so that a suspension of paper stock can be pumped in and caused to flow radially from the center out, or vice versa between the rapidly moving ribbed surfaces of the disks, thus resulting in refining.

*Due to this compendiums' partial listing, the authors suggest that interested students investigate these terms in the publications listed at the beginning of this chapter.

Document Parchment — **1.** A paper made to resemble animal parchment and used for diplomas, commissons, acts of Congress, and treaties where animal parchment was formerly used. It is made from high-quality linen and cotton fibers on a Fourdrinier machine; it may or may not be engine sized with rosin, but is surface sized with the highest quality animal glue or with a special tub sizing. The paper should possess maximum durability and permanency. **2.** A vegetable parchment paper used for diplomas and documents.

Doctor — A thin plate or scraper of wood, metal, or other hard substance placed along the entire length of a roll or cylinder to keep it free from paper, pulp, size, etc., and thus maintain a smooth, clean surface (Creped).

Double Calendered — Paper that has been run through the supercalenders twice, generally coated paper.

Double Coated — A term applied to a paper or board that has been coated twice on the same side with the same or different materials. The term is also used (incorrectly) to designate a paper or board with a heavy coating (but not necessarily two coatings).

Drag Spots — Imperfections in the paper sheet that appears as irregular thin streaks or lumpy spots caused by agglomerations of stock adhering to the slice. These agglomerations, while adhering to the slice, reduce the volume of flow of the stock at that particular point, thereby causing a thin streak in the formation. As the agglomerations break loose, they may be carried into the sheet and appear as lumps.

Draw Down — A method of surface application for testing purposes utilizing a wire-wound rod coater, a machined metal block, or other instrument to wipe an excess of Coating color or ink from a sheet of paper thus leaving a metered quantity on the surface.

Drawing Paper — **1.** The general term for paper used for pen or pencil drawings by artists, architects, and draftsmen. It is usually a machine-made paper in the United States, but in other countries most of it is handmade. There are a number of papers in this class or type that have certain properties emphasized to fit a special need. There are architect's, art, charcoal, crayon, detail, drafting, manila, matte art, rope, school, and vellum drawing papers. Chemical wood pulps, cotton, or mixtures of these fibers are used in the manufacture of drawing paper in basis weights of 80 to 100 pounds (24 × 36-500). This paper has a good writing surface for pencil, good erasability, and a dull or low finish. **2.** A grade of paper containing about 75 percent mechanical pulp with the balance unbleached chemical wood pulp. The sheet is principally used by school children for sketching, crayon, or watercolor work. It is hard sized and has a "toothy" surface. The usual basis weights are 56, 64, and 72 pounds (24 × 36-500). It is usually supplied in manila and gray colors.

Driers — A series of steam-heated metal cylinders, 30 to 60 inches in diameter, varying in number up to 130 or more, and arranged in two or more tiers. The cylinders are gear driven, and the wet paper or board passes over and under successive cylinders.

Dry End — The mill term for the drying section of the paper machine, consisting mainly of the driers, calenders, reels, and slitters.

Duplex Paper — Any paper showing different colors, textures, or finish on the two sides. Such paper is made by pasting two different kinds of paper together or on a cylinder machine or a combination cylinder-fourdrinier machine.

Duplicating Paper — **1.** Generally speaking, any paper that is designed for the reproduction of multiple copies by processes such as Mimeograph, spirit duplicating, Ozalid, etc. **2.** Specifically applied to paper for copies produced by transfer of small portions of aniline ink from a master copy to many sheets of copy paper (e.g. "Ditto").

Dynamite-Shell Paper — A well-formed, smooth, highly finished sulfite or kraft sheet, usually in basis weights of 60 to 90 pounds (24 × 39-500) to be converted into tubes for packaging of dynamite, powder, etc. Tensile and tearing strength and moisture resistance, as well as finish and uniformity, are important characteristics.

Embossed — A term applied to paper on which a raised or depressed design is pressed (a) by passing the paper between an engraved steel roll or plate and another roll or plate of soft or compressible material, such as paper or cotton, or (b) by pressing between strong coarse fabrics, or (c) by passing between etched male and female iron or steel rolls. The operation is used for decorative effects and is generally applied to book, blotting, cover, and wallpapers.

Enameled — Originally a term applied to supercalendered coated papers in which the coating pigment was largely satin white or blanc fixe. Today the term is used generally for any coated paper.

Envelope Paper — *Manila* — A Fordrinier M. F. paper made in manila color of chemical wood pulps, usually with some percentage of mechanical wood pulp. The basis weight ranges usually from 16 to 40 pounds (17 × 22-500). It is used for conversion into envelopes, mainly for commercial purposes.

Envelope Paper — *Kraft* — A Fordrinier M. F. or M. G. paper made of unbleached, semibleached, or full-bleached sulfate pulp, used in the manufacture of envelopes when strength is a primary requirement. The basis weights range normally from 16 to 44 pounds (17 × 22-500). Other desirable properties include smooth fold, strength at crease, good printability, and lack of tendency to curl or cockle.

Erasability — That property of a sheet which is concerned with the ease of removing typed or written characters and impressions of both from the sheet by mechanical erasure, the cleanliness or the amount of abrading on the erased portion, and the suitability of the erased portion for re-use.

Esparto — A coarse grass from Southern Spain and Northern Africa, obtained from two species-*Lygenum spartum* and *Stipa tenacissima*. It is generally cooked with caustic soda alone or with sodium sulfide. Fibers are short and relatively fine and wiry. It is employed principally by English and Scottish papermakers for the production of better grades of book paper. It is also known as alfa, esparto grass, and Spanish grass.

Extensible Paper — A smooth-appearing stretchable paper with high energy absorption properties. A controlled amount of stretch to meet specifications may be imparted in a number of ways, either on or off the paper machine by methods generally differing from those used to produce creped papers. Extensible papers, made in a variety of basis weights and grades, are used for multiwall sacks, packaging, converting, laminating, wrapping, etc.

Fastness — That property of a paper or dyestuff which renders it resistant to change in color. Depending upon its use, a paper or paperboard may be required to show good resistance (fastness) to change in color after exposure to destructive influences such as light, acids, alkalies, bleaching agents, or water usually under specified test conditions.

Feather Edge — **1.** A thin, rough edge, like a deckle edge. **2.** A term applied to papers made with a thickness tapering from that of the body sheet to the edge. Such edges are used on fireworks papers, e.g., so that, when rolled, the outer edge will paste down smoothly.

Felt Roofing — A term sometimes used in reference to sheet roofing in the form of heavy mineralized, wide selvage edge, smooth roll roofing or universal base sheet.

Felt Side — That side of the paper which has not been in contact with the wire during manufacture. It is the top side of the sheet.

Festoon Drying — A method of air drying. The paper is hung in a single continuous web in short festoons or loops on traveling poles or slats moving through a drying chamber in which the temperature and humidity are controlled. This type of drying is used for paper after tub sizing or coating and for wallpaper after printing.

Fiber — The unit cell of vegetable growth that is many times longer than its diameter and that is the unit of paper pulps. Fibers are sometimes divided into two classes, bast and wood, but they are best designated by means of the tissue or region in which they occur, as cortical fibers, pericyclic fibers, phloem fibers, wood fibers, leaf fibers, etc. Other types of fiber such as mineral, animal, and synthetic are also used to a certain extent in making special types of paper.

Fiber Drum — A cylindrical, convolute, or spiral-wound container made in various sizes from paperboard or from combinations of paperboard with paper, plastic films, plastic coatings or metal foil, with fiber, metal, or wooden ends. These containers may be designed for packaging fluid or dry products.

Fibrillation — A term commonly associated with refining of pulp. It results in the loosening of threadlike elements from the fiber wall to provide greater surface for forming fiber-to-fiber bonds. This is also called brushing out.

Fill — The maximum trimmed width of paper or paperboard that can be made on a given paper machine.

Filler — **1.** A material, generally nonfibrous, added to the fiber furnish of paper. **2.** In paperboard, the inner ply or plies of a multiple layer.

Filter Paper — A porous, unsized paper for filtering solid particles from liquids or gases. It is made from cotton fiber or chemical wood pulp or both, in basis weights from 15 to 200 pounds (20 × 20-500). Important properties are uniformity of formation, moderate strength when wet, high retention of particulate matter, high filtering rate and, usually, in high chemical purity. For most purposes, the pore size is carefully controlled, since this determines the speed of filtration and the size of particles removed from the fluid (liquid or gas).

Fine Papers — A broad term including printing, writing, and cover papers, as distinguished from wrapping papers and paper not generally used for printing purposes, which are generally referred to as coarse papers.

Fines — Very short pulp fibers or fiber fragments and ray cells. They are sometimes referred to as flour or wood flour.

Finish — The surface property of a sheet determined by its surface contour, gloss, and appearance. It is a property that is usually determined by inspection.

Finishing — The various operations in the manufacture and packaging of paper performed after it leaves the paper machine. Finishing operations include supercalendering, plating, slitting, rewinding, sheeting, trimming, sorting, counting, and packaging. Ruling, punching, pasting, folding, and embossing are also sometimes considered as finishing operations.

Firecracker Paper — A paper made to give sheets with deckle edges from which strips can be cut counter to the machine direction. In wrapping the firecrackers, the deckle edge serves to terminate the roll without leaving a sharply cut edge.

Fireproof Paper — Any paper that is treated with chemicals so that it will not support combustion. It is not actually fireproof but will not carry a flame.

Fish Eyes — Small, round, glazed, or transparent spots caused by slime, undefibered portions of stock, or foreign materials which are crushed in calendering the sheet. The term also applies to round, transparent spots in the coated surface of coated board, which may be caused by excess defoamer of an oil-base type.

Flax — The bast fiber of the flax plant (*Linum usitatissimum*) has been the source of linen for several millennia. Linen rags, cuttings, thread, etc., have long been used in papermaking. More recently the straw from flax cultivated for seed has been used for the manufacture of cigarette paper and similar papers.

Flint Glazing — A method of imparting a hard, brilliant polish to paper, more especially to coated papers, by means of rubbing with a smooth stone or stone burnisher on a flint glazing machine.

Flow-On Coating — Flow-on coating consists of flowing a suspension of pigment and adhesive directly onto the wet web as it is being formed on a Fourdrinier papermaking machine.

Fluorescence — **1.** That property of substances that causes them to emit radiation as the immediate result of, and only during, the absorption of incident radiant energy of different wavelength. **2.** The radiation emitted in this process. It is also called fluorescent radiation. The fluorescent radiation is usually of longer wavelength that the exciting radiation. Nearly all the constitutents of paper exhibit fluorescence to some extent when irradiated by ultraviolet light. The color and brightness of the fluorescent radiation are characteristic of the fluorescing materials. This fact is the basis of fluorescence analysis. Some constituents, notably certain dyes, show fluorescence when irradiated by visible light. The color of paper containing materials that fluoresce strongly under the stimulus of visible light is more than usually sensitive to the nature of the illuminant under which it is viewed.

Fluorescent White — **1.** A term descriptive of fluorescent dyes or pigments, colorless as applied to "white" paper or paperboard but which increase the brightness by absorbing the ultraviolet energy of daylight and re-emitting it as visible light. **2.** "White" paper or paperboard containing such fluorescent material.

Folio — A ream or sheet in its full size. When used in connection with books, folio means that the sheet has been folded once, producing four pages.

Formation — A property determined by the degree of uniformity of distribution of the solid components of the sheet with special reference to the fibers. It is usually judged by the visual appearance of the sheet when viewed by transmitted light. This property is very important, not only because of its influence on the appearance of the sheet but because it influences the values and uniformity of values of nearly all other properties.

Freeness — A measure of the rate with which water drains from a stock suspension through a wire mesh screen or a perforated plate. It is also known as slowness or wetness, according to the type of instrument used in its measurement and the method of reporting results.

Furnish — The mixture of various materials blended in the stock suspension from which paper or board is made. The chief constitutents are the fibrous material (pulp), sizing materials, wet-strength or other additives, fillers, and dyes.

Fuzz — **1.** That property which causes a sheet to exhibit fibrous projections on its surface or to develop such fibrous projections in use. (These two interpretations of the property might more descriptively be called "fuzziness" and "fuzzability," respectively.) **2.** Fibers projecting from the surface of a sheet or paper.

Gampi — A shrub (*Wikstroemia canescens*) of the family Thymelaeaceae, which grows wild in the mountain forests of central and southern Japan. The bast fiber of the inner bark is used in papermaking.

Gelatin — An albuminous material present in bones, ligaments, and skins, which may be extracted by boiling water (the water may be slightly acidified with hydrochloric acid). It differs from glue in its purity and in the care observed in its manufacture. It is used in the tub sizing of paper.

Glassine Paper — A supercalendered, smooth, dense, transparent, or semitransparent paper manufactured primarily from chemical wood pulps that have been beaten to secure a high degree of hydration of the stock. This paper is grease resistant, and has a high resistance to the passage of air and many essential oil vapors used as food flavoring and, when waxed, lacquered, or laminated, is practically impervious to the transmission of moisture vapor. It is made in white and various colors; opaque glassines are produced by the addition of fillers. The basis weights may range from 12 to 40 pounds, the ordinary range being from 15 to 40 pounds (24 × 36-500).

Glazed — Paper with a high gloss or polish, applied to the surface either during the process of manufacture or after the paper is produced, by various methods such as friction glazing, calendering, plating, or drying on a Yankee drier. It is used in connection with bond, book, cover, certain wrapping papers, and paperboard.

Gloss — That property of the surface which causes it to reflect light specularly and which is responsible for its shiny or lustrous appearance. Gloss may be measured at various angles of illumination. For most printing papers specular gloss is usually measured at 75° which is the angle between a line normal to the surface of the specimen and the direction of reflected and incident light. For waxed paper a lower angle (generally 20°) is used.

Glue — Organic colloids of complex protein structure obtained from animal materials such as bones and hides in the meat packing and tanning industries. It is used for gumming, tub sizing, and as a general adhesive. It also serves as a coating adhesive for specialty products. The term is sometimes loosely used in a general sense synonymous with Adhesive.

Grade — **1.** A term applied to a paper or pulp that is ranked (or distinguished from other papers or pulps) on the basis of its use, appearance, quality, manufacturing history, raw materials, performance, or a combination of these factors. Some grades have been officially identified and described; other grades are commonly recognized but lack official definition. **2.** A term sometimes referring to one particular quality, differing from another only in size, weight, or grain.

Grease Spots — **1.** Dirt spots in paper caused by grease or oil. **2.** Those portions of the paper where there is a paucity of pulp, frequently caused by the refusal of water to stay on a grease spot on the wire.

Grinder — A machine for producing mechanical wood pulp or groundwood. It is essentially a rotating pulpstone against which logs are pressed and reduced to pulp.

Groundwood Printing Papers — Groundwood papers of the same general type as *Book Papers*. The mechanical wood pulp used is a carefully prepared clean, bright, and rather slow pulp (book grade). The use of mechanical pulp instead of all chemical wood pulps facilitates the retention of loading materials and produces characteristics such as higher bulk and opacity for equivalent basis weight, softness and smooth finish, which are valuable from the standpoint of low-cost and high-speed printing. These papers are less permanent and somewhat less bright than book papers made of all chemical wood pulps. Groundwood printing papers are made in a variety of furnishes ranging from approximately 75 percent of mechanical wood pulp to as little as 20 to 25 percent and are sized, finished, colored, loaded, and coated in various ways to make them suitable for virtually all types of printing.

Guar Gum — A polysaccharide, mainly mannogalactan, derived from the seed endosperm of the guar plant, *Cyamopsis tetragonolobus*, grown in India and the United States — used as a beater or wet-end additive primarily for improving strength properties. It may also be used as a surface sizing agent.

Gum — Either a hydrophobic or hydrophilic high molecular weight substance, usually with colloidal properties, which in an appropriate solvent or swelling agent produces a gel, highly viscous suspension, or solution at low solids content. More commonly, however, gum refers to plant polysaccharides or their derivatives which are dispersible in either cold or hot water to produce viscous mixtures or solutions (see *Guar gum*).

Gummed Paper — A general name for any paper coated on one side with adhesive gum, the adhesive being a dextrin, fish, or animal glue, and resin or a blend of any of these. The usual basis weight is in the range of 38-45 pounds (24 × 36-500). Gummed papers of various types are used for stickers, labels, seals, stamps, splices, tapes, etc. They should be flat and noncurling and adhere firmly to the surface.

Handsheet — A sheet made from a suspension of fibers in water, with or without the addition of sizing, loading, or coloring agents. The sheetmaking operation is not continuous as in a commercial papermaking operation, but each sheet is formed separately by draining a pulp suspension on a stationary mold called a sheet mold. It is generally used for testing the physical properties of the pulp and/or the combinations of pulp with other material, in which case the sheet must be formed in accordance with standard procedures to eliminate variables that affect results. It is also called test sheet.

Hanging Paper — The raw stock used in the manufacture of wallpaper.

Hardness — **1.** That property of a sheet which resists indentation by objects of specified size, shape, and hardness. **2.** When applied to pulp, a term usually referring to the degree of cooking, a hard pulp resulting from milder than normal digesting conditions.

Hard Paper — **1.** Usually a kraft paper, although other stocks may be used, which is impregnated with artificial resins of the type of bakelite. It is used in the form of plates, pipes, and molded pieces for electrical insulating purposes. **2.** A paper with a hard, smooth surface, mostly writing paper, which, because of its sizing, is harder to print upon than ordinary book paper.

Hard Sized — A relative term indicating a high degree of water resistance, to be contrasted with slack sized.

Hardwood — A term applied to wood obtained from trees of the angiosperm class. The hardwoods are obtained from dictyledonous trees such as birch, gum, maple, oak, and poplar. The leaves are broad except in rare instances and are usually deciduous in the temperate zones. The seeds are enclosed in a fruit which is either fleshy or dry at maturity. Hardwoods are also designated as porous woods.

Harper Machine — A type of Fourdrinier machine in which the machine wire travels away from the presses, the flowbox being placed between the breast roll and the first press, and the wet sheet is couched from the wire by a pickup felt and carried back above the wire to the first press. It is generally used in the manufacture of lightweight papers [under 20 pounds (24 × 36-500)].

Headbox — **1.** On Fourdrinier machines: a large flow control chamber which receives the dilute paper stock or furnish from the stock preparation system and by means of baffles and other flow evening devices, maintains sufficient agitation of the mixture to prevent flocculation of the fibers, spreads the flow evenly to the full width of the paper machine and provides delivery of stock to the Fourdrinier wire uniformly across its full width. The height of the liquid in an open headbox or the air pressure in a closed headbox provides the requisite speed of flow of the stock onto the Fourdrinier wire. The present design trend for high-speed machines is towards enclosed headboxes. **2.** On cylinder machines: a flow-regulating device that controls the volume of stock flowing to the screens and mixing boxes before the vats.

Hectograph Paper — A smooth-surfaced (or coated with glue-glycerol composition) noncurling paper used for making transfer copies with hectographic inks from a gelatin surface. The paper should be relatively nonabsorbent and free from loose surface fibers. A type of duplicating paper.

Heliograph Paper — A carbon photographic printing paper for which the exposures are made by sunlight.

Hemicelluloses — Any of number of cell-wall polysaccharides occurring in nearly all vegetable fibers. They are not extractable by water or by most neutral organic solvents, but are gradually extracted by aqueous alkali.

Hickies — Plain or doughnut-shaped spots in printed matter, especially in solids. In lithography, plain white spots are caused by paper dust or pick-outs that adhere to the offset blanket, become saturated with moisture, and refuse to transfer ink. Doughnut-shaped white spots are caused by particles of ink skin or other ink-receptive material usually adhering to the printing plate, that depress the offset blanket and cause it to bear off the plate in the surrounding areas.

Holdout — The extent to which a paper or board surface resists penetration by aqueous or nonaqueous fluids. Where the fluid involved is water or water vapor, this property is usually termed *Sizing*. Nonaqueous fluids of concern include printing inks, lacquers, and various oils or waxes.

Holocellulose — The term applied to the total carbohydrate fraction in extractive-free wood, straws, grasses, and other plant materials.

Hollander — The original name given to the *Beater*.

Hydration — **1.** In the physical sense, the condition of materials containing water of adsorption or inhibition. **2.** In papermaking, the treatments, essentially mechanical refining, that increase the amount of water held by the fibers. Increased hydration results in slower drainage rate and rather profoundly influences sheet properties, especially increased physical strength and decreased opacity. **3.** The pulp characteristics resulting from the above treatment.

Hydrotropic Pulping — A pulping process in which the cellulosic raw material is digested with an aqueous solution of a hydrotropic substance, i.e. one that has the property of markedly increasing the solubility of materials which ordinarily are but slightly soluble in water, e.g. sodium *m*-xylene sulfonate for the removal of lignin.

Hygroexpansivity — The change in dimension of paper that results from a change in the ambient relative humidity.

Inch-hour — A term indicating the rate of operation over a period of time one or more paper machines taking into account machine width but not speed. The figure is arrived at by multiplying inches of machine width by the number of hours in the period.

Index Bristols — Bristols used principally for index records, business and commercial cards. They are a group of cardboards made on the Fourdrinier or cylinder machine of homogeneous stock (such as bleached chemical wood pulps and/or cotton fiber), or by pasting together two or more plies of the same kind of paper, and finished and sized for pen and ink work. The usual basis weights are 180, 220, 280, 340, and 440 pounds (25.5 × 30.5-1000).

Index Pressboard — A general term applied to those boards used for the manufacture of filing materials — guides, folders, etc. — and for book covers — composition books, receipt books, etc.

Industrial Papers — A very general term used to indicate papers manufactured for industrial uses as opposed to those for cultural purposes.

Inkometer — An instrument for measuring the tack of inks in terms of the force required to split an ink film between rollers with controlled speed, temperature, and ink-film thickness.

Ink Receptivity — That property of a sheet of paper (or other material) that causes it to accept an ink film in a printing process. Wetting of the surface by the ink is essential; in many cases, the absorbency for the ink vehicle is important.

Ink Transfer — The amount of ink film transferred to a receiving surface as the result of a printing impression, expressed as a percentage of ink available.

Insulation Paper — A paper, usually kraft, used in the manufacture of insulation batts. Open-face batts are made with a layer of paper on one side only. Also known as the vapor barrier sheet.

Integrated Mill — A paper or board mill that produces substantially all its own pulp. A partially integrated mill is one that produces some but not all of its pulp.

Internal Revenue Stamp Paper — A special paper manufactured for the United States government for printing internal revenue stamps. It is made of bleached chemical wood fiber in a basis weight of 42. 5 pounds (24 × 36-500). The paper is either white or blue, the color of which is fast to light and water. It is printed on an intaglio press.

Inverform — A papermaking device used to manufacture single or multi-ply grades of paper and paperboard. The stock flows from a headbox to a bottom wire (similar to a Fourdrinier) and is then joined by a top wire so that water removal from the stock is accomplished through the top wire as well as the bottom wire. In multi-ply operation the bottom wire and formed web continue under subsequent headboxes where additional plies are laid down. Each headbox is followed by another top wire. For each additional ply thus laid down virtually all of the water removal is upward through the top wire. The machine is capable of extremely high speeds of operation.

Job Lot — **1.** Paper produced in excess of an order or small lots of discontinued lines. **2.** Paper rejected because of defects or failure to conform to specifications, or paper which, although of standard quality at the time of manufacture, has become nonstandard because of a change in standards subsequent to manufacture.

Jordon — A *Refiner* whose working elements consist of a conical plug rotating in a matching conical shell. The outside of the plug and the inside of the shell are furnished with knives or bars commonly called Tackle. In operation, the rotating conical plug is pushed into the shell to press against the shell knives or bars and gives a macerating action on the fibrous material in water suspension that is passed between them.

Jute — 1. An Indian bast fiber, white jute (*Corchorus capsularis*) and tossa Jute (*C. olitorius*) used for the manufacture of coarse sacking and bags (gunny sack). Old gunny and sacking are used as raw materials in papermaking. **2.** A general term that now indicates a furnish consisting substantially of paper stock reclaimed from waste papers.

Jute Paper — Any paper made from jute fiber or burlap waste with various proportions of kraft or sulfite pulp. The basis weight is from 20 to 300 pounds (24 × 36-500). Jute papers are used extensively for envelopes, folders, tag stock, wrappers, cover stock, bristols, pattern papers, and a variety of specialties; also hydrated lime and cement bags, flour sacks, etc.

Kaolin — A white-firing clay mass composed primarily of the clay mineral, kaolinite. The kaoline clays have the approximate chemical formula $Al_2O_3 \cdot 2SiO_2 \cdot 2H_2O$ specifically ascribed to the kaolinite clay mineral.

Kappa Number — The Permanganate number of a pulp measured under carefully controlled conditions and corrected to be the equivalent of 50 percent consumption of the permanganate solution in contact with the specimen. It gives the degree of delignification of pulps through a wider range than does the permanganate number.

Karaya Gum — An acetylated polysaccharide obtained from the dried exudation of the *Sterculia urens* tree grown in India. In the deacetylated form, it is used as a fiber deflocculating agent for long-fibered pulps.

Knots — An imperfection in paper or lumps in paper stock resulting from (a) incompletely defibered textile materials (the term applies especially to ragpaper manufacture), (b) small undefibered clusters of wood pulp, or (c) the basal portion of a branch or limb that has become incorporated in the body of the tree.

Kraft — A term descriptive of the sulfate pulping process, the resulting pulp, and the paper or paperboard made therefrom.

Kraft Paper — A paper made entirely from wood pulp produced by a modified sulfate pulping process. It is a comparatively coarse paper particularly noted for its strength and, in unbleached grades, is used primarily as a wrapper or packaging material. It is usually manufactured on a Fourdrinier machine with a regular machine-finished or machine-glazed surface. It can be water-marked, stripped, or calendered, and it has an acceptable surface for printing. Its natural unbleached color is brown, but, by the use of semibleached or fully bleached sulfate pulps, it can be produced in lighter shades of brown, cream tints, and white. Kraft paper is most commonly made in basis weights from 25 to 60 pounds (24 × 36-500), but may be made in weights ranging from 18 to 200 pounds. In addition to its use as a wrapping paper, it is also converted into a wide variety of products, such as grocers' bags, envelopes, gummed sealing tape, asphalted papers, multiwall sacks, tire wraps, butchers wraps, waxed paper, coated paper, cable sheathing, insulating and abrasive papers as well as all types of specialty bags and sacks. Many paper grades including tissues, printing and fine papers, formerly manufactured from bleached sulfite are now made from bleached kraft.

Laid — The ribbed appearance in writing and printing papers produced by the use of a dandy roll on which the wires are laid side by side instead of being woven transversely.

Laid Dandy Roll — A dandy roll made with wires parallel to the axis of the roll and attached to the frame and kept in position by chain wires evenly spaced and encircling the circumference of the roll.

Lap — Folded sheets of wet pulp as they come from the wet machine for shipment or for storage. The pulp usually contains from 35 to 55 percent by weight of airdry pulp.

Lapping — The operation of extracting water from screened pulp by a wet press and collecting the fibers in sheets dry enough to enable them to be folded or lapped into a bundle.

Latex-Treated Papers — Papers manufactured by two major processes: in one, rubber latex is incorporated with the fibers in the beater prior to formation of the sheet and, in the second, a preformed web of absorbent fiber is saturated with properly compound latex. Papers made by the beater process can be produced on any of the regular types of papermaking machinery including cylinder, Fourdrinier, and wet machines. Latex-impregnated papers made by the saturating process are manufactured on specially designed equipment consisting essentially of a suitable bath for impregnation, a pair of squeeze rolls for removal of excess latex, and drying equipment. Fibers commonly used consist of rags and chemical wood pulp. Latex-impregnated products range from approximately 0.004 to 0.250 of an inch in thickness. They vary widely in their physical and chemical characteristics. As a class, they are characterized by toughness, folding endurance, flexibility, durability, and resistance to splitting and abrasion in varying degrees as may be necessary to meet end-use requirements. The heavier products find use in the shoe industry as innersoles and midsoles. The mechanical and process industries use them as gaskets. The thinner products are used variously: by the artificial leather industry in coated form as simulated leather; by the pressure-sensitive tape industry as a base for masking, holding, and protective tapes; by the automobile manufacturing industry as antisqueak and facing materials.

Ledger Paper — Originally a paper used for writing purposes and especially for pen and ink records. Such paper is commonly made from cotton fiber, bleached chemical wood pulps, or a mixture of these. Most ledger papers are surface sized or treated in some manner to enhance the properties required in the use of such papers. Normally it is made in basis weights ranging from 24 to 36 pounds (17 × 22-500). It is subjected to appreciable wear and requires a relatively high degree of durability and permanence. Significant properties include strength, especially tearing resistance, erasability, water and ink resistance, uniformity of surface and color and smoothness. A good surface for ruling is important.

Lignin — The noncarbohydrate portion of the cell wall of plant material. Lignin is more or less completely removed during chemical pulping operations; in the alkaline processes it appears in the spent liquors as alkali lignin; in the acid or neutral sulfite process, the legnin is sulfonated to lignosulfonic acids and occurs in the spent liquors as calcium, ammonium, magnesium, or sodium salts of these acids.

Liners — 1. The outside layers, i.e. the vat-lined or sheetlined surface-of a built-up or combination board. 2. A protection sheet inserted along the sides of a box as contrasted with a pad which protects the ends. 3. Various grades of light- and medium-weighted sheets, generally waxed, used as inner or protection wrappers in packaging food such as crackers, cookies, and powdered milk.

Lint — Particles of fibers that separate or "dust off" from paper during manufacturing or converting operations.

Lithograph Paper — A paper for use in lithographic printing made of bleached chemical wood pulp alone or in combination with mechanical wood pulp or deinked paper stock. Essential characteristics are surface cleanliness, a degree of water resistance sufficient to inhibit penetration into the paper of water encountered in the printing process, relative freedom from curl, and high pick strength. The paper is made both uncoated and coated in either sheets or rolls and with machine, supercalendered, or duplex finishes. Usual basis weights are uncoated, 45 to 79 pounds; coated, 50 to 100 pounds (25 × 38-500).

Loading — 1. The incorporation of finely divided relatively insoluble materials, such as clay, calcium carbonate, etc., in the papermaking composition, usually prior to sheet formation, to modify certain characteristics of the finished sheet, including opacity, texture, printability, finish, weight, etc. 2. Mineral matter, such as clay, used as a filler in paper.

Localized Watermark — A watermark arranged to appear at definite intervals in a sheet of paper.

Locker paper — Flexible sheet materials used for the wrapping and protection of frozen foods and meats during freezing and storage. The wide assortment of grades including waxed papers and wax laminated combinations. All grades must be resistant in some degree to moisture vapor, grease, and moisture. Pliability at low temperatures, nontoxicity, and lack of odor are important characteristics. High bursting strength and cleanliness are desirable features.

Locust Bean Gum — A polysaccharide derived from the seed endosperm of the locust bean or carob tree, *"Ceratonia siliqua,"* grown in the Mediterranean regions of Africa and Europe — used as a beater or wet-end additive primarily for improving strength properties.

Machine Direction — The direction of paper parallel with the direction of movement on the paper machine. It is also called grain direction. The direction at right angles to the machine direction is called the cross-machine direction or simply cross direction.

Machine Glazed — The finish produced on a Yankee machine, where the paper is pressed against a large, steam-heated, highly polished revolving cylinder, which dries the sheet and imparts a highly glazed surface on the drier side.

Magazine Paper — Paper used for periodicals. A wide range of grades and finishes are used, both coated and uncoated. There are no definite quality requirements separating these papers from the other printing papers.

Manifold Paper — Paper used for copies by interleaving with carbon paper on the typewriter.

Manila — A term generally used to indicate a color and finish comparable to that formerly obtained with paper manufactured from manila hemp (rope) stock; unless definitely stated, no manila fiber is present. Under present usage, it has no definite significance as to furnish.

Mannogalactan — Also called galactomannan. A reserve polysaccharide or gum, found in the seeds of certain plants, which yields mannose and galactose as the only sugars upon acid hydrolysis. The product is used as a beater or wet-end adhesive for improvement of sheet formation and fiber bonding (see *Guar Gum* and *Locust Bean Gum*).

Manufacturer's Joint — The body joint or joints of corrugated shipping containers, made by the manufacturer or corrugator. It may be lapped, butted, or spliced at the option of the customer. In the folding and set-up box industry, it is generally called a seam.

Map Paper — Paper used for the making of maps in sheet, book, or pamphlet form. It is made from cotton fiber or chemical wood pulps or a mixture of these, depending upon its use. It is made in basis weights of 16 to 28 pounds

(17 × 31-500) and is sometimes supercalendered. Significant properties are finish, printing quality, dimensional stability (to avoid poor register), good folding properties, and in some cases (road maps) high opacity. For special uses, map papers are treated to impart high wet strength, water repellency, mildew resistance, luminescence, abrasion resistance, and other properties pertinent to a particular use.

Melamine Resin Acid Colloid — A cationic colloidal solution of melamine-formaldehyde resin in dilute acid, used for imparting wet strength by addition to the furnish prior to sheet formation.

M. G. — (see *Machine Glazed*)

Mill Blanks — Mill blanks are cylinder-machine products, generally consisting of top and bottom liner of white stock, vat lined on a filler of mechanical pulp, news, or similar stock. Principal uses are for menus, posters, advertising cards, etc. Standard thicknesses are 3, 4, 5, 6, 8, and 10 ply. Thicknesses such as 12 and 14 ply and heavier are usually made by pasting together two thinner plies, which are white on one side only with a news back. No. 1 mill blanks have liners consisting of bleached and unbleached chemical wood pulps, deinked paper stock, and soft white shavings in varying amounts. The center is usually blank or printed news, though it may consist of mechanical pulp in the better grades. No. 2 mill blanks are, in general, characterized by being of poorer color and quality and not as bright as the No. 1 mill blanks, or as is more usual, it may contain a larger proportion of printed news.

Mill Bristol — A term applied to a group of bristols, usually made on a cylinder machine. The basis weights range from 90 to 200 pounds (22½ × 28½-500). They are normally made for printing purposes.

Mill Wrapper — A general term to designate grades of paper used by paper mills for wrapping purposes. The grade depends on the quality of the contents to be wrapped and upon the custom of the mill.

Mimeograph Paper — A grade of writing paper used for making copies on the mimeograph machine. A wide variety of furnishes ranging from cotton fiber and bleached chemical wood pulps to those containing mechanical pulp are used in varying proportions. Opacity, finish, absorbency, lack of fuzz, and mimeographing qualities are significant properties. The basis weight is usually 20 pounds (17 × 22-500) but may range from 16 to 24 pounds. Originally a slack-sized paper unsuitable for a pen and ink signature; at present practically all mimeograph papers have good writing qualities.

Mitsumata — A low shrub (*Edgeworthia papyrifera*) that grows in temperate Asia and is cultivated in Japan for its bark, the fibers of which are used in papermaking.

Moisture Welts — Defects in paper that occur as ridges in rolls or reams of paper caused by surface expansion resulting from uneven moisture content in the paper. They usually run in the direction of the grain of the paper.

Motted Color — Nonuniform coloring of a sheet of paper caused by irregularities in formation, calender pressure, dye application, drying or plating.

Mullen — An expression used for bursting strength. It is so called from the name of the instrument used in the test.

Newsprint — A generic term used to describe paper of the type generally used in the publication of newspapers. The furnish is largely mechanical wood pulp, with some chemical wood pulp. The paper is machine finished and slack sized, and it has little or no mineral loading. It is made in basis weights varying from 30 to 35 pounds (24 × 36-500), the great preponderance being 32 pounds.

Nip — The "line" of contact between two rolls, such as press, calender, or supercalender rolls. Owing to the compressibility of the felt and/or the web of paper, the "line" of contact is actually a narrow zone. *Wet nip* refers to those at the presses; *dry nip* usually refers to those at the calenders.

Offset — **1.** A type of printing which utilizes a lithographic plate. The image area of the plate is ink receptive, the balance of the plate is water receptive. The ink is transferred from the plate to the rubber blanket and thence to the material being printed. **2.** Undesirable transfer of ink from a printed surface to an adjacent surface, sometimes referred to as set-off to differentiate it from offset.

Offset Paper — An uncoated or coated paper designed for use in offset lithography. The kind, type, and combinations of pulps used in its manufacture depend upon the sheet qualities desired. Important properties are good internal bonding, high surface strength, dimensional stability, lack of curl, and freedom from fuzz and foreign surface material.

Onionskin — A paper used for making duplicate copies of typewritten material, for interleaving counter order books, for permanent records when small bulk is desired, and for airmail correspondence. It is a durable lightweight writing (bond-type) paper, thin and usually quite transparent, so called from its resemblance to the dry outer skin of the onion. Some grades are 100 percent cotton fiber content; other grades may contain up to 100 percent bleached chemical wood pulp. The pulp is beaten until the stock is slow and greasy, keeping the fibers long. It may be sized with rosin or tub sized with starch or glue. It is made on a Fourdrinier machine and usually given a high finish on a supercalender or plater, although it is also made with a cockle finish. The range of basis weights as 7 to 10 pounds (17 × 22-500). It may be considered a typical manifold paper.

Oven dry — Containing no moisture. A pulp or paper that has been dried to a constant weight at a temperature of 100 to 105° C (212 to 221° F) in a completely dry atmosphere. It is also termed bone dry or moisture free. In practice, the atmosphere in the oven usually is not completely dry, and the pulp or paper retains a few tenths of one percent of moisture even when constant weight is attained.

Overlay Paper — A high purity paper for impregnation with a synthetic resin and molded as the top layer of a decorative laminate.

Paperboard — One of the two broad subdivisions of paper (general term), the other being Paper (specific term). The distinction between *Paperboard* and *Paper* is not sharp but broadly speaking, paperboard is heavier in basis weight, thicker, and more rigid than paper. In general, all sheets 12 points (0.012 inch) or more in thickness are classified as paperboard. There are a number of exceptions based upon traditional nomenclature. For example, blotting paper, felts, and drawing paper in excess of 12 points are classified as paper while corrugating medium, chipboard, and linerboard less than 12 points are classified as paperboard. Paperboard is made from a wide variety of furnishes on a number of types of machines, principally cylinder and Fourdrinier. The board classes are (1) Container board, which is used for corrugated cartons; (2) Boxboard, which is further divided into (a) Folding boxboard, (b) Special food board, (c) Setup boxboard; and (3) all other special types such as Automobile board, Building board, Tube board, etc.

Papeterie Paper — **1.** A class of writing papers normally cut to size, boxed, and used for correspondence. These papers are made from cotton fiber or chemical wood pulps or mixtures of these are given many special treatments, such as embossing, motting, watermaking, aniline printing, etc., to obtain attractive and striking colors and appearance. The majority of them have low strength, high bulk, and good folding qualities — i.e. they have the ability to fold without cracking and to give what is known as a smooth, soft fold. They normally carry a considerable percentage of filler, for the purpose of giving the desired finish and opacity, and are sized to give satisfactory pen and ink writing qualities. They are normally made in basis weights from 16 to 32 pounds (17 × 22-500). **2.** A class of papers used for greeting cards.

Patch Mark — A watermark made with a wire mark patch sewed into the wire of a mold on a cylinder machine or into a dandy roll of a Fourdrinier machine.

Peeling — **1.** Removal of bark from pulpwood by either of two manual methods as distinguished from mechanical methods used in Barking. Sap peeling consists in stripping bark from wood during the relatively short season when sap flowing in the tree has loosened the bark from the wood. Chemical peeling (frequently called chemical debarking) consists in stripping bark from wood at any time after it has been loosened as a result of the application of appropriate chemicals to the tree. **2.** A defect in paper in which the surface scales or peels off.

Permanence — The permanence of paper refers to the retention of significant use properties, particularly folding endurance and color, over prolonged periods. The permanence is affected by temperature, humidity, light, and the presence of chemical agents. The probable permanence of paper is estimated by an accelerated oven-aging test or by tests under other specified conditions of temperature, light, and humidity. The evaluation of permanence is based on measurement of folding endurance, resistance to water penetration, color, solubility in aqueous alkaline solutions, and viscosity of a solution of the fibers in a cellulose solvent.

Photocopying Paper — A high-grade base paper, coated with a fast light-sensitive emulsion and used for photographing records, as well as designs and layouts. The base paper varies from 100 percent cotton fiber content to 100 percent bleached chemical wood pulp, usually papermaking alpha grade, but differs from ordinary papers in purity and chemical treatment, being made with special precautions to exclude metallic residues. It is specially treated with wet-strength agents to offer resistence to acid, alkaline, and other chemical solutions used in the photographic process.

Photographic Paper — Paper used as the base material for the various photosensitive systems employing silver halide crystals as the light-sensitive receptors. This paper is always manufactured specifically for this end use from either cotton or highly purified wood cellulose. It must be free from all foreign substances and chemical impurities that would affect the photosensitive emulsion. Photographic papers must have sufficient wet strength to withstand processing in both acid and alkaline solutions. They are usually classified as (1) light weight, (2) single weight, (3) medium weight, and (4) double weight, which covers a range of thicknesses from 0.0025 to 0.015 in. Most photographic paper is coated first with baryta (barium sulfate) to obtain a smooth high-reflectance surface on which the photosensitive emulsion is coated (up to 60 grams of baryta per square meter are used for high-gloss papers). Embossing rollers are sometimes used to obtain textured surfaces, and calendering is often used to obtain a high-gloss surface.

Pick — 1. (see *Picking*). 2. The adhering of pulp or fibers to the wet or drying sections of the paper machine.

Picking — The lifting of coating, film, or fibers from the surface of a body paper or body stock. It occurs in printing when the lifting stress due to the tackiness of the ink exceeds the bonding strength of the materials comprising the sheet.

Pinholes — 1. Defects in paper caused by fine particles of sand, clay, alum, etc., which, when the paper is calendered, are crushed and fall out, leaving holes. Very hard grit may be imbedded in the steel rolls and produce pinholes at each revolution. 2. Large pores in thin papers where fine fiber materials fails to fill the voids between large fibers. Pinholes are visible when looking through the sheet toward a light. 3. Minute and almost imperceptible pits in the surface of coated papers.

Pitch — The material (largely a mixture of fatty and resin acids and unsaponifiable organic substances) that can be extracted from wood, mechanical, or chemical pulps means of organic solvents, such as alcohol and ether. Pitch is associated mainly with the ray cells of the wood, and under certain conditions it accumulates on the Fourdrinier wire or the press section and causes trouble in the papermaking operation.

Pitch Spots — Dirt specks in paper that have their origin in the resins contained in the wood used in pulp manufacture. Pitch may accumulate on the Fourdrinier wire, causing spots in the paper.

Plasticizer — An agent added in the manufacture of certain papers, such as glassine, or employed in papermaking compositions or protective coatings, such as nitrocellulose lacquers, to impart softness and flexibility. Typical plasticizers of interest to the paper industry are glycerol, sorbitol, invert sugar, phthalic acid esters, various types of mineral oils, organic esters of phosphoric acid, and the like.

Ply — 1. One of the separate webs which make up the sheet formed on a multicylinder machine. Each cylinder adds one web or ply, which is pressed to the other, the plies adhering firmly upon drying. 2. One of the sheets that are laminated to build up a pasted board of given thickness. 3. One of the separate layers which together make up a multilayer aggregate such as milti-ply tissues, multiwall shipping sacks, and carbon-interleaved business forms.

Point — One thousandth of an inch. It is used in expressing the thickness of paper or board.

Postage Stamp Paper — Paper used in the production of various types of postage stamps. It is usually made from a mixture of various bleached chemical wood pulps, and its special properties include offset or intaglio printing qualities, noncurling characteristics, and good perforating and gumming qualities. Some grades must also have wet strength. It is usually made in an off-white color in basis weights ranging from 16 to 24 pounds (17×22-500) or 40 to 60 pounds (25×38-500).

Postal Money-order Paper — A paper used by the United States Government Post Office for money orders. Bleached chemical wood pulps are used in making the base stock in a basis weight of 32 pounds (17×22-1000). The surface of the paper contains a dye or other substance sensitive to the action of chemical reagents, such as ink eradicators, to show clearly any attempt at mechanical erasure. The dyed or impregnated fibers from a pattern only on the surface of the paper. Sensitivity and bond paper characteristics are significant properties (see also *Safety Paper*).

Poster Paper — 1. A term applied to a paper especially suited for billboard poster work. It is generally made of chemical wood pulp in basis weights of 32 to 63 pounds (24×36-500). It is strong and well sized to enhance water resistance. It possesses wet strength and should not curl after paste is applied. It should have good light fastness. The paper is usually rough on the underside in order that it may accept paste more readily. (2) A term applied to a special mechanical-pulp printing paper, the major use of which is in printed flyers, throw-aways, and similar inexpensive advertising pieces and publications, although it is sometimes used in the converting trade in manufacturing sales books, order forms, etc. This grade commonly contains a substantial portion of refined mechanical pulp mixed with unbleached pulp. It is normally unsized for high-speed flat-bed presses, has a smooth printing surface, and is almost entirely used in a range of six standard colors. The usual basis weights range from 32 to 45 pounds (24 × 36-500).

Powder Paper — **1.** Manila paper, sometimes waxed or treated, for wrapping charges of powder used in mining. The basis weight is 50 pounds (24 × 36-500) and heavier. **2.** A paper similar to cigarette paper, but which is coated with a facial powder that is easily rubbed off.

Press — In a paper machine, a pair of rolls between which the paper web is passed for one of the following reasons: (1) water removal at the wet press, (2) smoothing and leveling of the sheet surface at the smoothing press, (3) application of surface treatments to the sheet at the Size press.

Primer Paper — A strong, single or double deckle-edged sheet similar to *Cartridge Paper*; it is usually red in color and is made in basis weights of 80 to 100 pounds (24 × 36-500). It is used for sealing the open end of the primer.

Printability — That property of paper which yields printed matter of good quality. This complex property is not accurately defined. Printability should be distinguished from runnability, which refers to the efficiency with which the paper may be printed and handled in the press.

Pulper — A machine designed to break up, defiber, and disperse dry pulps, mill process broke, commercial waste papers, or other fibrous materials into slush form preparatory to further processing and conversion into paper or paperboard. It normally consists of a tank or chest with suitable agitation to accomplish the dispersion with a minimum consumption of power. It may also be used for blending various materials with pulp.

Pulp Sheet — Pulp, usually market pulp, in sheets from a pulp drier prepared in this form for convenience in shipment and handling.

Quire — One twentieth of a ream. Twenty-five sheets in the case of a 500-sheet ream of fine papers, and twenty-four sheets in the case of a 480-sheet ream of coarse papers.

Rag-Content Paper — Papers containing a minimum of 25 percent rag or cotton fiber. These papers generally are made in the following grades: 25, 50, 75, 100 percent and extra No. 1 (100%). They are used for bonds, currency, writing, ledgers, manifold and onionskin, papeteries and wedding, index, carbonizing, blueprint, and other reproduction papers, maps and charts and other industrial specialties.

Railroad Board — Clay-coated, white lined paperboard, the coating raw stock being a cylinder-machine product made of over-issue news. The clay coating is usually applied to both sides of the raw stock and is tinted to give a wide range of colors. The board is generally waterproof to withstand handling by damp or wet hands. The basis weight ranges from 130 to 300 pounds (22 × 28-500). It is used in general for mailing cards, showcards, tickets, checks, tags, and car signs. It is also known as car-sign board, colored railroad ticket, colored ticket stock, colored railroad stock, and ticket stock.

Ramie — A plant of the nettle family native to tropical Asia, but cultivated in other sufficiently warm regions. The bontanical name is *Boehmeria nivea* (especially important is variety *tenacissima*). The bast fiber from the decorticated material is commercially known as Chian grass and is used as a textile fiber. It is a potential source of papermaking fibers.

Rattle — That property of a sheet which produces noise when the sheet is shaken.

Ray Cells — Short cells, chiefly parenchymatous, which make up the wood ray. The wood ray is a ribbonlike strand of tissue extending in a radial direction across the annual rings of the wood. A large proportion of these cells are located in the sapwood.

Ream — A number of sheets of paper, either 480 or 500 according to grade.

Refiner — A machine used to rub, macerate, bruise, and cut fibrous material, usually cellulose, in water suspension to convert the raw fiber into a form suitable for formation into a web of desired characteristics on a paper machine. The many types of refiners differ in size and design features but most can be classified as either jordans or disk refiners. Beaters are not usually referred to as refiners although in a broad sense they serve a similar function. Refiners may be used in various combinations of types and numbers of units depending on the type of stock to be treated and the capacity required.

Register Bond — A bond-type writing paper generally made of chemical wood pulps in basis weights of 9, 10, 11, 12, 13, 14, and 15 pounds (17 × 22-500). For the top sheets of multicopy printed forms sub. 16, 20, and 24 are sometimes used. Register bond is characterized by good printing properties, high tensile strength and tearing resistance, good perforating, folding and manifolding qualities. The principal use is for printed business forms of all types including the so-called snap-apart forms, marginally-punched carbon-interleaved form sets, and related multicopy items.

Resin — A general term applied to various amorphous solid or semisolid organic substances insoluble in water but soluble in organic solvents, and classified as natural or synthetic. The natural resins are excretion or exudation products chiefly of plant origin (a familiar exception being shellac), fusible, usually yellowish to dark brown in color and transparent to translucent. The chemical composition varies widely, but characteristic acids, esters, and inert substances, termed resins, are present together with extraneous fatty, mineral, or other materials. Gum resins contain carbohydrate gums and oleoresins are mixtures of resins and volatile oils. The nonvolatile residue of the combined resins is called *Rosin*, which is the most important natural resin used in the paper industry. Copal and dammar are natural resins employed in varnish.

Retention — The amount of filler or other material which remains in the finished paper expressed as a percentage of that added to the furnish before sheet formation.

Rice Paper — A misnomer for the sheet material cut from the pith of a small tree (*Aralia papyrifera*) that grows in the swampy forests of Formosa. The cylindrical case of pith is rolled on a hard flat surface against a knife, by which it is cut into thin sheets of a fine ivorylike texture. Dyed in various colors, it is used extensively for the preparation of artificial flowers; the white sheets are employed by native artists for water-color drawings.

Ring Stiffness — The resistance of edgewide compression of a short cylinder (ring) of paper or paperboard. It is usually measured as the force, in pounds, required to cause collapse of the ring (short cylinder). Ring stiffness is also called ring compression (strength) resistance.

Roe-Genberg Chlorine Number — The number of grams of chlorine gas or of bleaching powder (expressed as its equivalent in chlorine) absorbed by 100 grams of oven-dry pulp in a definite time under specified conditions. It is an indication of the bleach requirement of the pulp.

Roofing Paper — A general term used to designate any material used in waterproofing upper decks of buildings. There are several varieties: (1) prepared roofing — felts saturated and coated with asphaltum, plain or crushed slate or other grit, embedded in an asphalt-coated surface; (2) built-up roofing — felts saturated but not coated with asphaltum; used in plies or layers and coated or built up at the time of application; (3) roofing shingles — prepared roofing cut into various sizes and styles of shingles.

Rope Marks — Diagonal welts appearing in a web drawn from a roll of nonuniform hardness, the welts being formed in paper from the area of the roll that is softer than the areas on either side.

Rope Paper — Any paper made from manila hemp (commonly called rope). It may be composed entirely of rope fibers or it may contain some chemical pulp. Such papers are made on both cylinders and Fourdrinier machines in practically all weights and thicknesses. They are used as cable papers, shipping tags, saturating papers, and for other purposes where strength is an important property.

Roping — The longitudinal wrinkling of a web of paper caused by tension as the web is drawn over the drying drums and also by the tendency of the web to creep transversely upon the drum surface.

Rosin — The residue obtained after distilling off the volatile matter (turpentine) from the gum of the southern pine (chiefly from longleaf and slash species). Gum rosin is obtained from the gum which exudes from the living tree. Wood rosin is obtained from the gum which exudes from pine stumps or other resinous woods by the steam and solvent process. Rosin is the commonly employed material for internal (beater) sizing.

Rosin Size — The solution or dispersion obtained by treatment of a suitable grade of rosin with alkali.

Rotoformer — A paper-forming device used to manufacture single or multi-ply grades of paper and paperboard. It consists essentially of a wire-covered drilled shell on which the stock is formed, suction boxes inside the shell to remove water, and a restricted forming area in the upper quadrant of the up-turning side of the cylinder.

Rotogravure Paper — A general term used to describe paper manufactured for rotogravure printing. The outstanding characteristic of the paper is the highest possible printing smoothness for both coated and uncoated grades. Consequently, a supercalendered sheet is frequently used although English finish and machine finish papers are also used.

Rubber Spots — Dirt specks in paper, composed principally of rubber. They originate (1), in rag-content papers, from elastic yarns in the rags or cuttings used; (2), in papers or paperboards containing reclaimed paper stock, from latex type adhesives used on mailing labels, etc., present in the waste paper furnish.

Safety Paper — A special grade of paper having a surface design or hidden warning indicia or both of such chemical composition as to make obvious any attempt at fraudulent alteration of the writing thereon by ink eradicators, mechanical erasure, etc. Such a paper is used for bank checks, tickets, postal money orders or other papers having a negotiable value. Safety paper is made by either a wet or dry process. In the wet process the surface design is applied to the paper by immersing it in a dye bath and then removing the excess dye solution usually by passing the paper through a press comprising one steel engraved pattern roll and a rubber composition backing roll. Wet process safety papers have a positive surface pattern on one side and a reverse pattern on the other. Such papers must be dried after processing. In the dry process the surface design and warning indicia if any, are applied by a flexographic press employing spirit-soluble inks or dyes. Dry process safety papers can be produced with positive-reading patterns on both sides of the sheet, with positive and negative patterns on the top and bottom of the sheet, or with multicolor or multi-pattern combinations of the two. Dry process safety papers require little or no drying during conversion because of the fact that alcohol instead of water is the principal ink (i.e. dye) solvent. The English equivalent of safety paper is cheque paper.

Saturating Papers — A general term for open, porous papers that are to be saturated or impregnated with solutions or compounds of various types. Tensile strength and degree or rate of penetration are important qualities.

Saveall — An apparatus used for reclaiming fibers and fillers from white water. It usually operates on a filtration, sedimentation, flocculation of flotation principle.

Scoring — The production of a score or crease in a sheet of heavyweight paper or paperboard by pressing it between two metal surfaces, one of which has a recessed groove and the other a tongue.

Scuffing — The raising of the fibers on the surface of a paper or paperboard when one piece is rubbed against another or comes in contact with a rough surface. Paper and paperboard are more susceptible to scuffing when wet.

Secondary Stock — Fibers that have been previously used in the papermaking process. The term includes paper stock reclaimed from waste papers as well as wet or dry broke.

Semichemical Pulp — A pulp produced by a mild chemical treatment of the raw material followed by a mechanical fiberizing operation.

Shake — A device that causes oscillation of the Fourdrinier wire in the plane of the wire, but at right angles to the machine direction. Its purpose is to assist in securing the desired formation of the sheet. The oscillations may be varied in frequency and length of stroke to obtain the desired result.

Shearing Strength — The maximum shear force required to produce failure in a paper or paperboard member. The shear force is the internal force acting along a plane between two adjacent parts of a body when two equal forces, parallel to the plane considered, act on each part in opposite directions.

Shoe Board — A fiberboard formed from a single web on a wet machine from wood pulp, reclaimed paper stock, leather waste, or other waste materials, or a combination of such materials, with or without the addition of chemicals. Depending upon their end use, shoe boards may be termed counterboard, heeling board, innersole board, leather fiber, midsole board, reinforcement board, shank board, or tuck board.

Shot-shell Top Board — A paperboard used as a round plug at the top of a shotgun shell. It is made of reclaimed paper stock and/or chemical wood pulp in thicknesses of 0.0030 of an inch and up. The fibers must be sufficiently short so that the small circles may be readily punched out of a larger sheet. The product must be water resistant.

Silicated Paper — A paper coated with sodium silicate to give hardness and finish.

Single Coated — A term used to indicate that a paper or paperboard has been coated once, either on one or both sides. The term is sometimes used (incorrectly) to designate a paper or board that is coated on one side only;

such a product should be called "coated one side."

Sisal — A plant (*Agave sisalana*) and the fiber obtained from its leaves and used for hard fiber cordage. Native to Central America, it is grown extensively in the West Indies and Africa. Some is used in rope papers and is obtained from cordage waste. The fiber has also been called sisal hemp.

Sizing — 1. Relates to a property of paper resulting from an alteration of fiber surface characteristics. In terms of internal sizing it is a measure of the resistance to the penetration of water and various liquids. In terms of surface sizing it relates to the increase of such properties as water resistance, abrasion resistance, abrasiveness, creasability, finish, smoothness, surface bonding strength, and printability, and the decrease of porosity and surface fuzz. 2. The addition of materials to the surface of paper and board to provide resistance to liquid penetration and, in the case of surface sizing, to affect one or more of the properties listed in 1.

Skating — A form of flow-streaking of the stock on the Fourdrinier wire whereby small irregularities at the slice discharge grow into definite streaks which migrate across the wire, frequently at a diagonal angle to the machine direction. It is caused by headbox deficiencies, wire ridges, pressure pulsations, etc.

Slack Edges — 1. A defect in paper rolls that shows up on rewinding, web printing, or in a converting operation, one or both edges of the paper web being soft or slack, usually resulting from the sheets being thin at the edges. 2. An unsatisfactory condition in the process of coating paper, in which the middle of the paper web leaving the coater and passing through the drying operation carries all the tension, the edges being slack.

Slice — That part of a Fourdrinier machine which regulates the flow of stock from the headbox or flowbox onto the Fourdrinier wire in a sheet of liquid of even thickness or volume.

Slime — An aggregation of heterogeneous material, sometimes having a slippery feel, found at various points within a pulp or papermaking system. It may be caused by microbial growths or deposits of nonbiological materials.

Slime Hole — A hole in a paper web caused by slime which was incorporated inadvertently during the formation of the web, breaking out of the dried web when it is run through the calender stack. A slime hole is often identified by the occurrence of translucent fragments around the edge of the hole.

Slime Spots — Spots or smears in paper caused by fungi or bacterial growths in the pulp stock.

Slimicide — A toxic material to control microbiological growths in pulp and paper mill systems.

Slip — A fluid or semisolid mixture of a pigment, such as clay, and water.

Slitter Dust — Small particles of fibers or coating or both, which are chipped off during the slitting operations, that may adhere to the edge of the sheet and later work their way into subsequent converting operations.

Slow Stock — A pulp suspension from which the water drains slowly. It usually results from refining.

Slush — A suspension, usually aqueous, of pigments or other insoluble materials used in coating or papermaking.

Smoothness — The property of a surface determined by the degree to which it is free of irregularities. In printing, the smoothness of paper in the printing nip is important and is referred to as printing smoothness. Smoothness improves as the paper is compressed and locally deformed under mechanically applied pressure.

Snailing — A term applied to streaks or marks on machine-made paper, caused air bubbles, which form in front of the dandy roll and disturb the alignment of the fibers. It may also be caused by froth bubbles formed at the slice or by an excess of water in the web when it reaches the dandy roll.

Soda Pulp — **1.** A chemical pulp produced by high temperature digestion using sodium hydroxide. **2.** A semichemical pulp.

Softwood — The softwoods, otherwise known as coniferous woods, come from coniferous trees such as the pines, spruces, and hemlocks. The leaves are needlelike, linear, awl-shaped, or scalelike, and the seeds are borne either in cones in the axil of a scale, or naked. Softwoods are also designated as nonporous woods.

Solid Fraction — The fiber, filler, sizing material, etc., that constitute what is generally thought of as paper. It is the ratio of the volume of solid material to the total volume of the measured sample of paper (see also *Void Fraction*).

Specific Gravity — The ratio of weight of a specimen to the weight of an equal volume of water. It is obvious that the specific gravity of paper cannot be measured in the usual way — i.e. by dipping paper into the water to obtain its volume by displacement — consequently, it is better to speak of the density of the paper.

Speck — A particle of contrasting appearance in pulp or paper.

Spirit Duplicator — A reproduction process in which a master copy is prepared on a sheet of paper by means of a special carbon paper. The master sheet is clamped to a cylinder and the paper, slightly moistened with a special duplicating fluid, is fed to the cylinder. The moistened sheet disolves a small amount of the ink from the master copy, giving an impression on the paper (see also *Duplicating Paper*).

Standard Brightness — A standard adopted by the paper industry originally for grade differentiation and specification and currently for specification and control. It is expressed as reflectivity for blue light when measured on instruments employing C.I.E. geometry with specified spectral, geometric, and photometric characteristics. It is sometimes called G. E. Brightness after the manufacturer who made the original instruments.

Stenographers Notebook Paper — A paper for stenographers' notebooks, normally made from mechanical pulp and/or bleached chemical wood pulps. Most paper for this purpose is beater-sized and made with a smooth writing surface. The normal basis weight is 16 pounds (17 × 22-500). Significant properties include smooth writing surface, water and ink resistance, a bright color, and opacity (sufficient to prevent show-through from previous page).

Stevens Former — A paper-forming device used to manufacture a wide variety of papers in weights ranging from tissues to heavy paperboard grades. It consists of a wire-covered suction roll, or a vacuum cylinder upon which the stock is formed, and a unique approach flow section that brings the stock to a restricted forming area under pressure. The forming area is located in the upper quadrant of the upturning side of the cylinder.

Stiffness — Stiffness is the ability of paper or paperboard to resist deformation under stress. The resistance to a force causing the member to bend is termed bending or flexural stiffness. This may be defined as the product of the modulus of elasticity and the moment of inertia of the section. The former is a material property, and the latter depends on the configuration of the test member. All other things being equal, the stiffness of paper varies as the cube of the thickness and directly with the modulus of elasticity.

Strike-In — The penetration of liquid into a sheet of paper. The term is commonly used in printing where it refers to absorption of ink vehicle by the paper. Inks used in printing newspapers "dry" by strike-in or absorption. In other cases strike-in may be objectionable as the absorbed vehicle increases show-through.

Suction Blanket Mark — An undesirable mark produced by the endless perforated blanket that runs over the suction box on a conversion coating machine.

Suction Box — A device used to remove water from the sheet being formed on the Fourdrinier wire of the paper machine or from the wet felt of a cylinder machine prior to pressing. It is a box with a perforated top over which the wire or felt passes. Water is removed from the stock or web by induced suction within the box.

Suction Box Mark — Streaks in paper produced by uneven suction.

Suction Roll Mark — A defect in a paper produced by excessive suction in the suction couch roll under the Fourdrinier wire or suction press roll. The marks may occur in the form of patterns in the paper.

Sulfate Paper — (see Kraft Paper)

Sulfite Bond — Originally a bond paper made entirely from sulfite pulp. Today the term *Sulfite Bond* is usually interpreted to apply to any bleached and chemical wood pulp bond paper that meets the particular physical specification.

Sulfite Pulp — Although some bleached sulfite is made from hardwoods, it is manufactured usually from softwoods of low resin content such as spruce, balsam fir, and hemlock. Traditionally, sulfite pulping has been accomplished by digestion of the wood with calcium acid sulfite cooking liquor (mixture of calcium bisulfite and excess sulfuric acid). By the use of the more soluble bases and their related recovery systems, several modifications which include (a) Bisulfite process (no excess suffurous acid at pH near 4.5) called Magnefite in the case of magnesium base and Sodafite or Arbiso when sodium base is used, (b) Neutral sulfite or Monosulfite processing using soda base with an initial pH in the range of eight to nine, and (c) Two-stage processes involving pH changes in the two digestion phases which develop distinctive pulp quality features.

Supercalender — A calender stack used to increase density, smoothness, and gloss of paper. It is constructed on the same general principle as a calender, except that alternate chilled cast-iron and soft rolls are used in the supercalender. The soft rolls are constructed of highly compressed cotton or paper. It is not an integral part of the paper machine, whereas the calender is.

Surface-active Agent — A substance which tends to reduce surface tension. The common term is Surfactant.

Surface Sized — A term applied to paper or paperboard whose surface has been treated with a sizing material applied to the dry or partially dried sheet either on the paper machine or as a separate operation.

Tablet Paper — A general term descriptive of any of the grades of paper used in the manufacture of tablets, but chiefly applied to book and writing grades of paper. For ink, the basis weight is betweeen 16 and 20 pounds (17 × 22-500); for pencil, it is usually 32 pounds (24 × 36-500).

Table Rolls — A series of rolls over which the Fourdrinier wire passes after leaving the breast roll. They maintain the working surface of the wire in a plane and aid in water removal through the wire. The tubes or rolls create a vacuum on the downstream side of the nip.

Tag Stock — A cylinder of Fourdrinier sheet ranging in weight from 100 to 270 pounds (24 × 36-500 — suitable for the manufacture of tags. It may be made from a wide variety of furnishes, such as rope fiber, sulfite, sulfate or mechanical wood pulp, and various types of waste papers, such as manila clippings, bottle-cap waste cuttings, and reclaimed shipping sack kraft. The more durable tag stocks, such as those used in foundries, machine shops, laundries, nurseries, etc., are made of rope and jute. Tag stock, depending upon its intended use, has the following properties to a greater or lesser extent: good bending or folding qualities, suitable bursting and tensile strength, good tearing and water resistance, and a surface adaptable to printing, stamping, or writing with ink.

Talc — Hydrous magnesium-silicate Mg_2 $(Si_2O_5)_2$ • $Mg(OH)_2$ • The commercial talc is never pure talc mineral and therefore chemical and physical properties vary over a wide range. The forms of commercial talcs (such as soapstone), when ground to a fine powder, usually have a soft, greasy feel and are mostly of a creamy to greenish-white color. Talc is used as a filler in some printing papers and certain writing tablet, papeteries, and similar grades. It gives the paper a raglike appearance and feel.

TAPPI — Technical Association of the Pulp and Paper Industry.

Tearing Resistance — The force required to tear a specimen under standardized conditions. There are three terms in common usage: (1) Internal (or continuing) tearing resistance, wherein the edge of the specimen is cut prior to the actual tear — the value is commonly expressed in grams of force required to tear a single sheet; (2) edge tearing resistance; and (3) torsion tearing resistance of paper or paperboard — the energy expended in propagating a tear when the tearing force is applied in such a manner as to create a twist or torque.

Templet Board — A stencil board that is treated with wax and resins or other materials. Dimensional stability is important.

Tensile Strength — The force, parallel with the plane of the paper, required to produce failure in a specimen of specified width and length under specified conditions of loading. This definition must be distinguished from that which is commonly used in engineering practice which expresses the tensile strength in force per unit area. In the paper industry, it is expressed as load per unit width or as breaking length.

Tissue Paper — A general term indicating a class of papers of characteristic gauzy texture, in some cases fairly transparent, made in weights lighter than 18 pounds (24 × 36-500). The class includes sanitary tissues, wrapping tissue, waxing tissue stock, twisting tissue stock, fruit and vegetable wrapping tissue stock, pattern tissue stock, sales-book tissue stock, and creped wadding. Tissue papers are made on any type of paper machine, from any type of pulp including reclaimed paper stock. They may be glazed or unglazed and are used for a wide variety of purposes.

Titanium Dioxide — The white oxide of titanium, TiO_2• There are two crystalline forms useful to the paper industry: the anatase form employed primarily as a filler pigment and the rutile form used primarily in pigmented coatings. Both types are particularly useful because of their white color, high brightness, and high refractive index (2.52-2.76), which makes them highly effective for improving both brightness and opacity.

Tooth — A term applied to the grain in the surface of various papers. Tooth may be caused by wove marks of the wire on the underside of the paper, by the minute depressions between the fibers or groups of fibers in the surface of a sheet of paper, or by the mesh of the felt fabric impressed upon the web when passed through the press rolls. It is sometimes referred to as bite.

Top — **1.** The correct term for the so-called felt side of machine-made paper. **2.** In paperboards composed of different stocks, the better quality side is usually referred to as the "top," and the rest of the board, composed of another stock, as the "back."

Top Sizing — Surface or tub sizing of paper that has already been internally sized.

Tough Check — A very strong paperboard made on a cylinder machine from extra-strong, usually unbleached, chemical wood pulps which may be blended with rope stock. It may be coated on one or both sides and comes in a variety of colors. The usual thicknesses are, 3-, 4-, 6-, and 8-ply, corresponding to 12, 18, 24, and 30 points, respectively. It is used principally for tickets, shipping tags, and wherever toughness is essential.

Translucency — That property of a material which permits it to transmit light with strong scattering of the light so that transparency does not obtain. This property must be carefully distinguished from transparency — a sheet of bond paper is translucent, whereas a sheet of high-grade glassine paper is fairly transparent.

Transparency — That property of a material which transmits light rays so that objects can be distinctly seen through the specimen. Transparency ratio is a measure of transparency as judged when a space separates the specimen and the object viewed through the specimen. Transparency should be carefully distinguished from opacity; the later property is measured by the show-through of light and dark objects placed immediately behind the specimen.

Trim — **1.** The widest sheet of paper, trimmed to remove deckle edges, that can be made on a given machine. **2.** To cut true to exact size, by cutting away the edges of paper in the web or sheet. **3.** The paper trimmed off the edges of a continuous web of paper or from the edges of sheeted paper.

Tube Board — Paperboard made of various raw materials in thickness from 0.009 of an inch up, generally unsized and fairly smoothly finished. It is suitable for slitting into narrow rolls for winding and pasting into spiral or convolute mailing tubes, cores, etc.

Tub-Sized — A term applied to paper or paperboard that has been surface-treated and/or impregnated with natural or synthetic sizing materials in a tub-sized press. The term is often incorrectly applied to surface-sized papers where a tub-size press, as such, is not used.

Tuck Board — (see *Shoe Board*).

Turned Edge — An edge on a sheet of paper that has been doubled back, creased, and held in that position by subsequent layers.

Turpentine Test — The procedure used to measure the time required for turpentine penetration as an indication of grease resistance of paper.

Twin Wire Paper — **1.** Duplex paper made as two separate sheets on two different wires of the papermaking machine and later combined, thus giving twin sides or two top sides to the paper at the end of the machine. **2.** Paper made on a Fourdrinier machine fitted with one top wire of the *Inverform* type so that drainage of water from the sheet during formation is partly from the top of the sheet and partly from the bottom to permit higher operating speeds. Such a sheet can be considered to have two wire sides.

Two-sidedness — The difference in shade or texture between the felt and wire sides of a sheet of paper. The term is commonly used in connection with dyed papers and refers to a difference in color depth between the usually darker felt side and lighter wire side. Two-sidedness may also occur in papers prepared from a mixed furnish, containing long- and short-fibered stock, the latter being more evident on the felt side, or filled sheets where more pigment is retained on the felt side. The degree of two-sidedness increases significantly with increase in machine speed.

Typing Paper — An oiled or unoiled paper used on printing presses for packing between the platen and the printed sheet.

Typewriter Paper — Most typewriter paper is bond paper cut to $8^1/_2 \times 11$ inch size. It requires regular bond sizing with no special surface, other than the usual bond-paper texture.

Underliner — A brighter furnish formed immediately above the middle of a multicylinder paperboard to assist in obscuring the dark color of the filler. It is covered with a better grade of stock, called the topliner, which serves as the surface of the board.

Unit — A term most frequently used in the Southern states in the measurement of pulpwood. It refers to a pile of wood eight feet long, five feet wide, and four feet high, containing 160 cubic feet, or 25 percent more volume than one cord.

Vapor Permeability — That property of paper or paperboard which allows the passage of vapor. This property must be measured under carefully specified conditions of total pressure, partial pressures of the vapor on the two sides of the sheet, temperature, and relative humidity. Because paper has specific affinity for water vapor, vapor permeability should not be confused with air permeability or porosity.

Varnish ability — The measure or ability of a sheet of paper to accept varnish. A sheet with a high degree of varnishability would generally be smooth, of low absorbency, and would have a minimum amount of color change on varnishing.

V board — Either solid or corrugated fiberboard (more usually the former) having certain designated properties as defined by the United States Government specifications (JAN-P-108). This board is characterized by the unusually high percentage of its dry bursting strength and effective lamination of components remaining after immersion in water for twenty-four hours.

Vehicle — The liquid portion of a material such as ink, paint, or coating composition, including the binders or adhesives and modifiers.

Void Fraction — The ratio of the volume occupied by voids or air spaces to the gross volume of a sheet of paper. It may also be expressed as unity minus the *Solid Fraction*.

Wad Stock — A paperboard spun into a small, tightly wound, compact coil to form the base of a shotgun shell. It is made of reclaimed paper stock or chemical wood pulp, usually 0.01 to 0.012 of an inch in thickness. It has uniform thickness and density, a high water finish, and water resistance (see also *Shot-shell Top Board*).

Washboard Marks — Soft sections of a roll of paper, which appears as corrugations at angles to the axis of the roll. They are caused by uneven caliper across the web.

Waterleaf — An unsized paper.

Watermark — (see Chapter 12).

Water-Soluble Paper — A combination of carboxymethyl cellulose (CMC), cellulose fibers, and various inorganic substances. This paper is not actually soluble in water, but it disperses very quickly and finely, leaving a residue or suspension. This paper is also known as "flash" paper, or by its' trade name, Dissolvo®. Basis weights vary with this paper; approximate basis for tissue weight being 25 × 38 34. Watersoluble paper is frequently encountered regarding unlawful wagering activities, or any type of clandestine operation where the rapid disposal of the writing medium is desirable. To counteract such attempts the authors refer the reader to "Analysis for Water-Soluble Paper," by A. H. Lyter, published in the *Journal of Forensic Sciences*, 24(4):380-381, 1979.

Water Streaks — Streaks in paper, appearing in long, light areas that run with the grain. They may be observed by holding the paper to the light.

Wavy Edges — A term applied to book and other printing paper to designate an effect similar to warping in boards. It is usually caused by the more rapid rate of change in the moisture content of the edges of the sheets in a pile as compared with the center.

W Board — Solid or corrugated fiberboard which is basically similar to *V Board* except for lower bursting strength and caliper requirements.

Web — The sheet of paper coming from the paper machine in its full width or from a roll of paper in any converting operation.

Wedding Bristol — A term applied to a group of high-grade bristols made by pasting together two or more sheets of finished or unfinished paper in different thicknesses or plies. It may be plated to give various finishes; it is used for cards, announcements, etc. The basis weights are 2-ply, 120 pounds; 3-ply, 180 pounds; 4-ply, 240 pounds, ($22\frac{1}{2} \times 28\frac{1}{2}$-500).

Weddings — A kind of superfine writing paper of medium to heavy substance, slightly modified for better folding. Appearance is the most important factor to be considered.

Welts — Defects consisting of elongated areas of deformation in paper or paperboard, in sheets or rolls, which appear as a continuous hump or a series of alternate humps and indentations parallel to the machine direction.

Wet End — That portion of the paper machine between the headbox and the dried section.

Wet-End Additive — Any material that is added to a papermaking furnish prior to formation of the web. It may include beater adhesives, waxes, rosin, dyes, alum, fillers and other pigments, antifoams, pitch-control agents, retention aids, etc.

Wet Machine — A machine used to form pulp into thick rough sheets sufficiently dry to permit handling and folding into bundles (laps) convenient for storage or transportation.

Wet Mullen — The Mullen bursting strength of paper or paperboard after complete satuation with water.

Wet Rub — The resistance of wet paper to scuffing.

Wet-Strength Broke — Paper that has been treated chemically to increase its wet strength and which has been discarded in the process of manufacture. Because of its high wet strength, this paper presents special problems in defibering. When the wet strength is produced by urea-formaldehyde or melamine-formaldehyde resins, it is normally defibered by means of mild acid and elevated temperatures. Some high wet-strength papers cannot be defibered by any feasible means. Similar defibering problems occur in the recovery of waste papers containing papers of high wet strength.

White Water — A general term for all waters of a paper mill that have been separated from the stock or pulp suspension, either on the paper machine or accessory equipment, such as thickeners, washers, and savealls, and also from pulp grinders. It carries a certain amount of fiber and may contain varying amounts of fillers, dyestuffs, etc.

Wild — A term used to describe a sheet with irregular formation of poor distribution of fibers. It has a mottled appearance on look-through.

Winder Welts — Grain-direction ridges in the paper, sometimes formed in the surface of the paper roll in the process of winding, that are caused by uneven expansion of the paper due to moisture variation or excessive tension of the web or both. *Winder welts* often remain in the paper after sheeting. In certain instances they disappear after conditioning or printing. *Winder welts* can run into *Winder Wrinkles.*

Winder Wrinkles — Long grain-direction crease marks sometimes formed in the surface of the paper in the processes of winding. These marks are due to various causes, such as uneven moisture content in the paper, improper tension in the paper web, or imperfect alignment of the roll shaft. Since these marks are set in the paper, it is seldom possible to eliminate them.

Wire Hole — A defect in the form of a hole in a paper web caused by a hole in the Fourdrinier wire that prevents retention of the papermaking materials at that spot.

Wire Side — That side of a sheet of paper which was formed in contact with the wire of the paper machine during the process of manufacture.

Wire Spot — A defect in a sheet of paper caused by imperfections in the Fourdrinier wire.

Wove — The usual type of wire mark on a sheet of paper. Wove papers do not exhibit the wire marks known as laid lines.

Writing Paper — A paper suitable for pen and ink, pencil, typewriter, or printing. It is made in a wide range of qualities from chemical and mechanical wood and rag pulp, or mixtures of rag and chemical pulp or chemical and mechanical pulp. Distinctive finishes and colors produce variations in this class of paper that, through long usage, have established them as well-known grades of paper. Thus, we have fine and extra-fine writing, azure laid, azure wove, boxed, chemical manila, commercial, flat, folded, industrial, laid, machine-dried, manila, railroad, superfine, tablet, etc., each in a form, finish, or color to meet a particular use, but all fairly typical of this class of paper. It is made in basis weights of 13 to 24 pounds (17 × 22-500). The most significant class property is good writing and ruling surface. For some uses, good strength and erasability are also necessary.

Yankee Machine — A paper machine using one large steam-heated drying cylinder for drying the sheet instead of many smaller ones. It produces a glazed finish (machine glazed) on the side of the sheet next to the drier.

Yoshino — A Japanese tissue paper made from the fibers of the paper mulberry. It is used extensively as a stencil tissue.

Z-Direction Tensile Strength — The tensile force per unit area required to rupture a paper or paperboard specimen when the direction of the force is perpendicular to the plane of the sheet. It is one of the several measurements used as a measure of bonding strength.

Zero-Span Tensile Strength — The tensile strength of a sheet of fibrous material, measured with special jaws, at an apparent initial span of zero. It is an indication of the strength of the material comprising the fiber.

CHAPTER 12

WATERMARKS

DEFINITIONS

THE Institute of Paper Chemistry, located in Appleton, Wisconsin has defined *watermarks* as the following:

> A true watermark is a localized modification of the formation and opacity of a sheet of paper while it is still quite wet, so that a pattern, design, or word group can be seen in the dried sheet when held up to the light. So-called impressed watermarks are made with metal or rubber letterpress-type marking or rubber letterpress-type marking devices on the topside of the sheet at a point beyond the press section of the paper machine and are not true watermarks. Simulated watermarks can also be produced by printing dry paper with transparentizing compounds.[1]

B. L. Browning who, in his *Analysis of Paper*,[2] defined *watermarks* in this manner:

> A watermark is produced in handmade papers by forming a nonpermeable design on the wire screen. When the sheet is made, the pulp is thinned in areas imposed by the design. A watermark can be made to appear in light-and-shade gradations if depressed and raised patterns are impressed in the screen.

The American Paper and Pulp Associations' *The Dictionary of Paper*[3] defines the term *watermark* as follows:

> A true watermark is a localized modification of the formation and opacity of a sheet of paper while it is still quite wet, so that a pattern, design, or word group can be seen in the dried sheet when held up to the light. Such modifications can be accomplished in several ways. The most common method is through the use of a bronze letterpress-type dandy roll riding on top of the sheet at or near the suction-box position of the Fourdrinier wire. When an impression of such a roll is made on the top surface of a wet sheet, such an impression will contain less fiber at the point of impress and hence, more translucency. Another method is through the use of a bronze intaglio-type dandy roll at the same location on the Fourdrinier wire. The image resulting from such a dandy roll is characterized by having more fiber at the point of impress and hence, more opacity. Such a watermark is often referred to as a "Shadecraft" watermark. A third method is a variation of the letterpress marking

method except that a soft rubber, letterpress device is used on the first press of the paper machine with the result that a watermark is produced on the underside (i.e., wire side) of the sheet from the topside. So-called impressed watermarks are made with metal or rubber letterpress-type marking devices on the topside of the sheet at a point beyond the press section of the paper machine where the water content of the paper has been reduced below the level required for a true watermark. Impressed watermarks are actually a form of embossing and are not true watermarks. Simulated watermarks can also be produced by printing dry paper with transparentizing compounds.

Donald Carpenter and Dale A. Lindens, in their *Identification of Paper*[4] devote a section pertaining to watermarks and wiremarks.

> Various steps are involved in producing these marks. First of all, the pulp, suspended in liquid, is floated onto a gauze mold or sheet on a conveyor belt; by this means, a high percentage of the liquid is rapidly drained off. Next, the pulp is placed under a "dandy roller" which packs it and further reduces its liquid content. If the paper is to be the "wove" variety (i.e., impressed with an interlaced wire network to create a woven appearance the dandy roller is covered with material similar to the gauze on the conveyor belt; otherwise, one side would appear smooth. If the paper is to be "laid" (i.e., have closely spaced parallel lines), the dandy roller will impress thin, flexible parallel wires into the pulp, displacing the fibers in such a way as to mark the paper without reducing its thickness and if the paper is to be watermarked with a symbol, letters, or numbers, the wires affixed to the dandy roller will have the shape of the watermark. This process is quite similar to that used in making "laid" paper.

HISTORY

As the reader has witnessed, there are several competent definitions of the term *watermark*. But what are watermarks, wherein lies their meaning, their origin?

It has been suggested that these archaic devices may have been used solely as marks of identification for sizes of moulds and the paper formed thereon, or as trademarks of the papermakers who fashioned them.

Harold Bayley has written extensively upon this subject of watermarks.[5] Mr. Bayley notes that, at the suspected time of origin of the watermark, Europe was overrun with mystic and puritanical sects, and the art of papermaking was one of the most developed trades of these religious bodies. Bayley attached symbolic importance to each of the watermarks used by these mystical people and believes that the papermarks carried with them signals of hidden meaning.

Another reasonable explanation of the conception of the watermark is that it was an attempt to satisfy the artistic urges of the papermaker. These designs and emblems may have soothed the fire in their artistic souls.

Perhaps the early use of these papermarks served the purpose of depiction.

It has been written that many of these early papermakers could not read or write. It may have been necessary to inform them (the workers) of their duties by the creation of "pictures," i.e. the watermark. Or was it an early form of advertisement? Early craftsmen, shopkeepers and merchants often resorted to an art form to describe their work, thus illustrating what function they performed without resorting to the written word.

The first use of the watermark is said to have occurred in Italy about the year 1282.[6] The use of watermarks caught on and shortly thereafter there were literally thousands of differing designs describing everything imaginable that could be imprinted upon paper.

The art of forming the actual wire watermark emblems that were applied to the moulds has been modified very little since their origin in the late thirteenth century. The question as to why these indentations were called watermarks is not known, as the mark or device in paper is not caused by the use of water to any greater extent than it the sheet itself. In the French language, the appellation is *filigrane*; and, in Dutch language, *papiermerkein*: these two names are more suitable as accurate descriptions.[7]

The first use of the term *watermark* in English appeared at the beginning of the eighteenth century. By all appearances we are led to believe that its faulty meaning had its origin in the English language.[8]

With the introduction of a "continuous papermaking machine" by Nicholas-Louis Robert, utilization of the watermark had to undergo a few necessary changes. Prior to this invention watermarks, and the manufacture of paper as well, was done entirely by hand. An Englishman by the name of John Marshall solved the problem of marking machinemade paper with the invention of a wire-covered roll.[9] This roll imparted specific designs upon it in wire, which rode over the susceptible sheet of paper just after it left the travelling wirecloth of the machine. This device obtained the name "dandy-roll," reportedly an expression by an elated workman who, upon first seeing the skeleton roll declared his delight by exclaiming, "Isn't that a dandy!"[10] The expression took hold, and we know this watermark making device by that name today. These metal wire cylinders containing patches of specific patterns are generally of two types — wire or screen.

The early 1960s saw the introduction of a new method in which to impart paper with a watermark. This Customark® or chemical process did not require the rearrangement of the fiber in the wet paper in the design area. The Customark process is performed in the paper after it has been made. Instead of moving the fibers, the paper in the design area is made transparent by placing a patented transparentizing formulation into the sheet. It differs from the traditional method of watermarking in that it is chemically produced and reportedly takes a smaller amount of time in which to complete the process. This newer chemical process is said not to fade, spread, or discolor with age. In short, it has all the advantages of the dandy-roll capabilities with the additional one of being capable of being produced in smaller quantities if need be.[11]

The detection of changes of the watermark has, over the years, provided the questioned document examiner with innumberable instances of fraudulent activities. Running the gauntlet from the detection of fraudulent bills of sale, patents, wills, and documents in general, the correct identification of the watermark has proved to be an invaluable aid to those in the employment of forensic document analysis.

The recognized "father" of questioned documents, Albert S. Osborn, has written on this subject of watermarks. In his chapter pertaining to paper and questioned documents, Osborn enumerates various methods of analysis relevant to watermark identification.[12] It was Obsorn who first suggested that a careful study be made of every part of the watermark as well as of the wire gauze marking (dandy-roll) of the paper. Osborn informed his followers that many things could and did occur in connection with the watermark that would indicate the date of the paper. Osborn was among the first to recommend the use of the *Lockwood's Directory of the Paper and Allied Trades* when investigating watermarks.

Osborn noted several potential identifiers geared to the mechanics involved during the watermarking process:

> One such accident may occur by which the wire cloth under the paper or the wire covering on the dandy roll may be injured or "buckled" so as to mark every run of paper thereafter. The dandy rolls for the different styles of paper, although carefully handled, are sometimes thus buckled or twisted, causing streaks to appear in the paper in exact relation to certain watermarks, and this may mark the date of paper showing this characteristic.[13]

THE MAJOR METHODS OF WATERMARKING

The Institute of Paper Chemistry's Continuing Education Center provides us with a definitive analysis of the methods of watermarking. We have touched briefly on this subject in our introductory definitions; let us elaborate further on these points.

Wire Mark

This is the first method and remains one that has been little modified since its conception in the Fabraino mills of Italy. This was accomplished by sewing wire designs to the mould on which the moist paper stock was lifted from the vat. The wire serves as a mattrix whose impressions is formed in the paper. Because the part of the paper into which the wire was pressed becomes less opaque than the rest of the sheet, the design appears darker when held over a dark surface or conversely, lighter when cast in front of the light.[14] In photographic terms, it is the negative while the paper sheet is a kind of diapositive.

This type of mark is produced by bent wires or electrotypes closing wire mesh and raised above it. Based on the type of production utilized by the dandy roll manufacturer it may either be sewn or soldered to the dandy roll or forming wire. The wire mark will always impart a light line mark. In addition, this process leaves a clear edge definition.

Shadow or Shaded Mark

A design is impressed into a wire mesh. The paper is actually denser in the design area resulting from the surrounding pressure encircling this impressed area. More fibers blow into this section, which is not being pressed down by the surrounding wire mesh. As the result of this increase of fibers in the design area, the design becomes more opaque than the rest of the sheet. This method has been considered to have developed into a fine art due to the fact that the process requires more concentration and manual skills in both papermaking and metal working.

In this process the wire mesh is not closed. These marks can be light, dark or shaded. There is a distinctive shaded edge definition to this process.

Stamp Mark/Rubber Stamp Roll (Molette Process)

This is a method of watermarking that was developed as the result of the introduction of higher speeds to the paper machine apparatus. The web of paper, at this stage, is considerably drier than it was at the dandy roll section; the "stamp mark" is pressed against the damp paper as it is supported by a cylinder or drum. By pressing these fibers together it makes them more transparent than the remainder of the sheet.

This third method differs from the previously mentioned in two respects: (a) The paper is in a much drier state during this stamping process, and (b) a rubber stamp is used to press the design into the paper.

With this method there will always be a light line mark imparted to the sheet. An additional note of identification is the fact that this process gives you sharp edge definition.

Chemical Watermarks

This fourth and newest technique was, in the last two decades, added to the art of watermarking. This novel method of watermarking is applied to the paper after the paper has been manufactured, not during the process of manufacture, which is the customary procedure for the previously mentioned methods. One unique feature of this process and one which distinctly imparts it from the other watermarking procedures is this: the marking process does not sacrifice the strength of the paper because it does not make the paper any thicker or thinner than any other part of the sheet.

Discussions with the Fox River Paper Company of Appleton, Wisconsin, holders of the patent of the Customark suggests that this newest process is geared towards the production of smaller quantities of paper.[15] For example, if a company or individual requests a specific watermark that is uniquely and exclusively their own, this Customark process could provide this service. This process can be considered profitable in the amounts as low as 100 lbs. In the old, more familiar 8½ × 11 reems that would work out to about 20 reems of paper.

The chemical watermark is "limited" to white and off-white colored sheets; if not, and the chemical mark is placed upon a differently colored sheet, say a light blue or blood red, the watermark appears "wet." It has been stated that anything that can be conventionally watermarked can be accomplished by the chemical process as well.[16]

As holds true with conventional watermarks, the chemical watermark is almost always applied from the wire side — the reason being that most people print on the felt side of the finished sheet. This means that this chemical watermark has the preponderance of its chemical applied on the wire side of the sheet.

The chemical watermark is relatively stable to accelerated aging and has the tendency to discolor around the same time the finished sheet of paper would discolor.

Thomas Delain, an employee of the Fox River Paper Company who is largely responsible for the conception of the chemical watermark, was questioned by the authors in the following manner.

"Is it, from a forensic point of view, that easy to spot a chemical watermark as opposed to a watermark issued from a dandy roll?" His answer was the following:

> "Just visually it's next to impossible [to detect the difference]. . . . You can extract those marks with an organic solvent. If you heat up some potassium iodine crystals over a hot plate . . . or even iodine crystals will do it . . . the mark will turn yellow after it has been exposed to the air. It will look much different than the rest of the paper."[17]

Embossed Watermarks

A few words regarding the uses of embossed watermarks are in order at this point. This process imparts its watermark when the sheet is nearly dry. This involves an engraved steel roll compressing fibers, which gives a very sharp edge-definition. As suggested by its name, this process raises to the surface of the sheet of paper the design of the watermark. Diplomas or certificates of achievement, etc., supplies the need for such watermarking.

TRADE DIRECTORIES

When searching for the answers to questions pertaining to watermarks, papermaking, pulp identification, etc., it has been suggested that the examiner first consult the various trade directories of the paper and allied trades.[18] As mentioned earlier, Osborn was the first questioned document examiner to utilize these trade directories, *Lockwood's Directory of the Paper and Allied Trades*, to be precise. These directories can provide the examiner with a great deal of information concerning the various watermarks and brand names, as well as the names and addresses of the manufacturers in question. There are several such sources to which the examiner may begin his search.

TAPPI

A monthly technical journal (*TAPPI* is published by the Technical Association of the Pulp and Paper Industry (TAPPI). Published out of Atlanta, Georgia, this journal publishes the papers and leading discussions of the Technical Association, with technical data on the whole range of the industry — management, engineering, operations, science and other technical interest, on pulp, paper, paperboard, and converted paper and board products. It is geared to high-level technology, but many reports are applicable or adaptable to small-scale operations. This magazine, like all TAPPI materials, is generally limited to members, which include many libraries.

Thomas' Register of American Manufacturers

Thomas Publishing Company, 461 Eight Avenue, New York, NY annually puts out a general directory of manufacturers, classified by kind of product, including pulp and paper, arranged geographically, and listed alphabetically. It includes a trade name section, with registered trade names listed alphabetically.

Phillips' Paper Trade Directory of the World

The S. C. Phillips & Company, Ltd., Graham House, 3 Tudor Street, London E.C. 4, England, publishes each year a directory of the pulp, paper, paperboard mills, and converters of major producing countries of the world by name and address. It also lists production of type and grades and equipment; commonwealth and foreign classification by product list; and producing mills by countries.

Walden's A B C Guide

Walden, Sons and Mott, Inc., 41 Park Row, New York, NY publish their guide annually. It includes the paper distributors of the United States and Canada with the personnel of each company and the kinds of paper handled by each house and the manufacturers of paper products, classified according to product.

Lockwood's Directory of the Paper and Allied Trades

A regular edition and traveler's edition of this list is annually put out by the Vance Publishing Corp., 133 East 58th Street, New York, NY. It includes manufacturers of equipment and supplies purchased by paper and pulp mills; manufacturers of paper specialties; paper dealers; watermarks and brands; pulp testing chemists; trade associations; statistical information, and it pertains to American and Canadian industries and concerns.

DANDY ROLL MANUFACTURERS

Since chemical watermarks are still in a relative state of infancy, the vast majority of watermarks are still made by the dandy roll. Many examiners, when confronted with a watermark that, for the moment, mystifies them, find that traversing to the "ultimate" source of the watermark to be a wise selection of time. In 1975, H. M. Spencer (Co.) purchased the company of Cheney Bigelow, located in Springfield, Massachusetts. Cheney Bigelow had been in business since 1900. There are at present, only a handfull of watermarking dandy-roll manufacturers. If approached in a businesslike manner, these manufacturers will provide the patient examiner with invaluable information as to the origin of the watermark in question. Featured below is a complete list of these manufacturers:

H. M. Spencer (Co.)   (Est. 1869)
Post Office Box 965
Holyoke, Massachusetts 01040

Sinclair International   (Est. 1900)
60 Appleton
Holyoke, Massachusetts 01040

Plank Corporation   (Est. 1907)
Post Office Box 1955
Appleton, Wisconsin 54913

Spencer Johnson   (Est. 1953)
Post Office Box 1761
Appleton, Wisconsin 54913

The Johnson Company   (Est. 1957)
158 Maine
Lincoln, Maine 04457

CODING OF WATERMARKS

Within the industry, the coding of watermarks is a closely guarded trade secret, to the extent that it is usually unknown to the papermaker's distributors. At present, few papermakers employ some type of code included in their watermark. This was not always the case. Some date coding has been practiced, to a limited extent, for close to a century now; however, the past eighty years have seen gradual decline in their use.

The coding system in use today saw their advent in the 1920s. Initially some attempts to use changes in obscure watermark details as in decorative designs or the position of "tie marks" in the widely used outlined lettering.[19]   The codes of today generally fall into one of two classes:[20]

- A simple arbitrary mark such as *o, x,* or a comma (,) located near some element in the basic watermark, which can be relocated from year to year or other time period. Also known as a "floating" mark.
- One or more arbitrary symbols located as a portion of the overall design such as *xo-* which are changed from year to year or other time period.

These codes may be indicated by the style and/or arrangement in the design features of the dandy roll. This would indicate variations pertaining to logos or trade marks, letter styling, certain design elements, etc. Strict attention must be given to the arrangement of the principal text involved, as well as the actual wording utilized. Any intentional deletions or additions involving special terminology, such as proprietary terms, must not be overlooked. The examiner must be conscious of the possibility of the addition or subtraction of arbitrary marks. These marks may revolve around the design elements, logos or trade marks, etc. The simple method of spacing or the arrangement of that spacing of marks on the dandy roll is another possible indicator of coded watermarks.

Under ideal conditions, when attempting to date paper, the paper in question would contain a date-coded watermark. Conversations with forensic examiners of questioned document analysis[21-30] indicated that less than 10 percent of the cases encountered by this group contained a date-coded watermark. Therefore, it is within the realm of the noncoded watermark that the examiner will find the vast majority of his cases.

Although a watermarked sheet of paper may contain a date, this does not indicate, by any means, inclusive reliance as to the actual usage of that sheet of paper. Since the majority of modern paper is noncoded, there are a series of steps the examiner must follow in order to obtain the necessary information regarding that paper. These steps will be enumerated in Chapter 13.

FOREIGN WATERMARKS

European

Recently we addressed the Institute of Paper Chemistry with the following question:

"Is there an equivalent of the *Lockwood's Directory, Phillip's Directory, or the Thomas Register* that would pertain to watermarks from abroad?"

It was suggested that, when dealing with European watermarks, we consult *Europa Birkner*. The official name of the work is the *Directory of Producers and Converters of Pulp, Paper and Board*.[31] This publication comes from Birkner and Company, Vrleg., Wichmann Strausse-4, D-2000., Hamburg — 52 West Germany. They have editions written in French, German and English. This publication resembles the *Lockwood's Directory* — in other words it has the names of the mills and paper dealers and contains trade names, brand names, and logos.

If the suspected watermark is English, consult the *Phillips Paper Trade Directory of the World*.[32] Like *Lockwood's*, the *Phillips Directory* tends to promote the British paper market or their own markets' sphere of influence.

Although not in the same league with the trade directories the Hilversun Paper Publication Society, located in Holland, can provide the examiner with some information regarding watermarks from the Netherlands. It should be noted that this Society takes pride in the many papers they have published on historical watermarks.[33]

Asian

When this same question was addressed to the Asian countries, we ran into a little difficulty. Japan is the acknowledged leader of these Asian countries in pulp and paper production. The Japanese are reluctant to place into print the names of their paper and pulp manufacturers, for reasons that appear inherent with Japanese customs. The 1970s witnessed a startling rise in the number of Japanese interests in the forest regions of the Pacific northwest of this country, and Canada as well. The Japanese import pulp from their mills in Oregon, Washington, and Alaska, and it is turned into a host of paper products, some of which are sold back to the United States.[34] Despite this interest in the wilderness of our Pacific northwest, the Japanese have nothing of the caliber of a *Lockwood's* or a *Phillip's Directory*. To be sure, there are a few publications that pertain to that aspect of Japanese business. One such publication is *Japan Tappi*, a monthly vehicle that is printed in Japanese . . . with English summaries. *Japan Tappi* is published by Japanese Technical Association of Pulp and Paper Industry, 9-11, 3-Chrome, Ginza Chuo-ku, Tokyo, Japan, 104.[35] Another decent source is the quarterly publication of *Japan Pulp and Paper*. This publication is in English from Shigyo Times Sha Limited, Bunsei Blvd., 9-4, 3-Chome, Ginza Chuo-ku, Tokyo, Japan.[36]

The Miller-Freeman Company publishes *The International Pulp and Paper Directory*, although it is listed as being published by Pulp and Paper International. This publication has listings of pulp and paper concerns pertaining to Viet Nam and the People's Republic of China and has reserved some thirty-odd pages to the Japanese pulp and paper industries.[37]

A periodical entitled *Graphic Arts Japan* occasionally runs an annual edition on paper suppliers, but there is no guarantee of yearly repetition.[38] There are several periodicals of a similar nature, but they are directed towards the foreign and international market of paper consumption.

It is our understanding that in Japan the government regulations regarding printing are very strict. A license must be obtained prior to printing anything. Where there exists a need for a license there must exist a need for a government agency to regulate that licensing. We would suggest that you address your problem toward that end, stressing (if applicable) that your inquiries are from a law enforcement agency.

The city of Hong Kong serves as a form of a clearinghouse for many of the paper manufacturers in Japan. The Hong Kong police have a history of being very cooperative when addressed in the proper manner. To be sure, unless the matter is of the utmost importance do not "wear thin" this record of cooperation.

NOTES

1. *Paper Analysis for the Forensic Sciences* (Appleton, WI, The Institute of Paper Chemistry, 1979), p. 47.
2. B. L. Browning, *Analysis of Paper,* 2nd ed. (New York, Marcel Dekker, Inc., 1977), p. 13.
3. *The Dictionary of Paper*, 3rd ed. (New York, American Paper and Pulp Association, 1965), p. 466.
4. D. Carpenter and D. A. Lindens, "Identification of Paper." In American Jurisprudence's *Proof of Facts* (ann.), Vol. 18. (New York, Bancroft-Whitney Co., 1967), pp. 719-720.
5. D. Hunter, *Papermaking — The History and Technique of an Ancient Craft,* 2nd ed. (New York, Alfred A. Knopf, Inc., 1947), pp. 258-264.
6. See note 6 above.
7. See note 6 above.
8. See note 6 above.
9. See note 1 above, G. M. Jeffery's section on watermarks, p. 2.
10. See note 6 above, pp. 400-403.
11. Personal communication with T. Delain, Fox River Paper Co., June, 1981.
12. A. S. Osborn, *Questioned Documents*, 2nd ed. (Albany, NY, Boyd Printing Co., 1929), pp. 471-498.
13. See note 13 above.
14. See note 1 above, J. L. Yankoski's section on watermarks.
15. See note 12 above.
16. See note 12 above.
17. See note 12 above.
18. See note 13 above.
19. L. Godown, *Watermark Evidence*. Read before the American Society of Questioned Document Examiners conference. Colorado Springs, 1975, pp. 5-7.
20. See note 20 above.
21. Personal communication with M. G. Rennert, document examiner, ATF, Washington, D.C., May, 1981.

22. Personal communication with C. Eaton, document examiner, ATF, Washington, D. C., May, 1981.
23. Personal communication with G. Epstein, document examiner, INS, Washington, D. C., June, 1981.
24. Personal communication with D. A. Crown, Criminalist, Depart of State, Washington, D.C., Feb., 1980.
25. Personal communication with R. Lockhard, document examiner, INS, Washington, D.C., Feb, 1980.
26. Personal communication with C. L. Eggleston, document examiner, IRS, Washington, D.C., Oct., 1981.
27. Personal communication with S. Goldbatt, private document examiner, Arnold Beach, FL, June, 1981.
28. Personal communication with S. Cain, Document examiner, Secret Service, Washington, D.C., Sept., 1980.
29. Personal communication with E. Alford, document examiner, Secret Service, Washington, D.C., June, 1981.
30. Personal communication with C. T. Spitzer, document examiner, FBI, Washington, D.C., Oct., 1981.
31. Personal communication with C. Booher, Head Librarian, Institute of Paper Chemistry, Appleton, WI, Sept., 1981.
32. Personal communication with W. C. Krueger, Research Fellow, Institute of Paper Chemistry, Appleton, WI, June, 1981.
33. See note 32 above.
34. See note 33 above.
35. See note 32 above.
36. See note 32 above.
37. See note 32 above.
38. See note 33 above.

Suggested Readings

Baker, J. N.: *Law of Disputed and Forged Documents.* Charlottesville, VA, Mitchie Co., 1955.
Harrison, W. R.: *Suspect Documents, Their Scientific Examination.* London, Sweet & Maxwell Co., 1958.
Hilton, O.: *Scientific Examination of Questioned Documents.* Chicago, IL, Callaghan & Co., 1956.

CHAPTER 13

METHODS FOR THE FORENSIC
EXAMINATION OF PAPER

INTRODUCTION

PAPER, like ink, is of great interest to the examiner of questioned documents and forensic chemists because the examination of paper can often answer questions concerning the identity of paper, its source or origin and its date of manufacture. This information is often used to determine whether a document is authentic or fraudulent.

Numerous methods for examination of paper are found in the literature.[1-49] Publications concerning the forensic methods for comparison of paper are less abundant;[1,4,7,17,21,23] however many procedures used by the paper industry are applicable to the forensic sciences as well. The most extensive and complete compendia of methods are the TAPPI[8] and ASTM[9] standards. Bibliographies and books that describe analytical methods for the analysis of paper also provide excellent sources of information on this subject.

The complete forensic comparison of paper can require the use of essentially every laboratory technique and instrument available. Microscopy, paper chromatography, TLC, G. C., visable and U. V. spectrometry, I. R., spectrophotofluorometry, emission spectroscopy, x-ray diffraction, S. E. M., mass spectrometry, N. M. R., differential thermal analysis, N. A. A., and A. A. have all been utilized for the comparison of paper. It is important to understand, however, that seldom does the forensic chemist have the luxury of sufficient sample to conduct all these tests, nor is it always necessary. Since forensic examiners have a limited sample to work with (to minimize damage to the document), they must choose an approach that provides the maximum points of comparison with the amount of sample available.

This chapter provides a systematic approach to the forensic comparison of paper that has proven successful at the Bureau of Alcohol, Tobacco, and

Firearms' Forensic Science Branch and other crime laboratories throughout the United States. This procedure was designed to answer the most frequently asked questions about questioned documents,

Do the samples of paper have the same origin or manufacture?

When was the paper manufactured?

The answers to these questions are often important in cases involving counterfeiting, forgeries, contracts, wills, business records, and other documents when the authenticity is questioned and when the date of preparation of a document is in doubt.

PHYSICAL CHARACTERISTICS

The first examinations performed on questioned documents are usually those that are essentially nondestructive. The physical properties examined are generally color, thickness, weight, opacity, and fluorescence. This level of examination is fast and nondestructive and often is sufficient to prove that two or more samples of paper are different. Similarity at this level of examination does not prove the papers are the same, only that they could be the same.

THICKNESS — Thickness is measured with a calibrated micrometer. A precision machinist micrometer will suffice; however a dial micrometer is more convenient to use and easier to read.

WEIGHT — The weight of the paper is measured per unit area.

COLOR — While color can be noted subjectively visually, it is desirable to measure the color by spectral reflectance with a visible wavelength spectrometer. Paper containing different dyes can be distinguished in this manner.

OPACITY — This property can be measured subjectively by viewing the paper by transmitted light or by placing the questioned paper over a printed page. It can also be measured more precisely with an opacimeter.

FLUORESCENCE — Fluorescence can be measured simply by observing the papers being compared under long (320 to 400 nm) and short (250 nm) wave ultraviolet light. The color and intensity of the fluorescence is significant and can be useful for the comparison of papers. Intensity of fluorescence must be interpreted with caution however, because the intensity usually decreases with the age of the paper especially when the paper is exposed to light. Thin layer chromatography may also be utilized in the measurement of optical brightners.

Specific fluorescent components in paper can also be compared by spectrophotofluorometry. Excitation and emission wavelengths of fluorescent compounds are very specific and this technique can actually identify the fluorescent components if adequate standards are available. This examination, however, requires extraction of the fluorescent components with solvents; therefore, this procedure is semidestructive, although only a small sample of paper is required for spectrophotofluorometry.

WATERMARK EXAMINATION

When present on paper, watermarks provide the most positive means for the identification of the manufacturer of the paper, because every watermark is the trademarked property of a particular manufacturer of paper. *Lockwood's Directory*[23] is very useful to determine the source of a watermark. Some manufacturers of paper use coded watermarks, which not only help to identify the manufacture, but also allow the examiner to determine the year the paper was manufactured.

Information concerning the dates a particular design of watermark or a code was used can be determined from the paper manufacturers and the dandy-roll manufacturers. Producers of dandy rolls keep accurate records that identify the paper manufacturer that purchased the dandy roll and the date the dandy roll was manufactured. Dandy-roll manufacturers also can provide important information on minute details in the design of the watermark and dates of various design changes. All of this information is important for dating paper samples. Since there are only a few dandy-roll manufacturers in the United States, it is relatively easy to obtain necessary information from them.

Although a watermark can identify a manufacturer of paper, unless it is a coded watermark, caution must be exercised in the dating of paper by watermark examination. It is possible for manufacturers to revert back to an earlier design; watermarks can be forged; and wear on the dandy roll itself can produce small variations in the watermark produced on paper and details of the original design can be obscured.

Examination

Details of a watermark design can be observed by viewing through transmitted light and watermarks can be compared in this manner. For a permanent record and easier comparison, however, the watermark should be photographed. Normally contact prints are made using transmitted light through the paper where the paper is in direct contact with the photographic paper.

Soft x-rays (Grenz) are also very effective in place of light. The paper is placed between a source of soft x-rays and x-ray film. Reproduction of the design of the watermark on paper is very accurate using both of these methods of photography, and the techniques are nondestructive.

The examiner of watermarks should be aware of the fact that there are other watermarks besides those produced from the dandy rolls. For example, artificial watermarks can be made by wetting the paper and pressing it with a rubber stamp that contains the design of the watermark in relief. Also, the first drying cylinder of a paper machine can consist of a rubber marking roll.[4] These artificial watermarks can be detected because they compress the fibers instead of separating them. Also, water will penetrate a genuine watermark faster than the surrounding paper, whereas water on the paper and compressed watermarks will penetrate evenly.

To detect compressed artificial watermarks, sprinkle the paper with a dry mixture of 0.5 g of fluorescent dye (rhodamine red) and 100 g of finely powdered sugar. Float it on water and observe under an ultraviolet lamp. The dye will fluoresce as it becomes moist if it is a compressed artificial watermark.

Chemical watermarks are made by placing a polymer or other organic material into the sheet of paper. The watermark appears semitransparent and can sometimes be detected by dissolving the impregnated material in organic solvents. The Fox River Paper Company employs a polymer organic material that does not readily dissolve in organic solvents. Their Customark registered trademark was introduced around 1960.

Watermarks are sometimes forged using carnauba wax, linseed oil, turpentine, mineral oil, and other agents that tend to make the paper transparent. Like other artificial watermarks, they can be detected by observing the manner in which water penetrates relative to the surrounding paper. Also marking oils and similar transparentizing agents stand out clearly when viewed under longwave ultraviolet light.

FIBER EXAMINATION

Paper consists primarily of cellulose fibers from plant material. The most common sources of paper fibers today are cotton, wood, and mixtures of cotton and wood in various proportions. Other less frequently used fibers originate from rag, jute, straw, abaca, bamboo, bagasse, esparto and flax hurds.

The experienced examiner can not only identify the type of fibers in the paper but also the (a) relative proportion of each type of fiber, (b) the pulping process used, and (c) the origin of the fibers. Browning published a detailed description of the methods for fiber examination.[28]

Methods for fiber examination consist primarily of (a) morphological examinations, by polarized light microscopy to identify the type of fibers in the paper and (b) staining procedures to determine the pulping process and origin of the fiber species. Substantial experience and training is necessary to obtain accurate and reliable results and access to appropriate standards is essential. A large collection of standard fibers, known as the "Fibrary," are available from the Institute of Paper Chemistry[26] and procedures for fiber analysis are given in TAPPI standard T 401[8] and ASTM D 1030.[10] A detailed discussion of fiber analysis is given in *Pulp and Paper Microscopy*[69] by Graff and Isenberg.

It should be mentioned that there exists a large number of synthetically produced fibers and some animal fibers that are used primarily in the textile industry. Occasionally these fibers will find their way into paper products, and the examiner should know how to recognize these fibers as well. Techniques for the identifications of synthetic and animal fibers have been well described by Browning.[28] For this reason and because these classes of fibers are not often encountered by the examiner in the examination of documents, no further discussions on this subject will be given in this text.

Preparation of Paper for Fiber Analysis

A portion of the paper is used where no writing, typing, or printing appears on the document, so as not to destroy any evidence. A total of about 0.2 g is required and the following apparatus is used.

Apparatus
- A polarizing microscope equipped with a mechanical stage and Abbe condenser. Although only 100X magnification is necessary for staining techniques, magnification up to 300X is helpful for morphological examinations.
- Glass microscope slides (1 × 3 in) and No. 2 cover glasses.
- Hot plate capable of controlling surface temperature at 50 to 60° C.
- Dissecting or probe needles (stainless steel is adquate).
- C stain, Herzberg stain, Wilson stain and Selleger stain (available from the Institute of Paper Chemistry, Appleton, Wisconsin).

Procedures (Common Paper)
Fibers in most papers used for documents can be separated from the binder and filter material by distilled water. The sample is fragmented into small pieces, placed into a small beaker, covered with distilled water and heated to a boil on the hot plate. The water is then decanted off and the residual fibers are transferred to a test tube, shake vigorously with distilled water until the paper fragments are completely separated into individual fibers.

Resistant Papers
Some paper will not separate into the component fibers by the above procedure. In these instances, repeat the above procedure using a solution of 1% sodium hydroxide in place of distilled water. Decant the sodium hydroxide solution; even the paper with 0.05N hydrochloric acid and allow to sit for about 10 minutes. Decant the hydrochloric acid solution and wash with distilled water several times by decantation to remove all residual acid, place the residual fibers in a test tube and repeat as above.

The vast majority of all documents can be defibered by this processes. For special purpose papers containing asphalt, rubber, parchment, plastic and other water resistant papers, refer to Brownings' *Analysis of Paper*.[28]

Morphological Examination

Transfer a 0.5 ml of a uniform mixture of water-suspended fibers to a clean microscope slide that has been scored with a glass washing pen. The scoring prevents the solution from running off the slide. Allow the water on the slide to evaporate until the fibers are barely suspended and then distribute the fibers evenly on the slide with a probe needle. Next completely dry the fibers on a hot plate. Place a glass slide over the fibers on the slide and examine using polarized light microscopy. The various types of wood species (coniferous and non-coniferous) and cotton have very characteristic morphological characteristics that can be used for their identification. Pulps from coniferous trees have long, thin-walled fibers that have one or more rows of large, irregularly spaced, bordered pits and areas of smaller pits. Douglas fir is recognizable by the tracheids that show spiral thickening on the inner surface of the cell adjacent to the lumen. Tracheids of the southern yellow pines are distinguishable from most American softwoods by the presence of irregularly shaped and spaced cross-fields pits.

Groundwood is readily recognizable by the undisturbed groups of wood cells that appear at right angles to the tracheids. Hardwood fibers have a large number of different types of cells that contain small, scattered pits. The hardwood fibers are differentiated from different species primarily by cell size and shape and by their characteristic detail of pits and perforations. Vessel members in hardwood fibers are difficult to find in the microscopic examination, because they are lost during the washing of the pulp during the pulping process.

Cotton, rag, and linen fibers are easily differentiated from all wood fibers because of their twisting, ribbonlike appearances.

As mentioned earilier, identifications of fiber type and/or species type should not be made without first obtaining the necessary training and experience to make accurate and reliable conclusions. It is essential to practice using standards to develop proficiency in this area, and it is also vital to observe the fiber characteristics under different degrees of polarized light to observe all of the characterizing properties of the fibers. Reference materials such as *TAPPI* T8, "Identification of Woods and Fibers from Conifers,"[8] Panshin et al., *Textbook of Wood Technology*,[30] and McCrones' *Particle Atlas*[29] are essential for the fiber analyst.

Staining of Fibers

Iodine staining examinations are very helpful to differentiate among cotton, chemical wood pulps, and groundwood, between coniferous and hardwood pulp, and between bleached coniferous sulfate pulped fibers. The stains produce characteristic colors on the fibers that, with the aid of color comparison charts,[27] can be used to differentiate the various pulping processes and fiber species.

The most commonly used stain is the C stain. For confirmation, the Wilson stain is often used, the Hertzberg stain is used to distinguish among rag, chemical, and groundwood pulps. To distinguish coniferous and hardwood pulp, the Selleger and Alexandria stains are very helpful, and the Selleger stain will also differentiate between bleached and coniferous sulfite and sulfate pulped fibers.

Preparation of Stains

C Stain

The C stain is prepared from the following solutions made with reagent-grade chemicals and distilled water.

Solutions

- Aluminum chloride solution: $AlCl_3 \cdot 6H_2O$ (about 40 g) is dissolved in water (100 ml) to make a solution of 1.15 specific gravity at 28° C.
- Calcium chloride solution: $CaCl_2$ (about 100 g) is dissolved in water (150 ml) to make a solution of 1.36 specific gravity at 28° C.
- Zinc chloride solution: Water (about 25 ml) is added to dry $ZnCl_2$ (50) to make a solution of 1.80 specific gravity at 28° C. (Fused reagent-grade sticks in sealed bottles or crystals should be used; $ZnCl_2$ from a previously opened bottle should not be used.)
- Iodide-iodine solution: Dry potassium iodide (0.90 g) and dry iodine (0.65 g) are dissolved in water (50 ml). The reagents are mixed and crushed together with a little water, and water is added slowly with stirring until the solution is complete.

The first three solutions are thoroughly mixed (20 ml, 10 ml, 10 ml respectively). Then 12.5 ml of the fourth solution is added and mixed well. The mixture is poured into a tall, narrow vessel and placed in the dark. After twelve to twenty-four hours, when the precipitate has settled, the clear portion of the solution is pipetted off into a dark bottle and a leaf of iodine is added.

Notes

- The solution should be kept in the dark when not in use. Fresh stain should be made every two or three months.
- The C stain is very sensitive to slight differences in composition, and care should be taken in its preparation and use. The solutions should be of the exact specific gravity specified and measured accurately with graduated pipets. Dark-colored, glass-stoppered dropping bottles, preferably wrapped with black paper, should be used as containers.

- Prepared C stain can be purchased from the Institute of Paper Chemistry.

Herzberg Stain

The following solutions are prepared.

Solutions

- Zinc chloride solution: Water (about 25 ml) is added to dry zinc chloride (50 g) to make a solution of 1.80 specific gravity at 28° C. (Fused sticks of $ZnCl_2$ in sealed bottles, or crystals should be used).
- Iodide-iodine solution: Iodine (0.25 g) and potassium iodide (5.25 g) are dissolved in water (12.5 ml).

All of the second solution is mixed with 25 ml of the first solution. The mixed solutions are poured into a tall cylinder and allowed to stand until clear (12 to 24 hrs.). The supernatant solution is decanted into an amber-colored, glass-stoppered bottle and a leaf of iodine is added. The stain should be protected as much as possible from exposure to light and air.

Selleger Stain

Calcium nitrate $[Ca(NO_3)2 \cdot 4H_2O]$ (100 g) is dissolved in water (50 ml). To this is added 3 ml of a solution of potassium iodide (8 g) dissolved in water (90 ml). Iodine (1 g) is added, and the solution is allowed to stand for one week. The stain is then ready for use.

Wilson Stain

Iodine (1.5 g) and cadmium iodide (70.0 g) are dissolved in water (100.0 ml). The mixture is heated to 43° C (110° F) and the solids stirred and crushed with a stirring rod until all are in solution. Water (180 ml), 37% formaldehyde (15 ml), calcium nitrate $[Ca(NO_3)_2 \cdot 4H_2O]$ (140 g), and cadmium chloride $(CdCl_2 \cdot 2 \cdot 5H_2O)$ (40 g) are added and dissolved.

A portion of the stain is titrated with 0.01 *N*-sodium thiosulfate, with addition of starch indicator near the end point. The stain solution (10 ml) should be equivalent to the thiosulfate solution (12.0 ± 2.0 ml). If the stain is too strong, it can be heated at 43° C (110° F) until titration shows the proper strength (about 20 to 30 min).

The stain is stored in an amber stock bottle. The strength is checked by titration from time to time and the stain is discarded when it becomes too weak.

Miscellaneous Stains

The Lofton-Merritt stain[31] is used primarily to indicate the presence of unbleached pulp; it produces colors that depend on the amount of lignin in pulp. Lignin-free pulp remains colorless, whereas a highly lignified pulp is stained blue; the depth of color is related to the degree of delignification. The stain is prepared from two solutions:

Solutions
- Malachite green (2 g) is dissolved in water (100 ml).
- Basic fuchsin (1 g) is dissolved in water (100 ml).

The fibers (1.5 g) are stained in a beaker with a mixture of solution 1 (15 ml), solution 2 (20 ml), and concentrated HCL (0.09 ml). After two mintues at room temperature, the dye is poured off, and the fibers are washed. The fibers can also be dyed on a slide.

The Green-Yorston stain reagent[32] is 4,4'-azobis (*N,N*-dimethylaniline) (also called *p,p'*-azodimethylaniline). It does not stain mechanical pulps, sulfate pulps, or hardwood sulfite pulps, but is a specific reagent for unbleached coniferous sulfite pulps that are stained a strong red owing to their content of lignosulfonic acids. In well-cooked pulps, only the bordered pits are stained strongly, and the fiber walls may be a light pink. The reagent (15 mg) is dissolved in glacial acetic acid (100 ml), and water (300 ml) is added with stirring. The fibers (0.1 g) are treated with the reagent solution (30 ml) and stirred 5 min. A portion of the fiber suspension is transferred to a slide, and a cover glass is placed over the preparation for microscopic observation.

The following staining procedure[33] is specific for residual lignin, but does not distinguish between pulping processes used. The dried fibers on a slide are treated for 20 to 30 sec with a solution of 4-nitroaniline (2.0 g dissolved in 100 ml of 3 N HCL) and the solution is sucked off with filter paper. Herzberg stain is then added to the fibers. After 20 to 30 sec, a cover glass is placed over the preparation, and excess stain is removed at the side with filter paper. Unbleached groundwood is stained orange; unbleached semichemical pulps are stained yellow, dark green, or gray green, depending on the lignin content; and bleached pulps are stained blue to dark violet. The stain responds to residual lignin, but does not distinguish between pulping processes, whereas the Green-Yorston stain indicates the use of the sulfite process, whether acid, neutral, or alkaline.

Examination of Stained Fibers

Place 0.5 ml of the 5% water suspended fibers on each end of a microscope slide and bring to dryness. Place three drops of the stain to the fibers on the slide, cover with a glass cover and allow to stand for about two minutes. Remove the surplus stain by tilting the slide and examine as follows.

Identification

The stained slide is placed in position on the stage of the microscope. For illumination, a 15-W "daylight" fluorescent tube, placed 10 to 12 in. from the mirror of the microscope, is recommended. The slide is examined for the different fibers, with attention given also to morphological characteristics. It is often desirable to prepare slides of authentic fibers for comparison with the sample.

Determination

The field is moved with the mechanical stage so that the pointer is 2 to 3 mm from a top corner of the cover glass. Then the field is slowly moved horizontally, and the fibers of each kind are counted as they pass the pointer. A single tally counter may be used to record the number of each kind of fiber, and repeated passes may be made to count additional kinds until all are accounted for. With a multiple tally counter, fibers of the various kinds can be counted in a single pass.

When all the fibers in one line have been counted, the stage is moved 5 mm vertically, and the fibers are counted similarly in the second line. The fibers in a total of five separate lines, each 5 mm apart, are counted. If the slide has been properly prepared, the total fiber count will be between 200 to 300.

If a single fiber passes the center of the pointer more than once, one count is made for each pass. If the fiber follows the center for some distance, it is counted only once. Each fiber in a fiber bundle (e.g. as in groundwood) is counted. Very fine fragments are ignored, but large fragments are mentally added together to give the equivalent of a whole fiber.

The number count of each kind of fiber is multiplied by its respective weight factor to obtain the weighted count. The fiber composition for each kind of fiber is found from

$$\text{Fiber composition } (\%) = \frac{\text{Weighted count}}{\text{total weighted count}} \times 100.$$

Both fields on the slide are counted. If the results for the two fields vary for any type of fiber by more than the tolerances given, one or more additional fields should be prepared and the average of results from all fields reported.

PERCENTAGE OF TOTAL	TOLERANCE, %
20 and 80	± 2
20-30 and 70-80	± 3
30-40 and 60-70	± 4
40-60	± 5

The results are usually reported to the nearest 1%. A percentage of less than 2% is reported as a "trace."

Polychromatics Produced by Stains of Iodine

A. *Wilson Stain*
1. *Groundwood*
   a. Unbleached: bright yellow
   b. Bleached: greenish yellow
2. *Softwood pulps*
   a. Sulfite
      (1) Raw cooked: very pale yellow
      (2) Medium cooked: colorless
      (3) Well cooked: very pale gray
      (4) Bleached: pinkish lavender
   b. Alpha
      (1) Unbleached: orange-red
      (2) Bleached: pale violet
   c. Sulfate
      (1) Raw cooked: dull brown
      (2) Medium and well cooked: gray
      (3) Bleached: blue; some blue with reddish spots
3. *Hardwood pulps*
   a. Sulfite
      (1) Raw cooked: very pale yellow
      (2) Medium cooked: colorless
      (3) Well cooked: very pale gray
      (4) Bleached: lavender
   b. Alpha
      (1) Unbleached: greenish gray
      (2) Bleached: dark blue
   c. Soda
      (1) Unbleached: greenish gray
      (2) Bleached: pale purple
4. *Straw*
   a. Raw cooked: green
   b. Well cooked: blue
   c. Bleached: dark blue
5. *Cotton*: red
6. *Linen*: pink
B. *Herzberg Stain*
1. *Groundwood*: brilliant yellow
2. *Softwood* chemical pulps
   a. Raw: light olive gray to olive gray
   b. Unbleached: dark bluish gray to weak purplish blue
   c. Bleached: dark purplish gray to dark reddish purple

3. *Hardwood* chemical pulps
   a. Raw: weak olive to dusky blue-green
   b. Unbleached and bleached: dark purplish gray to deep reddish purple
4. *Rag*: brilliant purplish pink to vivid red-purple
5. *Abaca* (manila fiber)
   a. Raw: moderate yellow
   b. Unbleached and bleached: dark purplish gray to moderate purplish yellow
6. *Jute*
   a. Unbleached: moderate yellowish orange
   b. Bleached: strong greenish yellow
7. *Straw, bamboo, bagasse, flax hurds,* and *esparto*
   a. Raw: light yellow
   b. Unbleached and bleached: light bluish gray to pale purplish blue and strong purplish pink
8. *Japanese fibers*
   a. Gampi and mitsumata: light greenish yellow
   b. Kozo: pinkish gray

C. *Selleger Stain*
   1. *Groundwood*: yellow
      2. *Softwood* pulps
      a. Sulfite
         (1) Unbleached: yellow
         (2) Bleached: red
      b. High Alpha
         (1) Bleached: red
      c. Sulfate
         (1) Unbleached: yellow
         (2) Bleached: blue-gray
   3. *Hardwood* pulps
      a. Sulfite
         (1) Bleached: bluish red
      b. Soda and sulfate
         (1) Unbleached: blue
         (2) Bleached: blue
   4. *Rag*: red
   5. *Abaca* (manila fiber)
      a. Bleached: claret red
   6. *Straw* and *esparto*
      a. Bleached: blue

D. *C Stain*
   1. *Groundwood*: vivid yellowish orange

2. *Softwood* pulps
    a. Sulfite
        (1) Raw: vivid yellow
        (2) Medium cooked: light greenish yellow
        (3) Well cooked: pinkish gray
        (4) Bleached: light purplish gray to weak red-purple
    b. High alpha
        (1) Unbleached: very pale brown to brownish gray
        (2) Bleached: moderate reddish orange to dusky red
3. *Hardwood* pulps
    a. Sulfite
        (1) Unbleached: pale yellow-green
        (2) Bleached: weak purplish blue to light purplish gray
    b. High Alpha
        (1) Bleached: moderate reddish orange to dusky red
    c. Soda, sulfate, and neutral sulfite
        (1) Unbleached: weak blue-green to dusky blue-green and dark reddish gray
        (2) Bleached: dusky blue to dusky purple
4. *Rag*: moderate reddish orange
5. *Abaca* (manila fiber)
    a. Raw: light greenish yellow
    b. Unbleached and bleached: yellowish gray to weak blue medium gray
6. *Jute*
    a. Unbleached: vivid yellowish orange
    b. Bleached: light yellow-green
7. *Straw, bamboo, bagasse, flax hurds,* and *esparto*
    a. Raw: light yellow to weak greenish yellow
    b. Unbleached and bleached: light greenish gray to dark bluish gray and medium purplish gray
8. *Japanese fibers*
    a. Gampi and mitsumata: light greenish yellow to light bluish green
    b. Kozo: pinkish gray

IDENTIFICATION OF PAPER ADDITIVES

Although paper consists primarily of cellulose fibers, many possible combinations of ingredients are added to give the paper its desired quality, depending on how the paper will be used. For example, sizing materials such as rosin or synthetic resins are added to paper to create resistance to the penetration of water and ink. Loading of paper by the addition of white pigments or fillers such as clay, calcium carbonate and titanium dioxide are commonly put into paper and improve printing quality.

Sizing materials such as starch, and proteins, coating ingredients such as clay, talc, titanium dioxide, barium sulfate, and calcium sulfate are commonly added to improve appearance and printing properties.

Numerous other materials, such as proteins, resins, waxes, and oils are sometimes added to produce paper for special applications.

All of these components can be identified by appropriate chemical methods; however, since most applicable methods are destructive, tests for these substances are usually limited to sample spot tests on a small area of the questioned document. Browning gives detailed procedures for the identification of loading, sizing, filler, coating, and other common paper additives.[28]

The tests presented here are usually sufficient when performed in conjunction with the entire scheme of examination. For an exhaustive treatment of the numerous possible tests on paper, the reader is referred to Browning's *Analysis of Paper.*

Identification of Starch

Iodine Staining Test

Starch is easily detected in paper by formation of the characteristic blue color when a dilute aqueous solution of iodine-potassium iodide is added. The test has been described by many investigators.[34]

The paper can be tested directly by placing drops of 0.01 N-iodine solution on the surface. The blue color appears within a few seconds if starch is present. A very faint blue color should be disregarded. If the result by direct spotting is doubtful, the test should be applied to a water extract of the paper.

Reagent

Iodine (0.13 g) is dissolved in a solution of potassium iodide (2.6 g) in water (5 ml). The resulting solution is diluted to 100 ml. If desired, the solution may be diluted to 0.001 N just before use.

Procedure

The paper (about 0.5 g) is torn into small pieces and boiled for several minutes with distilled water (10 ml). The mixture is filtered, and the filtrate is cooled to room temperature. Iodine solution (1 drop) is added. Formation of a blue color indicates starch. A faint violet coloration should be disregarded.

Not many substances interfere with the test. Some regenerated celluloses, hemicelluloses, and highly beaten or parchmentized fibers may also give a blue color, but they do not appear to a significant extent in the water extract. Poly(vinyl alcohol) can give a blue color with iodine. Confusion with starch is not likely in most cases; if it becomes necessary to differentiate the two, this can be accomplished by hydrolysis under conditions such that the starch-iodine reaction no longer gives a blue color. In examining colored papers and many papers containing impregnating agents, it is necessary to test the water extract and sometimes to preextract possible interfering materials with alcohol or other solvents.

The amylose component of starch produces a deep blue color with iodine, whereas amylopectin gives a less intense and more reddish shade. Extensively modified starches may not give the color characteristic for unmodified products, and the color observed usually depends on the degree of modification. Modification can be carried so far that no color is produced with iodine, but most commercial products have not been so extensively treated. Dextrins prepared from starch yield red-violet to red colors.

Ninhydrin Test for Protein

Ninhydrin (triketohydrindene hydrate or 2,2-dihydroxy-1, 3-indandione).[36]

Reagent

- Sodium hydroxide (0.14 g) and citric acid (0.43 g) are dissolved in distilled water (49 ml).
- Ninhydrin (0.5 g) is dissolved in methyl Cellosolve (49 g).

Solutions 1 and 2 are combined. Activol DS® (alkyl naphthalene sodium sulfonate) (0.57 g) is added, and the solution is shaken until the Activol dissolves. The solution stored in a dark-colored bottle is stable for several months at room temperature.

Notes

- The test is extremely sensitive, and controls should be run on papers known to contain proteins and those free of proteins. Enough protein can be picked up by handling paper with the fingers to give a positive test.
- The ninhydrin test is also used to detect slime.[36]

Test for Waxes and Oils

When they are present in considerable quantity, the paraffin waxes and oils can usually be detected readily by the physical characteristics of the paper or paperboard, such as waterproofness, greasy feel, and fracture on creasing. Introduction of a solvent in a restricted area on the surface of the sheet (e.g. from a micropipet) produces a characteristic wax "ring." In heavily waxed products, the wax can be scraped from the surface. The hydrocarbons normally give a brilliant white or very light blue fluorescence upon illumination by an ultraviolet lamp.

The Dunlop test[35] can be used for the detection of waxes or oils. It is based on the observation that the hydrocarbons are soluble in hot acetic anhydride but precipitate out on cooling.

Procedure

About 0.1 g of paper is boiled in a test tube with a few milliliters of acetic anhydride for 2 to 3 min. The solvent is poured off and allowed to cool. In the presence of paraffin, flakes of wax separate out, while mineral oils yield droplets in the liquid.

Most natural waxes also give the test, as to montan wax and ceresin. For small quantities the carbon tetrachloride extract of the paper should be tested. The test can also be applied to the unsaponifiable portion separated from a complex mixture.

The Dunlop test has been applied as a quantitative method to extracts from paper and particularly for determination of wax in sizing products.[35]

Confirmation of the presence and nature of paraffinic hydrocarbons may be accomplished by infrared spectrometry or pyrolysis gas chromatography when these techniques are available. Paraffin waxes are easily characterized by gas chromatography on a column of SE-30 or Carbowax 20M with temperature programming. A regular series of simlar peaks is obtained corresponding to the homologous series of hydrocarbons present in the wax. Polyethylene is nonvolatile and does not interfere, but if subjected to pyrolysis (pyrolysis gas chromatography), it yields characteristic chromatograms similar to those of paraffin wax.

Determination of Kind of Filler or Pigment

The identification of fillers or pigments may be accomplished by chemical analysis, by x-ray diffraction methods, and by microscopic examination. The physical properties of specific gravity and refractive index may be of value; these can be determined on very small amounts of material by the methods of N. A. A. and A. A., and analysis by emission spectroscopy provides rapid and reliable identification of metallic ions present in paper ash and can be applied as a quantitative method. The cations from fillers can be separated and indentified by thin-layer[37] and paper chromatography.[38]

It is important to note that two or more fillers may be present in a single paper. Also, filler may be present in the base stock and a pigment of a different type may be in the coating.

Chemical Analysis

A complete chemical analysis according to a qualitative scheme is time consuming, and the results are often difficult to interpret because of the impurities present in commercial fillers and those introduced from the pulp, process water, etc. A complete qualitative procedure is given in TAPPI Standard T421 and in ASTM D686. The methods are designed to establish the cations and anions present in the paper and to provide a rough measure of their amounts. The procedures are too lengthy to be given in detail here and the standards must be consulted if additional information is desired.

If the fillers cannot be identified unequivocally from the results of the qualitative analysis quantitative or semiquantitative analysis may be required. However, it is often more profitable to supplement chemical analysis with the following procedures.

The following procedure is given in TAPPI Standard T439 for detection of titanium pigments in paper.

PROCEDURE Ash (about 0.5 g) is placed in a 250-ml beaker with concentrated H_2SO_4 (20 ml) and $(NH_4)_2 SO_4$ (10 g). The mixture is boiled for 5 min, cooled, diluted with water to 100 ml, heated to boiling, and filtered through ashless filter paper. To the filtrate is added 3% H_2O_2 solution (10 ml); a clear yellow or orange color indicates the presence of titanium.

Microscopic Examination

The identification of fillers by the methods of chemical microscopy is convenient and fast. The compound microscope capable of a magnification of 40 to 100 diameters is adequate for most purposes; sometimes magnification of 200 to 300 diameters is desirable. The following simple procedures are often helpful in identification.

DIATOMACEOUS EARTHS, TALCS, AND CLAY — Diatomaceous earths are composed of the siliceous skeletons of diatoms, which are recognized by their characteristic shapes and symmetrical structure.

Clay particles are very small and are usually not resolved at low magnification. Clay is identified by the characteristic flat plates of kaolinite and some larger plates of mica. The crystal form of the clay platelets is strikingly shown by the much greater magnification possible in electron micrographs.

Talc particles are usually larger than either of the above fillers and can be observed at low magnification. They are irregular in outline, whereas the "fibrous talcs" are longer in one dimension.

CALCIUM CARBONATE AND CALCIUM SULFATE — The ash is tested for calcium sulfate by adding a small quantity to one drop of dilute hydrochloric acid placed on one corner of a slide. The drop is evaporated to dryness by heating carefully above the flame of a microburner. A drop of water is added to the cooled residue, and the presence of calcium sulfate is indicated by the appearance of individual and radiating clusters of needlelike crystals during evaporation of the water. (Satin white also contains calcium sulfate.) If calcium sulfate is absent, another test is made in which dilute hydrochloric acid is added to the original paper. Calcium ions also form characteristic diamond-shaped crystals of iodate. A small amount of ash is added to one drop of water on a slide, and iodic acid is dissolved in a separate drop. The drops are mixed by drawing a glass rod from one to the other. The iodate readily forms supersaturated solutions, and the crystals may form slowly.

ZINC COMPOUNDS — A small quantity of ash is added to one drop of dilute nitric acid near one corner of a slide and evaporated to dryness. The evaporation with the dilute acid is repeated twice. Then, one drop of water is added and made slightly acid with acetic acid. Some potassium mercuric thiocyanate is dissolved in a second drop of water, and the drops are allowed to flow together. If zinc is present, colorless crystals in the shape of feathery crosses appear.

BARIUM COMPOUNDS — Barium sulfate recrystallizes beautifully from strong sulfuric acid. A small quantity of ash is added to a large drop of dilute sulfuric acid on one corner of a slide. The drop is concentrated by heating over a microburner until white fumes appear (the slide must be cooled somewhat, breathing on the drop will start crystallization). The presence of barium is evidenced by barium sulfate crystals, which appear as feathery crosses.

TITANIUM COMPOUNDS — Titanium dioxide appears as minute black particles under transmitted light. A microscopic color test is based on heating a little ash on a slide with a drop of sulfuric acid and some ammonium sulfate until white fumes appear. Upon diluting the drop and added hydrogen peroxide, a characteristic yellow-to-orange color appears if titanium is present.[39] A weak test may be given by the titanium dioxide from clay.

Staining

The ash of papers containing fillers is colored characteristically by aniline dyes. Some ash is placed on a slide and a mixture of acid and basic dyes (e.g. methylene blue as basic dye and azo acid red as acid dye) are added. The ash is mixed with a needle, and the excess dye is sucked away with filter paper. Kaolin, talc, and asbestine are colored blue; calcium sulfate and barium sulfate, red.

X-ray Diffraction Techniques

Nearly all fillers and white pigments are crystalline and produce a diffraction pattern when irradiated with a beam of x-rays. The characteristic pattern observed for each kind of substance having a regularly spaced molecular structure makes possible an unequivocal identification. If the necessary apparatus is available, the x-ray technique may be very useful because it is rapid, requires little material, and constitutes a nondestructive method of testing.[14,15]

Kaolin clay, calcium carbonate (calcite or aragonite forms), talc, mica, titanium dioxide (rutile or anatase forms), bentonite, calcium sulfate (both the mono- and dihydrates), and barium sulfate can be early identified at concentrations of 2% or less of the sheet weight. The presence of quartz in clay (which may lead to abrasion problems) can be established. Identification is more difficult when several pigments are present in the same sheet. The identification is made with the aid of the *ASTM Index*[40] or other standard reference.

Satin white is partly amorphous but the presence of calicum sulfate and the character of the diffraction pattern usually permits identification. Forms of alumina originating from the alum used in the furnish are amorphous. The presence of cellulose makes correct interpretation more difficult because the cellulose reflections may obscure patterns from some crystalline inorganic materials, particularly if they are present in small quantities.

Electron Microscopy

The presence of plastic or other organic pigments, microcapsules, and other noncrystalline materials in paper often presents difficult problems in analysis. The organic pigments have very small particle size (about 0.2 to 0.5 μ, although aggregates of urea-formaldehyde pigments may reach several μ in size) and are difficult to resolve with the light microscope.

The combination of data from x-ray diffraction with those from a scanning electron microscope equipped with a x-ray analyzer (EDAX/SEM) provides information about the morphology and composition not otherwise attainable.[41]

Pigments that are crystalline in nature can be adequately characterized by the x-ray diffraction methods. Amorphous pigments (calcined clays or alumina, some satin whites, sodium silicoaluminate or other zeolites, diatomaceous pigments, and precipitated silica) are not detected, nor are organic pigments or encapsulated materials. Noncrystalline pigments can frequently be characterized by scanning electron microscopy through visualization of minute form and structure. The EDAX/SEM technique permits analysis for elements without regard to crystallinity.

Other Methods

Infrared spectra can be used for identification of fillers, but analysis of mixtures is complicated; a method has been devised for analysis based on IR spectra mixtures before and after calcination at 600° C (the IR spectra of some pigments is altered at this temperature). The FTIR technique has been used for determination of kaolin in layers of paper. The kaolin bands are observed at 3,700, 920,700, and 475 cm -1; the CH band at 2,900 cm -1 was used as reference.

X-ray absorption and x-ray fluorescence provide analysis of ash content and composition, and can be used for on-line measurements.[42]

Neutron activation analysis has been used for identification and analysis of filler.[43]

Identification of Coating Adhesives

A quick test for a carbonate coating pigment (usually calcium carbonate) in coated papers (especially offset papers) is based on applying a drop of concentrated HCL and noting any effervescence.[44] If the coating adhesive or surface size protects the carbonate, strips of the paper are boiled in water for 1 to 2 min, cooled, and tested. Sulfur-containing pigments such as lithopone (ZnS) in coated papers are detected by boiling with dilute HCL in a test tube, and testing with lead acetate paper in the mouth of the tube.

General Identification Scheme

A scheme for dating paper by identification of coating adhesives[45] is summarized in Table 13-I. The tests can be supplemented by observation of solubility in various solvents and by additional tests given in later chapers.

NOTES ON REAGENTS AND TESTS (Table 13-II)

1. Tetrabromophenolphthalein ethyl ester, 0.1% in benzene. Drops of the reagent are spread on the coated surface.
2. Procedures similar to that of the basic iodine staining test for the detection of starch in paper; 0.01 N iodine solution applied directly to the surface of the paper. If the results of the direct spotting are doubtful, the test should be applied to a water extract of the paper, TAPPI Method T419.
3. Several drops of 66% sulfuric acid are placed on the coated surface and acetic anhydride is dropped into the acid. (Rosin gives a red-violet color.)
4. Morpholine is spread on the coated surface.
5. Test on the hot water extract, being tests on the most common agents applied for imparting wet strength to paper (i.e. ureaformaldehyde and melamine-formaldehyde, with melamine resins applicable when dealing with currency papers).
6. Ninhydrin, 0.25% in acetone. Drops are placed on the surface and the paper is warmed.
7. Millon's reagent, TAPPI Method T415 and ASTN D587.
8. Schmidt's reagent, TAPPI Method T417 (Ammonium Molybdate Test). The sample is extracted with 0.5% NaOH, the extract is adjusted to pH 8, and ammonium molybdate solution is added. It is recommended to preextract the sample with 95% ethanol.
9. Copper wire test for chlorine for the detection of vinyl resins.
10. Bromine water. The paper is extracted with methanol and the extract is saponified with alcoholic sodium hydroxide. The white precipitate [poly(vinyl alcohol)] is separated and dissolved in water. The water solution is used for the test.
11. Iodine-boric acid. Test is performed on the water solution prepared in

Table 13-I

DATING OF PAPER BY DETECTION OF CHANGE IN COMPOSITION

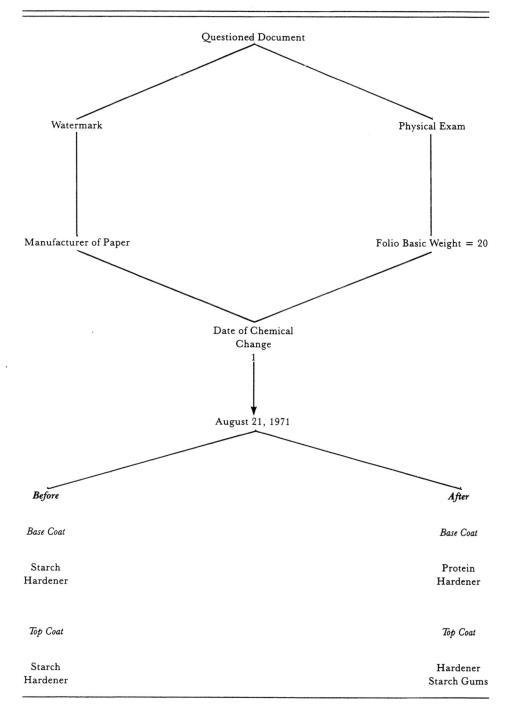

Table 13-II

TESTS FOR COATING ADHESIVES

Test	Result	Adhesive
Tetrabromophenolphthalein	Blue	Protein
ethyl ester (note 1)	Brownish yellow	Butyl rubber
Iodine (0.01 N) (note 2)	Blue	Starch
	Strong brownish red	Poly(vinyl acetate)
Storch-Morawsky (note 3)	Bluish or brownish gray	Styrene-butadiene
	Light green to blue to brown	Poly(vinyl resins)
Morpholine (note 4)	Brownish yellow	Poly(vinylidene chloride)
Iodine-boric acid (note 5)	Blue lake	Poly(vinyl alcohol)
Carbon tetrachloride extract (hot)	Fine, flaky ppt. after 24 hr (cold)	Polyethylene
Ninhydrin (note 6)	Bluish pink	Casein
	Bluish violet	-(soy) protein
	Bluish or brownish gray	Protein
Millon's reagent (note 7)	Brick red	Protein
Schmidt's reagent (note 8)	Heavy white ppt.	Protein
Copper wire test (note 9)	Sharp green	Poly(vinylidene chloride)
Bromine water (extract, note 10)	Yellow ppt.	Poly(vinyl acetate)
Iodide-boric acid (extract, note 11)	Blue lake	Poly(vinyl acetate)
Hot nitric acid (note 12)	Precipitate	Styrene-butadiene
Mercuric sulfate (note 13)	Brilliant yellow	Butyl rubber
	Dull brown	Natural rubber, styrene-butadiene

accordance with the previous note.

12. Nitric acid. The sample is digested in boiling concentrated HNO_3 (30 ml) for 5 min. The solution is cooled partially and filtered through an asbestos plug in a glass funnel; the beaker and asbestos are washed with hot HNO_3 (5ml). The filtrate is diluted to 100 ml in a graduate and the formation of precipitate observed after forty-eight hours. (The soluble portion of polystyrene gives a precipitate and acrylonitrile types give a very small precipitate.)

13. Mercuric sulfate, 5%. The reagent is dissolved in a little dilute H_2SO_4 (15 ml) in water (80 ml) is added, and the solution is diluted to 100 ml. Pieces of the coated surface are heated gradually in a test tube until the material starts to decompose. A strip of filter paper is wet with the reagent solution and exposed to the fumes.

14. Acrylic polymers give negative tests. They are soluble in dimethylformamide and formic acid and slightly soluble in hot nitric acid.

Special Tests for Adhesives

Casein

The following method has been used for detection of casein.[46] Paper (5-20 g) is extracted with borax or soda solution (2%) for 24 hr at 20° C. The extract is added to concentrated H_2SO_4 (1 ml) plus glacial acetic acid (2 ml). The presence of casein is indicated by a red-violet color produced by the tryptophan component of casein.

Carboxymethylcellulose

For detection,[46] paper (1 g) is digested with 6% ammonia solution (25 ml) for 15 min on a water bath. The mixture is filtered, and the paper is washed with water (5 ml). The filtrate is neutralized with H_2SO_4 (methyl orange indicator) and an equal volume of concentrated H_2SO_4 is added. The solution is heated on a water bath for 30 min. The cooled solution (1 ml) is mixed in a test tube with reagent solution (10 ml), and the test tube is suspended in a boiling water bath for 20 min. In the presence of carboxymethylcellulose, a violet coloration is obtained.

REAGENT — 2,7-Dihydroxynaphthalene (10 mg) is dissolved in concentrated H_2SO_4 (100 ml).

Styrene-butadiene

A very sensitive reaction is carried out as follows.[46] A portion of the paper is extracted with acetone and the solvent is evaporated. The substance is heated under reflux to complete decomposition with about ten times its weight of concentrated nitric acid. The reaction mixture is taken up in water (100 ml) and extracted with ether (3 × 30 ml). The combined ether extracts are washed with water (2 × 15 ml), which is discarded. The *p*-nitrobenzoic acid is extracted with 5% NaOH (3 × 15 ml), the solution is acidified with HCL (20 ml, d = 1.19), and the nitro group is reduced on the water bath with granulated zinc (5 g). Sodium hydroxide (20%) is added until the precipitated zinc hydroxide is just soluble again. The solution is extracted twice with ether, and the extract discarded. The solution is then acidified with HCL, cooled, and sodium nitrite solution (2 ml, 0.5 N) is added. The diazonium salt formed is then coupled with a 1% aqueous solution (3 ml) of N-(1-naphthyl)ethylenediamine hydrochloride. A violet color is obtained in the presence of polymers containing styrene.

Acrylics

Acrylic ester adhesives have been detected as follows.[46] A tetrahydrofuran extract of the paper is concentrated to a small volume and saponified with alcoholic KOH. (Ester-type softeners must be removed previously from the paper by extraction with ether.) A saturated solution of hydroxylamine hydrochloride in methanol is added, and the hydroxamic acid produced is chromatographed on paper (ascending) with isoamyl alcohol-glacial acetic acid-water (4:1:5). Acrylic acid produces a violet color upon applying a spray of ferric chloride solution. The test should be performed with a known material for reference.

Infrared Examination of Coatings

Infrared spectrometry has been applied to studies of coating composition. Because no preliminary preparation of the sample is required, the infrared procedure is relatively simple and rapid; components of mixtures can be identified without actual physical separation. Catalogs of reference spectra are available from several sources (e.g. a catalog that also includes spectra of plasticizers, solvents, and inorganic pigments).[49]

The identification of coating components can be found from infrared reflectance spectra obtained by the ATR or FTIR techniques.[47,48] The latter provides spectra that are comparable to transmission spectra obtained by the KBr pellet techniques. The reflectance spectra of water extracts can be examined by evaporating the extract on a thallium bromide-iodine plate.[47]

Starch, gum arabic, and poly(vinyl alcohol) can be distinguished easily and determined in coatings with pigment-adhesive ratio of approximately 5.5:1 and with clay greater than 90% of pigment. The absorption bands of clay can be used as a reference. The $CaCO_3$ band is at 1,435 cm-1; $BaSO_4$ bands at 632 and 605 cm-1. Poly(vinyl alcohol) and acrylic co-polymers absorb at 1,735 cm-1. Quantitative analysis for casein, acrylic, and styrene-butadiene adhesives by the FTIR technique is possible for intermediate concentrations of adhesives. Casein has characteristic absorption bands at 1,640 and 1,520 cm-1. The adhesive-pigment ratio (e.g. casein and acrylic resin emulsion-clay) and the ratio of adhesive components in mixtures can be determined to about ± 5%.[48] The concentration of adhesive components was found to be linear with the quotient of the absorption to the absorption of pigment when both were determined at appropriate wavelengths (1,000 cm-1 for China clay, 1,640 cm-1 for casein, and 1,728 or 1,230 cm-1 for acrylic emulsion "Acronal 500D").[48]

The proportions of white pigments (e.g. in mixtures of clay and calcium carbonate) can be found from reflectance spectra.[47] Other inorganic pigments (e.g. barium sulfate can be identified). The compensated reflection techniques aid in identification of components; for example, the spectrum of a coating containing clay and calcium carbonate is determined with a coating containing clay alone in the reference beam.

TRACE ELEMENTAL ANALYSIS

When it is considered necessary to further establish the similarity of paper samples or to try to determine the approximate time of production of the paper, trace elemental analysis is performed. Methods for determining the trace elemental compositions of papers are primarily neutron activation analysis (NAA), energy dispersive analysis, emission spectography, and atomic absorption.

Measurement of the trace elemental composition of papers provides highly individualizing information in that the trace elements are contributed to papers by the processing equipment used and through the impurities in the numerous additives of paper. Studies have verified that there is statistically little chance that any two manufacturers will produce a paper product containing the same trace elements present in the same relative concentrations. As a result, when two or more samples have the same trace elemental compositions and examinations performed in physical characteristics, watermark examinations, fiber analysis, and chemical analysis indicate similarity, it is possible to conclude with a high degree of certainty that the papers have the same origin (see Table 13-IV).

This level of examination can assist in the determination of the approximate period of time a paper sample was produced. This is accomplished by comparing the results of a questioned sample with known samples that have known production dates several years before and after the date of the questioned document. The known samples are obtained from the manufacturer, thus necessitating manufacturer identification prior to this examination of the watermark.

Differences found when comparing papers at any level of examination serve to indicate that the papers being compared are not the same. However, when the results of examinations performed in physical characteristics, watermark examinations, fiber analysis, chemical analysis, and trace elemental analysis fail to reveal any significant differences, it is then possible to conclude that the questioned and known samples came from the same source or from some other source which may possibly give the same results. The possibility of some other source of paper providing the same result, however, can be considered extremely remote.

DATING OF PAPER

A coded watermark enables the exact year of manufacture of paper to be determined (see Tables 13-I, and 13-II and Figures 13-1 and 13-2). No other method can be as definitive; however, there are three procedures that can be helpful under certain conditions to determine the age of paper. One method requires the identification of an additive not previously used by a particular manufacturer. A second method involves the comparison of the trace elemental composition of the questioned paper with production lot standards. A third method involves detection of a change in the design of an uncoded watermark.

A discussion of these approaches to the dating of paper follows.

Detection of New Additives

Technological advances often lead to the development of new and improved additions for paper to improve product performance and to meet the changing demands of the printing industry and other industries that require special types of paper. Anytime a new additive is added to paper, there exists a possibility to determine when that particular product was first produced. For example, a paper manufacturer might change a starch coating to a protein coating. Or, the amount of fluorescent whitener might be increased or decreased on a particular date (see Tables 13-I and 13-III).

Table 13-III

DATING OF PAPER BY FLUORESCENT PROPERTIES

Paper Sample	Fluorescence Measurement	Date of Production
Questioned (Dated Jan 1972)	6.14	?*
Known		
1	7.31	Jul 1974
2	6.85	Feb 1974
3	6.20	Aug 1973
4	6.04	Mar 1973
5	5.75	Dec 1972
6	5.53	Jul 1972
7	4.95	Jan 1972

*Data indicates questioned paper was made between March and August 1973.

Essentially the same methods are used to detect and identify these new additives as previously discussed in the "Identification of Paper Additives" section of this chapter.

Figure 13-1. Example of a Coded Watermark. Note the small circle beneath the *E* in BERK-SHIRE.

Figure 13-2. Example of a Coded Watermark. Note the Line below the *G* in Gilbert.

Comparison of Trace Elemental Composition With Standards

Studies have shown[7] that the trace elemental composition of paper are highly individualistic to a specific manufacturer. This is attributed to the contaminates that are accidentally present from the large variety of raw materials added to paper during the manufacturing process. Trace elements are also accidentally added to paper by the manufacturer's paper processing equipment. Therefore, papers with the same trace elemental composition most likely were produced by the same manufacturer.

Furthermore, these same studies have shown that batch variations of paper are detectable over a period of time as different lots of raw materials are used in the paper. When adequate paper standards can be obtained from the manufacturer (identified by means of a watermark) then a match of the trace elemental composition between the questioned paper and paper from a production lot of a known date is possible. A match of this type can determine an approximate date of production of the questioned paper.

The methods used to measure the trace elemental compositions in paper are primarily the N. A. A.,[7] and x-ray fluorescent spectrometry.[10] No attempt will be made in this text to describe these methods because they are described in detail in the references. (see Table 13-IV).

Table 13-IV

COMPARISON OF PAPER BY TRACE ELEMENTAL COMPOSITION
(Concentration of Elements in PPM)

Elements Found	Known Samples		Questioned Sample*
	Page 1	*Page 2*	*Page 3*
Manganese	350.1	362.0	106.8
Copper	58.2	51.4	25.3
Tantalum	0.8	0.8	not detected
Lanthanum	278.5	280.1	350.5
Gold	0.2	0.2	not detected
Chromium	6.3	5.9	36.4
Antimony	43.4	44.0	26.9
Scandium	7.1	7.4	10.7
Barium	10,105.0	10,059.0	10,120.0
Samarium	122.0	120.2	110.0

*Data indicates page 3 of a 3-page contract consisted of a different batch of paper indicating this page may have been substituted for the original page 3.

Detection of Changes in the Design of Uncoded Watermarks

A change in the design of an uncoded watermark can also be used to determine the first manufacturing date of paper if the change is detectable. Also when a dandy roll is subject to wear during use, standard, known-dated, reference samples of paper containing these watermarks of various production runs may aid in establishing the approximate date the paper was made.

It cannot be assumed however, that uncoded watermarks always provide conclusive evidence for dating. Identity and dating can be misleading because a paper manufacturer may use a watermark of an earlier date or even a copy.

Complete cooperation of the paper and dandy-roll manufacturers is essential for the dating of paper by these watermark procedures. Without their accurate records and reference samples no meaningful conclusions can be given (see Fig. 13-3).

Figure 13-3. Example of a Change in the Design of a Watermark.

INTERPRETATION OF RESULTS OF PAPER COMPARISONS

The systematic approach to the examination of paper evidence described in this chapter consists of several levels of examination. This examination primarily includes (a) the measurement of physical characteristics, (b) watermark examination, (c) microscopic fiber analysis, (d) chemical analysis of additives, and (e) trace elemental analysis. These procedures provide numerous points of comparison that can serve at any point in the examination to prove that paper samples are different. While it is not possible to conclude with absolute certainty that paper samples have the same origin, these examinations described can serve to provide valuable corroborative evidence to determine whether or not paper samples have a common origin. The procedure can also assist to disprove or verify the alleged preparation date of questioned documents.

NOTES

1. O. Johari and I. Corvin, eds., *Scanning Electron Microscopy* (Chicago, Illinois Institute of Technology, 1975).
2. E. Martin, in F. Lundquist, ed., *Forensic Science*, Vol. II (New York, Wiley-Interscience, 1963).
3. C. A. Mitchell, *Documents and their Scientific Examination* (London, Griffen and Co., 1922).
4. J. Grant, "Paper and Crime, Unusual Aspects of Paper Science," *The Paper Maker*, 1968, International Number, pp. 80-95.
5. G. F. Mesnig, *Physical Characteristics of Paper As a Means of Identification.* Read before the Questioned Document Section of the Annual Meeting of the American Academy of Forensic Science, Atlanta, GA, 1972.
6. W. C. Kruger, *Paper Analysis for the Questioned Document Examiner. Behavior Analysis — A New Concept.* Read before the 36th Annual Meeting of the American Society of Questioned Document Examiners and the 8th International Meeting of the International Association of Forensic Sciences, Wichita, Kansas, 1978.
7. R. L. Brunelle, W. D. Washington, C. M. Hoffman, and M. J. Pro, "Use of Neutron Activation Analysis for the Characterization of Paper," *JOAC, 54*(4):920-924, 1971.
8. TAPPI Monogram Series (Atlanta GA, Technical Association of the Pulp and Paper Industry)

    (a) #7, *Pigments for Paper Coating*, 1948
    (b) #13, *Wet Strength in Paper and Paperboard*, 1954
    (c) #19, *Paper Loading Materials,* 1958
    (d) #22, *Synthetic and Protein Adhesives for Paper Coating*, 1961
    (e) #29, *Wet Strength in Paper and Paperboard,* 1964
    (f) #30, *Paper Coating Pigments,* 1966
    (g) #57, *Retention of Fine Solids During Paper Manufacture,* 1975

9. *ASTM Standards,* Part 15 (Philadelphia, PA, American Society for Testing and Materials, 1963).

    (a) Standards for Paper and Related Products
    (b) Paper and Paperboard — Characteristics, Nomenclature, and Significance of Tests (Special Technical Publication 60-B).

10. I. H. Isenberg, *Pulp and Paper Microscopy,* 3rd ed. (Appleton, WI, The Institute of Paper Chemistry, 1967).
11. J. A. Radley and J. Grant, *Fluorescence Analysis in Ultraviolet Light* (London, Chapman and Hall, 1954).
12. R. A. Nyquist, *Infrared Spectra of Polymers and Resins* (Midland, MI, Dow Chemical Co., 1961).
13. American Society for Testing Materials, *Methods for Emission Spectrochemical Analysis,* 3rd ed. (Philadelphia, ASTM, 1960).

14. C. L. Garvey and J. W. Swanson, "X-ray Diffraction of Fillers," *TAPPI, 43*:813, 1960.

15. A. Breuning and H. Weninger, "Use of X-ray Diffraction for Identification of Fillers and Pigments," *Wochbl Papierfabrik, 102*(20):773, 1974.

16. R. A. Parham, *Proceedings on the Workshop on Scanning Electron Microscopy and the Law* (Chicago, ITT Research Institute, 1975), pp. 511-528.

17. D. E. Polk, A. E. Attard, and B. C. Giessen, "Forensic Characterization of Papers. II.: Determination of Batch Differences by Scanning Electron Microscopic Elemental Analysis of the Inorganic Components," *J Forensic Sciences, 22*(3):524-533, 1977.

18. W. W. Simons and M. Zanger, *Guide to NMR Spectra of Polymers* (Philadelphia, Sadtler Research Laboratories, Inc., 1973).

19. R. C. MacKenzie, Ed., *Differential Thermal Analysis,* vol. 1 (New York, Academic Press, 1970).

20. D. B. Blanchard and S. H. Harrison, "Trace Element Profiles and Ratios Determined by Instrumental Neutron Activation Analysis for Fine Paper Identification," *J Forensic Sciences, 23*(22)679-686, 1978.

21. G. J. Lutz, ed., *Forensic Science: A Bibliography of Activation Papers,* Technical Note 519 (Washington, D.C., National Bureau of Standards, 1970).

22. H. L. Schlesinger and D. M. Settle, "A Large-Scale Study of Paper by Neutron Activation Analysis," *J Forensic Sciences, 16*(3):309-330, 1971.

23. *Lockwood's Directory of the Paper and Allied Trades* (New York, Bulkley Dunton & Co.).

24. J. Grant, *Books and Documents, Dating, Permanence, and Preservation* (London, Grafton and Co., 1937).

25. B. L. Browning, ed., *The Chemistry of Wood* (New York, Wiley-Interscience, 1967).

26. *TAPPI Library Catalog* (Appleton, WI, Institute of Paper Chemistry).

27. J. H. Graff, *A Color Atlas for Fiber Identification* (Appleton, WI, The Institute of Paper Chemistry, 1940).

28. B. L. Browning, *Analysis of Paper,* 2nd ed. (New York, Marcel Dekker, Inc., 1977).

29. W. C. McCrone and J. G. Delly, *The Particle Atlas,* 2nd ed., vol. 1 (Ann Arbor, MI, Ann Arbor Science Pub. Inc., 1973).

30. A. J. Panshin, C. DeZeeuw, and H. P. Brown, *Textbook of Wood Technology,* 2nd ed., vol. 1 (New York, McGraw Hill, 1964).

31. B. E. Lofton and M. F. Merritt, *Lofton/Merritt Stain for Unbleached Pulp,* Technical Paper 189 (Washington, D.C., National Bureau of Standards, 1921).

32. H. V. Green and F. H. Yorston, "Staining Reagent for Unbleached Coniferous Sulfite Pulps," *Pulp Paper Mag Can, 53*(6):133, 1952.

33. G. Jayme and M. Harders-Steinhauser, "Staining Procedure for Residual Lignin, *Papier, 20*:684, 1966.

34. B. L. Browning, "Iodine Staining," *TAPPI, 39*(1):161A, 1956.

35. H. J. Donlop, "Detection of Waxes and Oils," *J Soc Chem Ind, 27*:63, 1908.

36. S. J. Buckman and V. Henington, "Ninhydrin Test for Protein," *TAPPI, 34*:302, 1951.

37. H. Hammerschmidt and M. Muller, "TLC Identification of Cations in Fillers," *Papier, 17*:448, 1963.

38. M. Luciani, "Separation of Cations in Fillers by Paper Chromatography," *Indicatore Grafico* (Suppl), *5*:1, 1961.

39. W. R. Willets, "Detection of Titanium in Paper," *TAPPI, 54*:1543, 1971.

40. American Society for Testing and Materials, *Index to the Powder Diffraction File* (Inorganic), PDIS — 17i (Philadelphia, ASTM, 1967).

41. R. A. Parham and J. K. Hultman, "Morphology and Composition of Fillers by X-ray Diffraction/SEM," *TAPPI, 59*:152, 1976.

42. J. Hill and K. H. Riergerl, "Ash Content and Composition by X-ray Absorption and

Fluorescence," *Svensk Papper Stid, 75*:535, 1972.

43. J. Kuusi and A. Leh Tinen, "Identification of Fillers by Neutron Activation Analysis," *Pulp Paper Mag Can, 71*(3):37 (T65), 1970.

44. W. R. Willets, "Test for Carbonate Coatings," *TAPPI, 55*:430, 603, 1972.

45. W. H. Boast and S. W. Trosset, Jr., "Identification Scheme for Coating Adhesives," *TAPPI, 45*:873, 1962 and Adhasion, *18*(9):276 and *18*(11):330, 1974.

46. H. Toepsch, "Detection and Identification of Adhesives," *Wochbl Papierfabr, 98*(17):788, 1970.

47. J. P. Deley, R. J. Gigi, and A. J. Liotti, "Identification of Coating Components by FTIR," *TAPPI, 46*(2):873, 1962.

48. G. Jayme and E. M. Rohmann, "Use of FTIR for Identification of Coatings," *Papier, 19*:497, 1965 and *20*(1):169, 1966 and *Wochbl Papierfabrik, 94*:855, 1966.

49. Chicago Society for Paint Technology, Federation of Societies for Paint Technology, *Infrared Spectroscopy, Its Use in the Coatings Industry* (Philadelphia, PA, 1969).

CHAPTER 14

COURT ACCEPTABILITY
Applications of Forensic Paper and Ink Analysis

HISTORICAL PRECEDENTS

THE scholarly efforts by Thomas Astle who, in 1803, penned "The Origin and Progress of Writing," has an application in this section. Astle pleaded with the ink manufacturers of his era to improve the standards of their respective art and science.

> The constant occasion we have for Ink evinces its convenience and utility. From the important benefits arising to society from its use, and the injuries individuals may suffer from the frauds of designing men in the abuse of this necessary article, it is to be wished that the legislature would frame some regulation to promote its improvement, and prevent knavery and avarice from making it instrumental to the accomplishment of any base purpose.[1]

As the forensic scientist is aware, it is useless to make comparisons with knowns and unknowns if one is uncertain of the standards of the knowns. If the ink industry did not insist on certain specifications, certain guidelines, for their respective products, it would prove futile to attempt any type of structural comparisons. Consistency among each respective manufacturer is a necessity. Effective notice when changes are made or about to be made is information of the utmost importance if any forensic examination is to be performed.

For decades, document examiners have searched for ways to detect fradulent documents other than by traditional methods such as handwriting analysis, typewriting identification, obliterated and indented writing, deciphering and determination of the sequence of writings. New methods for the detection of fraudulent documents developed slowly for several reasons: (a) analysis of ink and paper causes slight destruction to the document; (b) document examiners considered the preservation of the original condition of the document very important; and (c) document examiners with few exceptions were trained in the areas of handwriting and typewriting analysis but lacked the scientific training to explore chemical and physical methods for use in detecting fraudulent documents.[2]

Before we review a few of the recent cases that helped to solidify modern ink analysis, let us look briefly at a few cases from yesteryear — cases that broke the ground, so-to-speak, within our legal system.

Chemicolegal ink evidence has been employed in the trials of civil causes for many years; but it was not until the year 1889 that a precedent was established for the chemical examination of a suspected document preceding any trial.[3] The question under indagation is a common one now; a matter regarding an alleged will that was executed in triplicate. The purpose of determining the chemical composition of ink on these wills raised a few eyebrows in that New York courthouse. The Honorable Rastus S. Ransome, surrogate of the county of New York at the time, permitted David N. Carvalho to both photograph and administer chemical tests to the document in question.

> and it is further ordered and directed that such chemical test be applied to the ink
> or writing fluid on said alleged Will to the following specified portion, or any part of
> such portions, viz.[4]

The will of Thomas J. Monroe was not admitted to probate because of the efforts of Mr. Carvalho. Carvalho's experiments demonstrated beyond question that, exclusive of the date and names of the witnesses, Mr. Monroe's signature had been transferred from a gelatine pad (hektograph), a method of duplicating popularly in vogue at that time.[5]

Another case of interest involved the contested will of George P. Gordon of New Jersey. The decedent, who passed away in 1878, was the inventor of a then famous printing press and left a large fortune behind him. The Gordon will was not probated due to an oversight by the witnesses; they had failed to sign it in each other's presence. The draft of the will, which was on white paper, was also written in the main in black ink, but a copious quantity of red ink had been used in interlineations. Testimony for many weeks followed and finally the court declared the will a forgery. The court came to this conclusion as the result of a "scientific investigation" of the red ink on the will.

> With a view to testing the truth of this testimony the contestants submitted the
> draft to scientific experts, who pronounced the red ink to be a product of eosine, a
> substance invented by a German chemist named Caro in the year 1874, and after
> that time imported to this country.[6]

You are, no doubt, wondering "where's the rub?" Although Gordon had passed away in 1878, he had written his will ten years prior — something unknown to the perpetrators of this fraud. The real will of Mr. Gordon was handed over to the court, and the legitimate Gordon heirs counted their blessings.

Another instance where the identification of an ink was a crucial factor can be found in the famous *Throckmorton v. Holt* case (180 U. S. 552, 21 S.Ct. 474,

45 L.Ed. 663). This case also involved a disputed will — that of Joseph Holt, Judge Advocate General in Lincoln's administration. The attesting witnesses involved such public figures as Ulysses S. Grant, William T. Sherman, and his wife Ellen B. E. Sherman. The signatures of the above notables were verified by the respective members of the immediate families. This will "appeared" one year after the death of Joseph Holt. As J. Newton Baker observed:

> No other paper was in the envelope containing the will was received by the Register of Wills. The curious feature of this will was that the edges of the paper was burned as if retrieved from fire before any part of the writing had been damaged or destroyed. The address on the envelope had large irregularly printed letters indicating that it was sent by an illiterate person. An attempt was made to identify the printed address by comparison with other printing similar in character to the address on the envelope, but the comparison was ruled out by the United States Supreme Court although it would be admissible in modern practice.[7]

Three renowned experts were called in by the concerned parties; they testified both for and against the authenticity of this disputed document. An expert for the opposition declared the will to be a forgery, and he based his opinion on the fact that the ink used on the will was not in existence in the year 1873. Although a large amount of emphasis was placed upon the manufacture and composition of the ink in question, the court, at that time, felt that there were no facts to support the expert's conclusion. The jury, history informs us, found the will to be a forgery.

At the close of the nineteenth century, the famous Pinkertons', detectives of merit, had brought still another culprit into justice. Charles Becker, the then "king of forgers" and publicly acclaimed head of his "profession," had been captured by those skillful detectives. Arrested and taken to San Francisco, Becker had been brought to trial, and his alleged crime was that of a successful "raising" of a check by chemical means from $12.00 to $22,000.00. Becker, operating under the alais of A. H. Dean, took office space in the then Chronical building in San Francisco. Dean, under the ruse of a merchant broker, then payed a month's rent in advance. A day, or so, later he went to the Bank of Nevada and opened an account with $2,500.00 cash, saying that his account would run from $2,000.00 to $30,000.00, and he would want no accommodation. As the journal the *American Banker* noted:

> He (Becker) manipulated the account so as to invite confidence . . . (a week or so later) he deposited a check or draft of the Bank of Woodland, California, upon its correspondent, the Crocker-Woolworth Bank of San Francisco. The amount was paid to the credit of Dean, the check was sent through the clearing-house, and was paid by the Crocker-Woolworth Bank. The next day, the check having cleared, Dean called and drew out $20,000.00, taking cash in four bags of gold, the teller not having paper money convenient. At the end of the month, when the Crocker-Woolworth Bank made returns to the Woodland Bank, it included the draft for $22,000.00. Here the fraud was discovered . . . the Bank of Woodland had drawn no such draft, and the only one it had drawn which was not accounted for was one for twelve dollars, issued in favor of A. H. Holmes, who had called to ask how he could send twelve dollars to a distant

friend, and whether it was better to send a money order or an express order. When he was told he could send it by bank draft, he seemed to have learned something new; supposed that he could not get a bank draft, and he took it, paying the fee. Here came back that innocent twelve-dollar draft, raised to $22,000.00, and on its way had cost somebody $20,000.00 in gold.

The almost absolute perfection with which the draft had been forged had nearly defied the detection of even the microscope. In the body of the original $12.00 draft had been the words, "Twelve . . . Dollars." The forger, by the use of some chemical preparation, had erased the final letters "lve" from the word "twelve," and had substituted the letters "nty-two," so that in place of the "twelve," as it appeared in the genuine draft, there was the word "twenty-two" in the forged paper.

In the space between the word "twenty-two" and the word "dollars" the forger inserted the word "thousand," so that in place of the draft reading "twelve dollars," as at first, it read "twenty-two thousand dollars," as changed. In the original $12 draft, the figure "1" and "2" and the character "$" had been punched so that the combination read "$12." The forger had filled in these perforations with paper in such a way that the paper filled in looked exactly like the field of the paper. After having filled in the perforations, he had perforated the paper with the combination, "22,000.00."

The dates, too, had been erased by the chemical process, and in their stead were dates which would make it appear that the paper had been presented for payment within a reasonable length of time after it had been issued. The dates in the original draft, if left on the forged draft, would have shown that the holder had departed from custom in carrying such a valuable paper more than a few days.

That was the extent of the forgeries which had been made in the paper, the manner in which they had been made betrayed the hand of an expert forger . . . . It was the work of an artist, with pen, ink, chemicals, camel's hair brush, water colors, paper pulp and a perforating machine.[8]

Not content with their earnings in San Francisco, the Becker gang attempted the same actions in Minneapolis and St. Paul, Minnesota. Unfortunately for Becker, the Pinkertons captured two of his gang and they informed on him. Becker was arrested and brought to trial in San Francisco. When asked how Becker made it to the top of his "profession," Becker replied,

A world of patience, a heap of time, and good inks.[9]

Becker was a genius in the judgement of bank checks. He knew the value of ink and the correct chemical to affect them. His paper mill was his mouth, in which to manufacture specially prepared pulp to fill in punch holes, which when ironed over, made it most difficult to detect even with a magnifying glass.[10]

As the reader can see, forensic ink and paper analysis is over one hundred years old. These cases broke some of the ground for such analysis, and they are important for just those reasons.

THE ATF INK DATING PROGRAM

Based upon a survey of classical techniques for dating documents — techniques used by document examiners — it occurred to Brunelle that it might be possible to date documents by detecting changes in the formulation of inks — work had been done on this idea prior to 1968 by the Swiss. The Zurich Cantonal Police Department Laboratory had done a limited amount of work in the analysis of inks by Thin-Layer Chromatography. Researchers such as George Nakamura and Satoru Shimoda had experimented with the use of TLC, as well as had Joseph Tholl and others, to differentiate inks on documents. Very little work prior to 1968 had been done on the analysis of inks for the purposes of dating documents. Brunelle believed that TLC might provide an excellent approach to detecting the back-dating of questioned documents. He decided to conduct a survey of the ink industry. After contacting several ink manufacturers he found that, as of 1968 there existed some twenty-four manufacturers of ink in the United States. Of that number, only twelve manufactured ball-point ink. As the result of this survey he concluded the following:

- The ink industry is basically a very competitive industry. As the result of this intense competition, there existed very little chance of one company duplicating anothers' formulations regarding ball-point inks.
- The ink manufacturers said that they changed their formulas quite frequently and that they maintained very high quality control standards — in other words, every formula with the same number would be made in essentially the same manner everytime a batch was made.
- These ink manufacturers kept very accurate records on the changes of their formulations, the ingredients that they used and the dates in which these changes were made.
- That the ink industry, in general, is very cooperative — they mentioned the availability of several standard laboratory techniques that are currently in use by that industry for the analysis of inks for quality control purposes.

Based upon the feedback from the ink industry, Brunelle speculated that, if he could detect changes (minor changes within ink formulations as they pertained to a respective manufacturer), he could distinguish different inks made by different manufacturers.

Brunelle decided that if he were to compile these differences and place them in "library" form, he would have a ready reference in response to the question of dating documents. The compiling of a standard ink library would result in the addition of another method to be directed at the questioning of a back-dated document. This would correspond directly with an axiom known to all forensic scientists — that of matching standards with standards, with knowns to knowns and the resulting comparisons of these standard knowns with that of the unknowns. One would now be able to match questioned ink on documents with standards in a standard ink library and determine the first availability of the formula that had been identified.

On the basis of this theory, Brunelle decided to request ink samples from several ink manufacturers in the United States to run some tests in his laboratory. The tests he performed confirmed what the manufacturers had already told him, and what he had imagined he would find. It was possible to distinguish inks made by different manufacturers; one could distinguish among formulas manufactured by the same company as long as they were different formulations.

Brunelle found that, using relatively simple techniques (TLC and Infrared luminescence), he could, in a short period of time, distinguish inks of different formulations. As the results of these tests upon the standard inks that had been sent to IRS by the ink manufacturers (since he was able to confirm, with those tests, what the ink manufacturers had informed him), he decided to initiate the beginnings of a standard ink library.

The first step was to formally write a letter of request to each and every ink manufacturer in the United States. Brunelle requested their cooperation and assistance in sending to the IRS laboratory standards of all the inks they had manufactured to extend as far back as their stocks permitted. In addition, he requested that they keep the laboratory "updated" on new formulations as they were developed. Without exception, all of the manufacturers that were identified and contacted cooperated by sending the laboratory samples; a few companies sent samples dating back to the 1930s. Within a years' time the laboratory had accumulated approximately 1500 to 2000 standard ink samples. This "library of standards" was considered complete starting with the year 1968. It was essentially complete dating back to a period as early as 1960, but some gaps were to be expected from that time period. By 1969, the lab began to receive, from the ink manufacturers, new formulation samples as they were developed.

Between 1970 and 1975, the forensic laboratory had actually worked several hundred cases; the technique utilized for the back-dating of documents began to receive wide-spread recognition. As the result of this recognition, the technique of detection for the back-dating of inks in IRS fraud cases began to receive approval within our legal system. With several successful court cases under their belts from the period of 1970 to 1975, the laboratory began to receive requests for assistance from many agencies in the federal government.

In 1971, Brunelle was awarded the highly coveted John A. Dondero Memorial award, presented by the International Association for Identification, for his contribution toward the development of a new technique for the identification and dating of inks on questioned documents.

In 1975, the laboratory began to look at ways of improving the existing technique for dating documents by ink analysis. It was recognized, for example, that they were only dating documents by determining the first availability of a particular ink formula. In other words, if an ink was found that wasn't in existence at the time the document was dated, they felt they had been helpful in aiding the investigators. Since not all inks changed their formulations frequently, quite often an ink was found that was in existence at the time the document was dated even though it may have been written after the date had appeared on the document: some formulas and formulations do not change as frequently as others. When this situation arose, they were not always successful in being able to establish back-dating evidence.

After considerable research on how the laboratory might improve its dating capability, it was decided to launch a tagging program. This tagging program was accomplished in 1975 after a years' research conducted by Doctor Antonio Arnoldo Cantu and Richard L. Brunelle. It had been decided that, if they could get the ink manufacturers to add chemical "tags" or taggants to the ink during the manufacturing process and have them change this tag annually, they would be able to determine the exact year that the ink was manufactured.

When the laboratory initiated this tagging program, they hoped it would be the solution to all of their problems as they related to backdating, at least in a higher percentage of their cases, but problems began to arise. As the program developed, the laboratory encountered the presence of some stumbling blocks; the cost of their taggants, which was to be paid for by the ink manufacturers, proved to be one of the detriments to this program. This possibility of the taggant affecting the quality of the ink and the performance of the inks caused the tagging program to fall a little short of the goals they had set. At the time of this writing only about 40 percent of the inks manufactured in the United States are being tagged. Many of the manufacturers were very cooperative with us in tagging their inks, while others, for a number of reasons, elected not to participate in the tagging program.

This tagging program had been a major undertaking; a tremendous amount of research had gone into developing a technique that would keep the costs of the taggants to the manufacturers at a minimum. Tags had to be developed, in the laboratory, that could be detected in very small quantities in the ink. Tags had to be found that would be compatable with the various kinds of inks used for writing purpose such as ball-point, fibertip, and fountain pen inks.

By 1982, the ink library had acquired over 4,000 standards of inks. The tagging program, although not totally successful, did increase the number of cases in which ATF was able to establish back-dating. In addition, by 1982 the laboratory had worked a few thousand cases since the inception of this program in 1968.

Another new development was made in the ability to date inks on documents in 1980, which was the dating of inks by determining the "relative age," of the ink in question, on suspected documents. This landmark break-through, in the field of document examination, was achieved through the efforts of Doctor Antonio A. Cantu. His discovery has enabled, for the first time, the dating of an ink without requiring comparison standards. The basis of the theory is outlined in Chapter 9.

DISCUSSION OF CASES

The ATF systematic approach to ink identification and ink dating has been successfully applied to cases numbering in the thousands to date. With the exception of a single case, ink testimony has been accepted across the board throughout the land.

The courts have held that scientific methods of analysis are acceptable in the courts if the techniques used have general acceptance in the scientific community (*Frye v. U. S.*). The ink identification technique satisfies these criteria because all of the methods utilized to analyze inks are well established and proven analytical tools and these points have been conceded by experts for the defense in several cases.

Usually the ink testimony is offered as corroborative evidence, yet occasionally it has been used as primary evidence. Such was the case in *Stoller v. U. S.*, tried in Miami, Florida, in 1969.

Stoller v. U. S.[11]

In this case, testimony based on the ink dating technique was presented for the first time. Several inks were identified in travel and expense diaries for the years 1965, 1966, and 1967. Our analysis revealed that a large number of the inks used in the diaries were not available commercially until after the years in question, indicating the entries had been backdated. The testimony was used as a rebuttal to impeach the testimony of the defendant and placed considerable doubt on the authenticity of the diaries. Thousands of dollars of taxable income were involved and the defendant became liable for the tax assessed by the Internal Revenue Service.

U. S. v. Wolfson[12]

In *U. S. v. Wolfson*, tried in the Southern District of New York, the defendant charged the government with using a spurious document to prosecute him for violation of SEC regulations involving the Capital Transit Sytem. The defendant claimed that one of a seven-page document had been altered and was not the original instrument.

Analysis revealed that ink prepared from the same formulation was used on each of the seven pages. This test, together with the findings from paper analysis and watermark examination conducted on the documents, helped to substantiate the authenticity of the questioned document. The ink testimony was accepted by the court as valid and persuasive and the examinations conducted by the Bureau of ATF Identificaiton Branch were held in the balance of the court even though a large sum was spent on defense expert work and testimony.

U. S. v. Meyers[13]

In another case, an official of a large New York bank was accused of illegally awarding loans to small business concerns. In this case, tried in the Southern District of New York, ink and handwriting analysis assisted in showing that many of the loan application forms were prepared by the bank official rather than the loan applicant. The scientific testimony presented for the government was accepted by the court and was not challenged by the defense.

U. S. v. Sloan[14]

In Memphis, Tennessee, the defendant was charged with perjury resulting from testimony given at the defendant's federal income tax evasion trial. A conviction was obtained; during the trial, certain documents were offered as evidence. It was because of these instruments that perjury charges were made.

The defendant claimed he was investing money for an anonymous rich client through land purchases that were supposed to have been made from 1958 through 1966. The government claimed the defendant was investing his own money and was using the rich client scheme to avoid paying the tax.

In an attempt to prove his case, Sloan introduced a four-page agreement dated 1958, stating that the defendant was to invest sums of money for an anonymous client covering an indefinite period of time. Also introduced were a series of notes dating from 1958 to 1966, which presumably was the proof of these investments.

Ink analysis of the writing on each page of the agreement and the notes, showed that the same ink formulation was used on the documents. In addition, the findings revealed that the documents could not have been in existence in 1958, due to the fact that a unique dye identified in the ink was first synthesized by Ciba Chemical Corp., in 1959 and the ink formulation was not produced until 1960.

The testimony involving the ink analysis was primary evidence, and its use was sufficient to obtain a conviction of perjury even though three experts were employed by the defense to counter the ATF ink testimony.

U. S. v. Colasurdo[15]

The defendants in this case, tried in the Southern District of New York, were allegedly connected with organized crime operations and were charged with the formation and dissolution of companies to achieve personal financial gain at the expense of unknowing stockholders.

After almost two months of trial, testimony based upon ink identification and ink dating was introduced by a Bureau of ATF chemist. The findings, which were accepted by the court over objection of defense counsel, revealed that a document dated 1965 offered as evidence by the defense was backdated. The ball-point ink used to prepare the signature on this instrument was not produced until 1968.

The defense appealed the guilty verdict partly on the basis of the ink testimony, in the form of expert testimony by Richard L. Brunelle. Appellants argued forcefully that the weight of the evidence was that the Government's ink expert was wrong, and that the present (1971) state of the art ink analysis did not justify admission of this testimony. In support of this argument, appellants pointed out that the Government's expert was the only individual in the world who claimed to be able to identify inks and that testimony by Brunelle had been rejected in the Eastern District of Pennsylvania.[16] Nonetheless Brunelle's testimony was adduced without objection.

Appellants elected to battle it out regarding Brunelle's report on the then alleged backdating of the document in question. Regardless of the experts appellants paraded before the jury, that the same jury gave the affirmative nod to Brunelle's expert testimony.

The defense appealed the guilty verdict partly on the basis of the ink testimony, but the U. S. Court of Appeals for the Second Circuit affirmed the conviction. Later the United States Supreme Court denied certiorari.

U. S. v. Bruno[17]

Prior to the appeal of the *Colasurdo* decision, ink testimony was offered in *U. S. v. Bruno*, tried in Philadelphia, Pennsylvania. The request for laboratory assistance was initiated by the Criminal Tax Division of the Justice Department. The charge involved the evasion of income tax from the sale of certain vending machines and the premises on which the equipment was located.

Analysis revealed that ink used to prepare a signature on a document dated 1965 was not available commercially until 1967. A combination of ingredients that was unique to one ink manufacturer in all of the United States and in Europe was identified.

In this case, the presiding judge, after about two weeks of trial, ruled that the evidence was not conclusive because the ATF Laboraory did not have access to *all* foreign inks. In addition, the ink testimony was the primary evidence; and, in the judge's opinion, the state of the art of ink identification had not reached a reasonable degree of scientific certainty. This ruling was made despite five prior rulings by different courts in different jurisdictions upholding the ink identification techniques as valid and persuasive.

The U. S. Court of Appeals for the 2nd Circuit affirmed the conviction of Colasurdo after considering an appeal based on reasoning that the ink identification technique was not yet proven. In their opinion, the Court considered the ruling made by the Judge in the *Bruno* case, but were not particularily influenced by his failure to accept the ink identification technique.

U. S. v. Miller

The adverse Bruno decision encouraged the defense in this case, to file a motion to establish that the Government's witness was unqualified. In addition, the defense filed to exclude any testimony from Richard L. Brunelle in particular.

Basing their contention entirely upon *U. S. v. Bruno* (E. D. Pa. 1971), 333 F. Supp. 570, the defendants contended (a) that ink identification testimony had not achieved a degree of acceptance and was therefore inadmissible; (b) that the identification test employed by Brunelle was inadmissible; and that (c) Brunelle was unqualified as the result of their first two contentions.

The court in this case felt somewhat differently than that in the Bruno decision:

> Contrary to the holding in Bruno, it appears from the government's memorandum that Brunelle has been accepted and has testified as an ink expert in eight federal court trials, among which are *Stoller v. U. S.* (S. D. Fla.); *U. S. v. Gordon Thompson* (M. D. Fla); *U. S. v. Sloan* (W. D. Tenn.); *U. S. v. Colasurdo* (S. D. N. Y.); *U. S. v. Wolfson* (S. D. N. Y.); *U. S. v. Meyers* (S. D. N. Y.); and *Petition of William Wilson* (U. S. Tax Ct., N. Y. C.).[19]

The court in *U. S. v. Miller* went on to express:

> The trial court has the primary function to determine whether or not a witness is an expert or has sufficient knowledge to qualify as an expert. The determination of the competency and qualification of a witness offered as an expert is addressed to the judicial discretion of the trial judge before whom the testimony is offered. It is inconceivable to this Court that the trial judge in Bruno could have devoted three weeks merely upon the competency and qualifications of an expert witness with respect to the defendant's motion for a preliminary hearing or trial regarding Brunelle's qualifications. . . . to qualify as a witness, the expert is not required to prove that he has achieved a record of perfection or to testify with absolute certainty. See *U. S. v. Longfellow*, 406 F.2d 415 (C.A.4., 1969) *cert. den.* 394 U. S. 998. . . . Indeed, it is universally recognized that expert opinion testimony may be given in terms of an opinion that something might, could or would produce a certain result on the theory that an expert witness often is helpful in the determination involving matters of science or technical or skilled knowledge.[20]

The court in *U. S. v. Miller* concluded:

> Testimony such as Brunelle's regarding ink identification based upon the chromatogram technique has not been rejected by any appellate court in any case to me or which my reseach has found.[21].

With the Bruno decision kept in the perspective in which it fully deserves, ink identification and ink dating techniques, to date, are deemed generally acceptable for purposes of the court.

People v. Corona[22]

At the time of his trial, Juan V. Corona stood accused of perpetrating what was considered to be the largest mass murder in the history of the United States. The Mexican-born Corona operated in the capacity of a farm labor contractor for a pair of California ranches, namely the Kagehiro and Sullivan concerns. It was on the Sullivan ranch that the bodies of twenty-five immigrant workers had been eventually unearthed. The Sonoma County Prosecutor's office, faced with the task of prosecuting this case, searched all over the United States for forensic specialists to examine a large variety of evidence they felt may have linked the suspect to the twenty-five murders.

The Bureau of Alcohol, Tobacco and Firearms forensic laboratory played a major role in the examination of much of this evidence; a total of four experts from the BATF were involved in carrying out the various examinations deemed necessary by the state, all of whom eventually testified at Corona's trial. Several months passed before all of their examinations had been completed.

One expert identified all of the writings in a ledger book belonging to Juan Corona. This ledger book listed the names of the victims; in the opinion of this expert the handwriting belonged to the suspect.[23]

On other evidence, it was determined that the same type of bullets that were used to kill some of the victims were contained in the suspect's pistol.[24]

Actively growing head hair was found adhering to the end of a post-hole digger owned by Juan Corona. This hair matched the hair of one of the victims, indicating that the post-hole digger may have been used as a weapon to kill one of the victims.[25]

A plaster cast of tire tracks found near one of the victim's grave site was matched with the tires on a van; a van belonging to Juan Corona.[26]

This list of evidence went on and on, evidence that, admittedly, was circumstantial. Nonetheless the staff of the Sonoma County Prosecutor's office, headed by G. Dave Teza and Ronald W. Fahey, was able to construct the proverbial web of circumstantial evidence that was eventually to surround Corona and bring him to justice.

One item of particular interest to the prosecutor was a ball-point pen. This ball-point pen is one of Italian design, named the Universal V-6 ballpoint pen. The Government's expert in this case once again, was Richard Brunelle. Ink analysis revealed that this unique multicartridge ball-point pen owned by the suspect to be the same pen used to prepare much of the writing in, what was called by the district attorney, the "deathlist ledger."

In 1978 the California Court of Appeals, Third District, overturned Juan Coronas' conviction (see *People v. Corona* 1978 80CalApp3d 684, 23 CrL 212). This case was not reversed on the basis of the evidence submitted. It was appealed on the basis of Corona's attorney failing to provide an adequate defense, including possible mental illness (on the part of Corona). In 1982, this case was tried again, and, as before, the jury found Juan Corona guilty.

U. S. v. Jorgensen[29]

V. H. Jorgensen was convicted by a jury of knowingly and willfully making a false statement to the Internal Revenue Service in violation of 18 U.S.C. § 1001, and of aiding and abetting in the making of such a statement in violation of 18 U.S.C. § 2.

During 1970 and 1971 the IRS conducted an audit of Jorgensen's 1959 and 1960 income tax returns and as a result of such audit determined that Jorgensen owed additional taxes for those years. Accordingly, on June 25, 1971, the IRS issued Jorgensen a statutory Notice of Deficiency. In response to such Notice of Deficiency, Jorgensen filed a petition with the U. S. Tax Court, to which the IRS filed a response. Issue was thus joined in the Tax Court between Jorgensen and the IRS as to whether Jorgensen owed additional income tax for 1959 and 1960.

Jorgensen's position was that he owed no back tax for 1959 and 1960; alternatively and in any event, he was entitled to "additional" business deductions which he had failed to claim in his 1959 and 1960 returns. In this latter regard, Jorgensen's accountant presented fourteen invoices totaling some $85,000 to the IRS, such invoices representing alleged purchases by Jorgensen of gasoline in 1959 and 1960 from a local oil company. During the years in question Jorgensen was in the wholesale gasoline business, buying gasoline and then selling it at wholesale or at retail through several filling stations owned by him. In presenting these invoices, Jorgensen's accountant informed the IRS that Jorgensen had just found the invoices and that such represented additional business deductions for the years in question. The IRS took copies of these fourteen invoices, indicating that they would attempt to verify the transactions represented by the invoices.

Seven of these invoices bore dates August, 1959, and the remaining seven were dated in January, 1960. Jorgensen identified his signature each of the fourteen invoices and stated that each invoice was prepared on or about the date shown on the face of the invoice.

During the course of the trial, the Government offered expert testimony from Richard Brunelle, who testified that the fourteen invoices were all prepared by the same blue ball-point pen and that the ink contained fluorescent ingredients that were not in use until about 1969 or, at the latest, 1970.

Jorgensen at trial admitted that the fourteen invoices were prepared in about 1971, and not in 1959 and 1960, but he testified that each represented an actual transaction occurring in those same years, and that the invoices had been back-dated to what was believed to be the approximate date of his purchase of gasoline.

On appeal Jorgensen raised three issues: (a) the Government failed to show that Jorgensen made material misrepresentations to the IRS; (b) Jorgensen had no specific intent to defraud, and that the only evidence was that Jorgensen was merely trying to reconstruct actual records; and (c) the trial court erred in admitting expert testimony from the so-called ink expert.

The defense felt that the decision of the lower court should be reversed because of the so-called expert testimony offered by Richard Brunelle on behalf of the Government. However, the appellate court stated:

> In this regard the Government called a witness who was qualified as an expert in the analysis of inks and the age thereof. He testified that the same pen was used to prepare each of the 14 invoices, and that the same pen was used by Jorgensen in affixing his signature as was used to fill out the balance of the invoice. The expert also ascertained the source of ink used on the invoices by comparing the ink on the invoices with an ink specimen in his ink library. . . . We find no error in the admission of this line of testimony concerning the ink used in preparing the 14 invoices. The competency of a witness to give an opinion concerning a matter of expertise lies largely within the trial court's discretion. *U. S. v. Brumley*, 466 F.2d 911 (10th Cir. 1970), *cert. denied*, 412 U. S. 929 (1973), and *U. S. v. Kienley*, 415 F.2d 557 (10th Cir. 1969). In the instant case we find no abuse of that discretion.[30]

U. S. v. Durr [31]

This case was handled by the forensic chemists at ATF at the request of the United States Air Force Office of Special Investigation.

A United States Army Air Force Base Exchange, located near Madrid, Spain, had been the site of an armed robbery. It was the practice of the head clerk of this exchange to keep tract of the number of bills in his register at the close of each days' business; the bills were stacked according to denomination. The clerk then listed, on a ledger sheet, the number of bills on hand and the denominations of those amounts of currency. For example, the clerk would go through the cash register and count the number of twenty dollar bills they would have on hand, and then record the number. He then placed a paper clip or rubber band around the stack of bills and made a notation as to the number of the bills in that particular stack by writing that number on the top bill in the stack and circling that number.

The day of the armed robbery there were 16 ten dollar bills in the clerk's stack. During the course of the next few days the Air Force investigators searched a suspect's residence. They discovered, underneath his bed, a ten dollar bill; along with that ten dollar bill they found a number of other bills, but that specific ten dollar bill had the number 16 written on it.

Albert Lyter was asked to analyze the ink on the ten dollar bill, the ink that the clerk used, and the ink on the ledger sheet. All three ink samples matched with the highest degree of scientific certainty. Meanwhile the Air Force investigation team had ascertained that the clerk in question had used but three different types of pens in that ledger since being employed by the Department of Defense. To add some additional icing to the cake it was discovered that the clerk, since his employment, could recall only three other nights when there were only 16 ten dollar bills; the other two nights he had used different ink pens.

This case ended in a court-martial for Mr. Durr.

The Howard Hughes Will [32]

This next case involved the disposition of the vast wealth accumulated by the late Howard Hughes. It was a case that involved three testimonies; a deposition in Los Angeles, another one in Houston, Texas, and the third in Las Vegas.

A request for the examination of certain evidentiary items was submitted from the desk of the attorney general of the state of Nevada. An individual by the name of Melvin Dumar was being investigated on the charges of fraud and forgery. The attorney general's office wanted the forensic chemists at the BATF to examine this will and determine whether or not the will had been backdated.

Albert Lyter, then on the staff of forensic chemists at the BATF, was handed the case. Lyter's examinations did not show anything conclusively. What he was able to indicate was the type of ink that was used on the will, namely a Papermate formula numbered 307. In addition to that, Mr. Lyter was able to identify which of the particular types of dyes were used in that formula; scanning the Ink Library he was able to eliminate all the other inks in that Library on that basis.

Papermate formula 307 contained a particular dye that was available during the years 1966 through 1972; the will had been dated in 1968. This meant that this particular formula was available when the will was purportedly made.[33]

In addition to the will, the ATF chemists analyzed an envelope that contained some writing. This other writing on the envelope matched that on the will, that is they were of the same ink formulation.

As this case was progressing, the ATF chemists received the so-called outer envelope that had contained the before-mentioned inner envelope, which, in turn, had contained the purported will. This outer envelope had been examined by the Federal Bureau of Investigation for fingerprints. The latent print examiners at the FBI found several latents belonging to one Melvin Dumar. While being examined for fingerprints, the envelope went through a bleaching process and therefore the ink on this outer portion of the envelope could not be examined fully. The FBI had been following what is considered to be a normal procedure when examining the envelope for latents, after all, it was months after their examinations that the request came down for this particular ink examination.

Lyter was able to determine that the ink on the outer envelope fell within the same class of inks as that on the inside of the envelope and on the will itself. By class of inks it is meant that there were between eight and ten standards that had the same basic characteristics, one of them being the Papermate. Unfortunately, as the result of the bleaching of the outer envelope, he was unable to say that it was of the same formation as that used on the will.[34]

At the time of this civil trial in Las Vegas, Lyter testified to everything he had written in his deposition. The side that was purporting that this will was authentic used his testimony to argue that the ink was available at the time the will had been drawn up. In addition to that, they introduced testimony in an attempt to show that Howard Hughes had used some Papermate pens during that specific time sequence. Dumar's attorneys posed what appeared to be a hypothetical question — "What were the chances of an individual going out and buying a ballpoint pen that had been discontinued in 1972, using that pen to prepare a document essentially fraudulent in nature in 1977 and having the good fortune of using the "right" ink on the will?" In other words using an ink that Howard Hughes coincidently used in this purported will.[35]

The side of the people who were trying to discredit Dumar and prove that this will was indeed a fraud were first attempting to discredit Lyter as an expert witness because

- Lyters' testimony proved helpful to their opposition by showing that the will *may* have been authentic.
- They didn't want to discredit him too much due to the fact that they wanted Lyter to show that the ink on the outside envelope could have been the same as that on the will.[36]

Essentially both sides were attempting to elicit information that would help their case, with Lyter caught in the middle.

The questioned document personnel involved in this case had determined that the writing of the will was not in the hand of the late Howard Hughes.

What about the deposition from Houston? Howard Hughes was born in the sovereign state of Texas and had legally resided there for a number of years. As the result of his residing in Texas, Texas felt entitled to a portion of the inheritance tax, as opposed to the state of Nevada where the trial actually took place.[31]

The Los Angeles deposition? Hughes had lived and worked in California for a number of years prior to his "retirement" in Nevada. California felt, as did Texas, that they had a legitimate claim to that inheritance tax as well.[38]

These issues are still under litigation.

People v. Pryor [39]

It took the good people of Okaloosa County, Florida, a mere five hours to deliberate the innocence or guilt of a local real-estate developer in a case involving the attainment of land through the use/misuse of fraudulent documents.

This recent case (1981), involving the use of ink analysis to detect fraudulent documents, found a Fort Walton Beach developer guilty of thirty-two counts of forgery, utterance of forged documents, and grand theft.

This case involved, as deemed by the prosecutor in his closing argument to the jury, "the biggest land fraud scheme in the history of the state — maybe even the country . . . with the defendant claiming some thousands of acres of land, some of which belonged to the Federal Government."[40]

Larry F. Stewart, a forensic chemist with the BATF laboratory, testified that his studies indicated that various alterations were made with ball-point pen inks that became commercially available in 1949, 1958, 1966, and 1974. This proved to be items of exceptional interest to the prosecution in lieu of the fact that the documents involved were allegedly penned in the 1920s and 1930s.

"The 1949 ink was found on a purported 1925 document and the 1966 ink was on purported 1925 and 1928 documents; the 1974 ink was found on a purported 1935 document and the 1958 ink was used on the remaining 28 documents in question," reported Stewart.

Stewart had utilized his agency's Standard Ink Library to identify and date the inks used to alter land deeds in this Florida land scandal. His methods were in accord with agency policy; Stewart ran TLC on the questioned and known inks and compared his results with the Library. The rest is history.

As a possible note of irony, the defense attorney involved in this case attempted to sway the jury by stating that the defendant was far too intelligent to have made the mistake of using modern pens if it were his intention to forge official documents.[41]

The Investigation of Spiro T. Agnew

Another case, in the early 1970s, involved the investigation of the man who held the number two spot in the political structure of this country. The investigation of the Vice President of the United States of America, Spiro T. Agnew, rapidly deteriorated into what has been considered to be the biggest plea-bargaining negotiations in our history as a nation. While the newspapers reported that President Richard M. Nixon had adopted a strictly "hands-off" policy during Agnews' investigation, several of his top aides went scrambling to ascertain what turned out to be one of the more indigestible scandals in recent Washington history.

While serving as governor of the state of Maryland, Agnew selected a man by the name of Jerry Wolff as his chairman-director of the state road commission. One of Wolff's chief tasks was to control the selection of architects and engineers on every roads commission contract, subject to, and only to, Agnew's approval.

Bud Hammerman, one of Agnew's oldest friends, was asked to join Wolff in an "arrangement" in which engineering firms that were in line to receive state contracts would have to speak to him prior to submitting their bids on those contracts. For a year and a half Wolff told Hammerman which engineers were in line for state contracts, and Hammerman kept him informed of which engineers were "paying off." These engineers were expected to make "political contributions," almost always in cash, and even when there was no campaign requiring a contribution.

Wolff agreed to participate in the above-mentioned scheme with the understanding that he, Agnew, and Hammerman were to divide the proceeds in three even slices. Agnew wouldn't stand for that arrangement.[42] Initially Agnew wanted to cut Wolff off from these kickback funds; Hammerman was dispatched back to Wolff with the understanding that Agnew was to receive half of the funds, while he and Wolff were to divide the remainder between themselves.[43]

Sometime after Agnew's election as Vice President in November, 1968, but before his inauguration, Agnew asked Wolff to draw up a list of the contracts to Green Associated, Inc., a Maryland engineering company. Wolff discussed the list with the firm's president, Allen Green, revised it somewhat, and turned it over to Agnew. The clear inference to be drawn from this exercise was that Green had been paying off, and Agnew planned to use the list to persuade him to continue.[44] As one who had been around the Maryland state capitol for a number of years, Green knew the score. Agnew, as governor, had heavy financial burdens and was not a wealthy man. As governor of Maryland, Agnew received a yearly salary of $25,000. During his stay in the governor's mansion, Agnew hadn't managed to improve his financial matters to any large extent. Despite the fact that as Vice President he would receive a salary of $43,000 a year (later to be increased in 1970 to $62,500) Agnew wanted Green to continue his "payments" for services rendered.[45]

Green continued to pay Agnew off personally, delivering envelopes containing $2,000 four times a year either to the Office of the Vice President in the Old Executive Office Building or to Agnew's apartment in the Sheraton Park Hotel.[46]

Unfortunately for Agnew and associates, Jerry Wolff had been contacted by a team of Baltimore prosecutors who held it in their collective minds to bring Agnew to justice; this with the "unofficial" blessings of the U. S. Department of Justice. Wolff was, in the description of one of those prosecutors, "a pack rat, a guy whose nature is just to keep a lot of documents."[47] Wolff also kept diaries, small pocket-sized ledgers which he went to great pains to keep accurate. Wolff had, to the joy of the prosecutors, kept a little book of these alleged kickbacks involving himself, Hammerman, and Agnew for almost every month of the previous ten years.

At this point the Scientific Services Division of the Treasury Department's Bureau of Alcohol, Tobacco, and Firearms was called in on the case.

We ask the reader to consider the possible repercussions of the examinations to be performed by these BATF chemists. Jerry Wolff's notes alone were sufficient to convince a grand jury that the Vice President of the United States had probably committed a crime, both before and during the taking of his high office.

Wolff was able to produce the list he prepared of Green's business with

Agnew and numerous other documents all of which painted the Vice President in most unfavorable circumstances.

A fifty-two-page report by the BATF established that the inks Wolff used, of various colors, were on the market at the times the notations were said to have been made. Wolff and his omnipresent notebooks had incriminated Agnew in a dozen shades of ink.[48]

Agnew received formal notification that he was under investigation for possible conspiracy, extortion, bribery, and tax evasion. The Department of Justice had waited until they held what they considered to be more than sufficient evidence for conviction; after all, the reputation of a national leader was at stake.

The net result of many months of investigation proved to be the entering of a plea of *nolo contendere* by the Vice President of the United States regarding the criminal charges facing him.

On October 10, 1973, Spiro T. Agnew resigned from that high office.

U. S. v. Mitchell [49]

This case involved the combined efforts of the Internal Revenue Service and BATF. Mamie B. Mitchell, the defendant, was employed as the secretary to the comptroller of the state of Florida. During the course of her trial the Tampa press referred to her as the "Rosmary Woods" of Florida; she, allegedly, was trying to cover up certain items of evidence that would render her boss, one Mr. Fred O. Dickerson, in the poorest possible light.

The case involved the question of the true ownership of a certain amount of stock in a local bank, in addition to the questionable usage of certain promissory notes. The underlying question directed to Doctor A. A. Cantu was the following, "had a portion of the documents involved in this case been prepared at the alleged date . . . or had they been prepared somewhat earlier?"

Doctor Cantu proceeded to perform two different types of analysis; paper analysis and ink analysis. The results of the ink analysis showed that the inks utilized by Ms. Mitchell were available at the time of the alleged date of the documents.

During the course of his paper analysis, Doctor Cantu identified a watermark and proceeded to contact the paper manufacturer in question. The paper concern in this case, the Kimberly-Clark Corporation, notified him that there had been a slight change in the chemistry of the paper. At a specified date, the chemistry of the paper went from type *a* to type *b*, and that date was, essentially, nine months *after* the date of the document in question. Therefore the document could not have been prepared at the time of the alleged date, but at anytime *after* the date that the paper had been placed on the market.

The defense brought the jury to believe that Ms. Mitchell had suffered a "memory-damaging stroke" as the result of the federal perjury charges she was facing.[50] The net result of this line of defense secured a hung jury for the defendant. To date this case is still pending.

Md. v. Doe [51]

This recent case involved a number of original documents prepared by a medical doctor in an attempt to authenticate claims for Medicaid reimbursement.

Thirty-three original letters bearing the letterhead and handwriting of a physician, dated between January 1978 and June 1979, were submitted to the BATF. The pages consisted of handwritten notes dealing with Medicaid patients. The case investigator, operating out of the Attorney General's office in Baltimore, Maryland, felt that the documents he had forwarded to the BATF had actually been prepared a few weeks prior to their confiscation. Proof of his assertion would indicate Medicaid fraud.

Although the earliest alleged date on these documents was January 1978, Larry F. Stewart noted several "pecularities" within these documents. The appearance of extreme age in some of the documents indicated that the pages had been artificially aged. Certain pages had patterns of dark and light streaks. Under UV light, these documents had marking on the back in the form of parallel lines or bars. These bar markings did not consistently appear in the pages; on most of these pages the bars ran lengthwise but on one page the bars were essentially horizontal. These inconsistencies tended rule out the possibility that the bars had resulted from a manufacturing process. Stewart, in conjunction with Doctor A. A. Cantu, concluded that the bar marks on the back of these pages were similar to what would be expected to occur by heating the document on an oven rack. Studies comparing artificial aging by use of an oven with aging under normal conditions have led to the conclusion that oven aging at 212° F for three days is approximately equal to 25 years of normal aging.[52]

To test the above theory, the chemists at the BATF obtained paper of equivalent type and quality as that of the suspected documents. The samples obtained were heated in a "home-type" oven for one to four hours at temperatures ranging from 200° to 400° F. The pattern produced, in every instance, matched that on the questioned pages. To verify his conclusions, Stewart ran a spot check consisting of twenty ovens at local home appliance store; all had equidistant bars of the same approximate distance noted on the questioned pages.

The ball-pen inks used to prepare the documents were analyzed using standard ATF procedures; it was discovered that six different ink formulations were used to prepare the questioned documents. All were glycol-based ball-pen inks. The inks found on the "bright" sheets, although glycol-based, had the spreading appearance of the old oil-base inks. (In paper analysis, "bright" refers to the lack of yellowing of the paper.)[53] This suggested the possibility of induced aging through wet heat.

Upon consulting the Standard Ink Library in an attempt to match the six questioned inks to formulations, it was found that five of the formulas were available at the alleged dates of writing. The remaining formula, found among the nonbright documents only, did not match any ink in the Library, although it closely resembled one particular ink formula (Formulation A). The questioned ink had all the TLC characteristics of Formulation A in addition to others. The manufacturer of Formulation A (a unique two-dye component system) claimed that the components of the ink are sold to their company for exclusive usage in their ink formulation. If the questioned ink did match Formulation A, backdating would have been shown due to the fact that the formula was not available at the alleged dates of writing.

Because evidence had been found to suggest that the documents had been artificially aged by using heat, Formulation A was subjected to heat to determine if it thermodegrades into an ink similar to the unmatched questioned ink. Using a standard procedure, a Merck TLC plate was used to chromatograph the questioned ink versus the standard Formulation A, unheated as well as artificially aged at 400° F for intervals of one, two, and three hours. Not only did Formulation A change when subjected to heat, but each of the heated inks resulted in a different chromatogram from the unheated standard ink. The questioned ink matched the standard Formulation A that was heated at 400° F for one hour.

On the basis of the accelerated aging tests of both ink and paper, BATF chemists concluded that to create "old" looking documents, the physician artificially aged the thirty-three pages in question. Their analysis suggests that this may have been accomplished in the following manner:

> This documents were first heated with steam in one of two ways. Either they were hung on a line and steam heated (for example, in a large autoclave), or they were steam heated by use of a steam iron and hung to dry. This could account for the spreading of some of the inks. Ink spreading as a result of water or heat is formula dependent and thus certain inks are resistant. The paper clip-type markings could be due to the hanging process.
>
> Then, those pages that did not appear old enough were probably placed in an oven for additional heating. This would explain the bar markings, variations in the browness, loss of water (brittleness), and degradation of the ball pen ink.[54]

This case, to date, has not gone to trial. Doctor Doe, on the advice of her legal council, has elected to obtain a forensic scientist to attempt to refute the before-mentioned results of the BATF staff. When one takes into consideration the track record of the BATF chemists, this refutation does not seem likely.

U. S. v. Holland [55]

This last case involved the combined efforts of the United States Attorney's office, the Drug Enforcement Administration, and the BATF.

The defendant had been charged with the violation of continuing a criminal enterprise, possession of illegal substances (heroin and cocaine), and conspiracy to distribute those illegal substances.

The evidence submitted to the BATF chemists was a series of glassine bags bearing the following questioned ink impressions: a "happy face" rubber stamp, another rubber stamp bearing the impression "na no na no," with a self-contained ink pad, and one Carter's® inking pad.

Doctor Cantu performed both chemical and physical examinations on the questioned ink entries on these evidentiary items. The underlying question was this, "could the impressions made by both the 'happy face' and the 'na no na no' be matched with the rest of the submitted evidence?"

The results of Doctor Cantu's examinations concluded that the suspicions of the D. E. A. agents were correct; the "happy face" impressions on the number of glassine bags matched that of the seized ink pad. Likewise, "na no na no" impressions on the glassine bags matched that of the self-contained ink pad. This evidence, in addition to the fingerprint examinations performed by BATF personnel,* provided the prosecution with the necessary edge to obtain a conviction.[62]

The above case is currently under appeal, but not on the basis of the analysis of the evidence submitted.

COURT ADMISSIBILITY

Courts of law are traditionally conservative in nature and are very reluctant to change except with extreme caution. This resistance to change is in sharp contrast to the open-minded attitude of the scientific community toward the reception of new ideas.

Frye v. U. S.

The courts have viewed the problem of relevancy as the basic issue concerning the admissibility of scientific evidence. *Frye v. U. S.*, decided in 1923, established the standard concerning the admissibility of scientific and technological evidence.[56] The case has been followed by most jurisdictions. The court in the Frye case enunciated the test of general acceptance in the admissibility of polygraph results.

> Just when a scientific principle of discovery crosses the line between the experimental and demonstrable stages is difficult to define. Somewhere in this twilight zone the evidential force of the principle must be recognized and while courts will go a long way in admitting expert testimony based on well recognized scientific principles, these techniques must be sufficiently established to have gained general acceptance in the particular field in which it belongs.[57]

---

*B. L. Wilson and V. D. McCloud, fingerprint specialists, Washington, D.C., 1981.

The validity of the Frye definition as a reference to all scientific methods has, in the last two decades, been questioned. The trend to reject the application of legal relevancy in favor of logical relevancy is evident from treatment by the courts and by proposed legislation. It is only when a new "technique" is introduced into evidence that its relevancy to the criteria of the Frye decision is questioned. Cases such as *People v. Williams*[58] and *Coppolino v. Florida*[59] have added further refinements to that earlier Frye decision.

Currently, the courts do follow what is known as the "general approach" to admissibility tests. As the rules of evidence are, for all practical purposes, rules of exclusion, all evidence submitted is admissible unless, upon objection, it is subject to exclusion under some of the other rules.

Essentially, objections can be voiced in two broad catagories: (a) objections as to the form that the question or questions were asked and (b) objections as to the substance of the answer or answers submitted.

To avoid confusing the witness, the court will require that a question be clear and intelligent. Questions that are confusing, improperly phrased, misleading, or argumentative will not be allowed if objected to by opposing counsel. If there is no objection as to form or such objection is settled, the test of substance is applied.

RULES OF EVIDENCE FOR UNITED STATES COURTS
AND MAGISTRATES

With the codification of the Federal Rules of Evidence, express guidelines for the testimony from the lay witness and particularly that from the expert witness were obtained for the first time. As the reader knows, the expert witness possesses knowledge and skills that are not in the possession of the lay witness. Because of the necessary training and experience, the expert witness is in a position of superiority when testifying in our modern judicial system. Often it is within the discretion of the court to draw specific inferences and conclusions from the evidentiary facts submitted by the expert witness. Listed below are some specific federal guidelines for the opinions submitted by both the expert and lay witness.

Opinions and Expert Testimony (Article VII)*

Rule 701. *Opinion Testimony by Lay Witnesses*

If the witness is not testifying as an expert, his testimony in the form of opinions or inferences is limited to those opinions or inferences which are (a) rationally based on the perception of the witness and (b) helpful to a clear un-

---

*From the *Federal Rules of Evidence*, July 1, 1975, Title 28 U. S. C.

derstanding of his testimony or the determination of a fact in issue.

Rule 702. *Testimony by Experts*

If scientific, technical, or other specialized knowledge will assist the trier of fact to understand the evidence or to determine a fact in issue, a witness qualified as an expert by knowledge, skill, experience, training, or education, may testify thereto in the form of an opinion or otherwise.

Rule 703. *Bases of Opinion Testimony by Experts*

The facts or data in the particular case upon which an expert bases an opinion or inference may be those perceived by or made known to him at or before the hearing. If of a type reasonably relied upon by experts in the particular field in forming opinions or inferences upon the subject, the facts or data need not be admissible in evidence.

Rule 704. *Opinion on Ultimate Issue*

Testimony in the form of an opinion or inference otherwise admissible is not objectionable because it embraces an ultimate issue to be decided by the trier of fact.

Rule 705. *Disclosure of Facts or Data Underlying Expert Opinion*

The expert may testify in terms of opinion or inference and give his reasons therefore without prior disclosure of the underlying facts or data, unless the court requires otherwise. The expert may in any event be required to disclose the underlying facts or data on cross-examination.

Rule 706. *Court Appointed Experts*

(a) Appointment — The court may on its own motion or on the motion of any party enter an order to show cause why expert witnesses should not be appointed, and may request the parties to submit nominations. The court may appoint any expert witness agreed upon by the parties, and may appoint expert witnesses of its own selection. An expert witness shall not be appointed by the court unless he consents to act. A witness so appointed shall advise the parties of his findings, if any; his deposition may be taken by any party; and he may be called to testify by the court or any party. He shall be subject to cross-examination by each party, including a party calling him as a witness.

(b) Compensation — Expert witnesses so appointed are entitled to reasonable compensation in whatever sum the court may allow. The compensation thus fixed is payable from funds which may be provided by law in criminal cases and civil actions and proceedings involving just compensation under the fifth amendment. In other civil actions and proceedings the compensation shall be paid by the parties in such proportion and at such time as the courts directs, and thereafter charged in like manner as other costs.

(c) Disclosure of appointment — In the exercise of its discretion, the court may authorize disclosure to the jury of the fact that the court appointed the expert witness.

(d) Parties' experts of own selection — Nothing in this rule limits the parties in calling expert witnesses of their own selection.

QUALIFICATIONS FOR INK TESTIMONY

This last section is an attempt to give the reader an idea of the necessary qualifications for ink testimony. Each examiner must meet a certain number of these qualifications prior to his testimony being admitted into record. Ultimately it is at the discretion of the trier of fact to consider or not to consider those who meet these qualifications. We submit a "short list" of necessary qualifications that have been asked of Richard L. Brunelle in order to qualify as an ink expert.

Qualifications

- Please state your name and address.
- By whom are you employed?
- What position do you hold in the laboratory?
- What are your responsibilities in the laboratory?
- How long have you been employed by the Treasury Laboratory.
- Would you please state your educational background.
- What work experience did you have prior to joining the Treasury BATF Laboratory?
- Do you belong to any scientific societies?
- Have you ever received any awards for your work with the Treasury Lab?
- Have you published any scientific papers on research you have performed?
- Have you ever published a paper on ink identification?
- Do you ever give lectures at scientific meetings or at colleges or universities?
- Do other scientists consult you for advice in your field?
- What other professional activities are you involved in?
- Have you ever qualified as an expert in court before?
- About how many times have you qualified?
- Have you qualified and testified to ink identification before?

REPORT OF LABORATORY EXAMINATION (EXAMPLE)

The following are two samples of the "finished product" of a typical, routine

DEPARTMENT OF THE TREASURY
BUREAU OF ALCOHOL TOBACCO AND FIREARMS

Report of Laboratory Examination

EXAMPLE

FORENSIC SCIENCE BRANCH
NATIONAL LABORATORY CENTER
1401 RESEARCH BLVD.
ROCKVILLE, MARYLAND 20850
PHONE: FTS AREA CODE: 301
CHIEF: 443-1443
EVIDENCE ROOM: 443-5447
EXAMINER/ANALYST:

TO: *(Use window envelope. Begin typing two lines below dots.)*

Mr. John E. Doe
Criminalist
Sheriff-Corner's Department
Criminalistics Laboratory
2060 Happy Lane
Zenitram, California 94355

DATE:
May 20, 1981

YOUR:

RE:
Rape Case

OUR:
2I-256

DATE EXHIBITS RECEIVED: May 14, 1981

DELIVERED BY: Certified Mail PO2-72446797

TYPE OF EXAMINATION REQUESTED:
Ink

EXHIBITS:

G1 - Small sample of paper bearing a red stain.
G2 - Small sample of paper bearing a red stain.
G3 - Small sample of paper bearing a red stain.
G4 - Small sample of paper bearing a red stain.

RESULTS OF EXAMINATION:

Chemical and physical examinations were performed on the red stains from
Exhibits G1 through G4. The results were compared with each other and with
those from our Standard Ink Library.

The red stains were identified as writing ink. The inks matched each other
(Exhibits G1 through G4) and a standard from our ink library. The library
ink is available in fiber tip markers such as the Sanford pens Fiddlestick
and Mr. Sketch.

DISPOSITION OF EVIDENCE:

The evidence will be returned to you by United Parcel Service.

LARRY F. STEWART
Forensic Chemist

Reviewed by:
RICHARD L. BRUNELLE, Chief
Forensic Science Branch
Scientific Services Division

ATF F 7100.2 (11-78)   EDITION OF 4/78 MAY BE USED

DEPARTMENT OF THE TREASURY
BUREAU OF ALCOHOL TOBACCO AND FIREARMS

Report of Laboratory Examination

E X A M P L E

FORENSIC SCIENCE BRANCH
NATIONAL LABORATORY CENTER
1401 RESEARCH BLVD.
ROCKVILLE, MARYLAND 20850
PHONE: FTS AREA CODE: 301
CHIEF: 443-1443
EVIDENCE ROOM: 443-5447
EXAMINER/ANALYST:

TO: *(Use window envelope. Begin typing two lines below dots.)*

Barbara A. Bourgeois
Assistant U. S. Attorney
U. S. Department of Justice
Southern District of New York
Two St. Anthonys Plaza
New York, New York 10006

DATE: March 23, 1981

YOUR:

RE:

OUR: 1I-383

DATE EXHIBITS RECEIVED: March 19, 1981

DELIVERED BY: S/A William J. Parks, III

TYPE OF EXAMINATION REQUESTED: Ink

EXHIBITS:

Exhibit L - One document containing three entries at the bottom (June, July and August) each prepared with questioned ink

RESULTS OF EXAMINATION:

A chemical and physical examination was performed on the questioned ink entries appearing on Exhibit L and the results were compared with those from inks in our Standard Ink Library.

One ink prepared each of the three questioned ink entries found on Exhibit L and this ink matched a standard ink first commercially available in May 31, 1979. Commercial quantities of pens containing this ink became available in August 1979. However, a limited number of trial shipments of pens were made to special customers in the United States and Canada in May 1977. The U.S. customers were in Phoenix, Arizona; Van Nuys, California; Philadelphia, Pennsylvania; Hallandale, Florida; North Hollywood, California (two customers); Los Angeles, California; Charleston, West Virginia; and Baldwin, Montana.

The exhibit has been returned to you.

ANTONIO A. CANTU
Chemical Physicist

REVIEWED BY:

Richard L. Brunelle, Chief
Forensic Science Branch
Scientific Services Division

ATF F 7100.2 (11-78)   EDITION OF 4/78 MAY BE USED

report of a laboratory examination. The names, other than those of the Department of the Treasury BATF personnel are fictional; the addresses at the top of the lab report are mythical as well. In addition, it should be noted that the Certified Mail numbers have been exaggerated. All other facts, such as the results of examination and the nature of the case involved, are factual.

NOTES

1. T. Astle, *The Origin and Progress of Writing* (— — —, F. J. White Co., 1803), pp. 240

2. R. L. Brunelle and A. A. Cantu, *Ink Analysis — A Weapon Against Crime by Detection of Fraud.* ACS Symposium Series No. 13 Forensic Science, 1975, p. 134.

3. D. N. Carvalho, *Forty Centuries of Ink* (New York, Banks Law Pub., Co., 1904), pp. 217-244.

4. See note 3 above.

5. See note 3 above.

6. See note 3 above.

7. J. N. Baker, *Law of Disputed and Forged Documents* (Charlottesville, VA, Mitchie Company, 1955), pp. 357-361.

8. See note 3 above.

9. See note 3 above.

10. See note 3 above.

11. Stoller v. U. S., 69-974-CIV-CA, S. D. F.a, Miami, Fla. (1969).

12. U. S. v. Wolfson, 437 F.2d 862 (2d Cir. 1970).

13. U. S. v. Meyers, N.Y., N.Y., (1970).

14. U. S. v. Sloan, CR-69-137, W.D. Tenn., (1970).

15. U. S. v. Colasurdo, 453 F.2d 585 (1971).

16. U. S. v. Bruno, 333 F.Supp. 570, E.D. Pa. (1971).

17. See note 16 above.

18. U. S. v. Miller, S.D. Fla., No. 72-668-CR-WM, (1972).

19. See note 18 above.

20. See note 18 above.

21. See note 18 above.

22. People v. Corona, CalApp3d 684, 23 CrL 2212, (1980).

23. See note 22 above, testimony of S. Goldblatt, ATF document examiner, New York.

24. See note 22 above, testimony of C. M. Hoffman, ATF, Washington, D.C., 1972.

25. See note 22 above, testimony of C. M. Hoffman, ATF, Washington, D.C., 1972.

26. See note 22 above, testimony of R. L. Wilder, ATF, Washington, D.C., 1972.

27. See note 22 above, Sec 80.

28. See note 22 above, Sec 80.

29. U. S. v. Jorgensen, U. S. Ct.App.10.CR. No. 75-CR-75, (1975).

30. See note 29 above.

31. U. S. v. Durr, (U.S.A.F. Madrid, Spain) 1977.

32. Personal communcations with Albert Lyter, March, 1981, *re* the "Mormon" Will, or the Howard Hughes Will, Las Vegas, Nevada, 1977-78.

33. See note 32 above.

34. See note 32 above.

35. See note 32 above.

36. See note 32 above.

37. See note 32 above.
38. See note 32 above.
39. People v Pryor, Cr. Ct. Fla., 80-812 "C", 1981.
40. Personal communication with L. F. Stewart, Aug., 1981.
41. See note 40 above.
42. R. M. Cohen and J. Witcover, *A Heartbeat Away — The Investigation and Resignation of Vice President Spiro T. Agnew* (New York, Viking Press, 1974), pp. 113-136.
43. See note 42 above.
44. See note 42 above.
45. See note 42 above.
46. See note 42 above.
47. See note 42 above.
48. See note 42 above.
49. U. S. v. Mitchell, S. D. Fla., 1975.
50. C. Heck, article in *St. Petersburg Times*, St. Petersburg, FL, Jan. 17, 1975.
51. Md. V. Doe, 1981 (case is still active).
52. L. F. Stewart, *Artificial Aging of Documents* (unpublished manuscript, 1981).
53. B. L. Browning, *Analysis of Paper,* 2nd ed. (New York, Marcel Dekker, Inc., 1977), pp. 917-922.
54. See note 52 above.
55. U. S. v. Holland, J. 80 2032, 1981. This case is currently under appeal.
56. Frye v. U. S., 293 F. 1013, 1014 (D.C. Cir. 1923).
57. See note 56 above.
58. People v. Williams, 164 Cal. App. 2d Supp 848, 331 P. 2d 251 (1958).
59. Coppolino v. Florida, 223 So. 2d 68 (Fla. App. 1968), App. dismissed 234 So. 2d (Fla., 1969) cert. denied 399, U. S. 927.
60. R. W. Reed, unpublished paper, 1981.
61. J. C. Klotter, and C. L. Meier, *Criminal Evidence for Police,* 2nd ed. (Cincinnati, Anderson Pub. Co., 1978), pp. 29-44.
62. C. McCormick, *The Law of Evidence,* 2nd ed. (St. Paul, MN, West Pub., 1972), p. 319.
63. Weinstock v. U. S., 231 F.2d 699, (D.C. Cir. 1956).
64. *Black's Law Dictionary,* 5th ed. (St. Paul, MN, West Pub., 1979), p. 257.
65. See note 64 above.
66. *Federal Rules of Evidence,* July, 1975.
67. See note 62 above.
68. *Corpus Juris Secundum,* vol. 31 (St. Paul, MN, West Pub., 1957).

ABBREVIATIONS

AA   *Atomic Absorption (Spectroscopy)*

AEC   *Atomic Energy Commission (United States)*

ASQDE   *American Society of Questioned Document Examiners*

AOAC   *Association of Official Analytical Chemists*

ASTM   *American Society for Testing and Materials*

ATR   *Attenuated Total Reflectance*

BATF   *Bureau of Alcohol, Tobacco and Firearms*

BEP   *Bureau of Engraving and Printing*

C°   *Celsius degrees*

CMC   *Carboxmethyl cellulose*

DEA   *Drug Enforcement Administration*

EDXA   *Energy-dispersive x-ray analysis*

EPA   *Environmental Protection Agency*

ES   *Emission spectroscopy*

F°   *Fahrenheit degrees*

FBI   *Federal Bureau of Investigation*

FDA   *Food and Drug Administration*

FTIR   *Fourier Transform Infra-red*

g   *Gram*

GC   *Gas Chromatography*

HPLC   *High Pressure Liquid Chromatography*

IAI   *International Association of Identification*

INS   *Immigration and Naturalization Service*

INTERPOL   *International Police*

IR   *Infrared*

IRS   *Internal Revenue Service*

JTAPPI   *Japanese Technical Association of Pulp and Paper Industry*

LEAA   *Law Enforcement Assistance Administration*

ml   *Milli liter*

NAA   *Neutron Activation Analysis*

NAPIM   *National Association of Printing Ink Manufacturers, Inc.*

MG   *Machine glazed*

nm   *Nanometers*

NMR   *Nuclear Magnetic Resonance*

OCR   *Optical Character Recognition (Inks)*

OSHA   *Occupational Safety and Health Administration*

PGC   *Pyrolysis Gas Chromatography*

pH   *Hydrogen ion concentration*

ppm   *Parts per million*

RAR   *Revenue Agent's Report*

Rf   *Retardation Factor*

SCt   *Supreme Court*

SEC   *Securities and Exchange Commission*

SEM   *Scanning electron microscope*

TAPPI   *Technical Association of the Pulp and Paper Industry*

TLC   *Thin-Layer Chromatography*

TSCA   *Toxic Substances Control Act*

USDA   *U. S. Department of Agriculture*

μg   *Micro gram*

ul   Microliter (10-6 liter or 10-3 millimeter)

USAF   *United States Air Force*

UV   *Ultra Violet*

WIMA   *Writing Instruments Manufacturers Association, Inc.*

XREOF (XEOF)   *X-ray excited optical fluorescence spectrometer*

XD   *X-ray diffraction*

INDEX

287

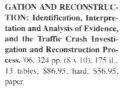
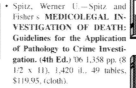
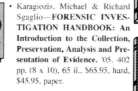
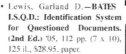

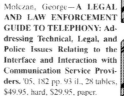

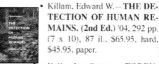
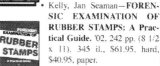
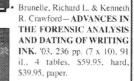
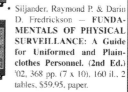

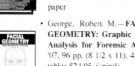
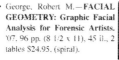
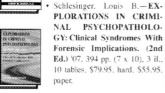
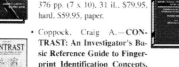